Beyond Suffrage

Beyond Suffrage

WOMEN
IN THE
NEW DEAL

Susan Ware

Harvard University Press
Cambridge, Massachusetts
and London, England
1981

Library of Congress Cataloging in Publication Data

Ware, Susan, 1950-
    Beyond suffrage, women in the New Deal.

    Bibliography: p.
    Includes index.
    1.   Women in public life—United States.
2.   United States—Politics and government—1933-
1945.   I.   Title.
HQ1236.W37   1981   305.4′2   80-25265
ISBN 0-674-06921-8

To Dorothy F. McConnell

ACKNOWLEDGMENTS

Many people and institutions made contributions to this study. The Franklin D. Roosevelt Library in Hyde Park, New York, and the Arthur and Elizabeth Schlesinger Library on the History of Women in America at Radcliffe College provided helpful and congenial atmospheres for my research. I would like to thank the Roosevelt Library, the Schlesinger Library, and the Columbia Oral History Collection for permission to cite from their collections; I would also like to thank Franklin D. Roosevelt, Jr., Clara M. Beyer, Hilda Worthington Smith, and Susanna Perkins Coggeshall for permission to quote from unpublished material. The Eleanor Roosevelt Institute at Hyde Park and the Charles Warren Center for Studies in American History at Harvard University provided research grants during the initial stages of the project. Professor Frank Freidel gave me the proper balance of encouragement and criticism throughout my years at Harvard as a student in history, and while writing this book. I have also benefited greatly from my association with Dr. Barbara Miller Solomon of Harvard, from whom I have learned much about the writing and teaching of women's history. Alan Brinkley and Warren Leon took time from their own work to help me with mine. Gale Halpern made helpful suggestions as she typed several versions of the draft. The editors at the Harvard University Press, especially Aida Donald, provided encouragement and assistance in the final stages of revision. And the entire manuscript profited immeasurably from close readings by Don Ware, lawyer, historian, and spouse. Finally, the book is dedicated to my great-aunt, Dorothy F. McConnell, who has been my own personal link with feminism in the 1930s (and beyond) for as long as I can remember.

CONTENTS

INTRODUCTION   1

1 THE WOMEN'S NETWORK   3

2 A GENERATIONAL APPROACH   18

3 THE CRITICAL YEAR, 1933-1934   43

4 WOMEN AND DEMOCRATIC POLITICS   68

5 WOMEN AND SOCIAL WELFARE POLICY   87

6 A GENERATION ON THE WANE   116

EPILOGUE   132

APPENDIX A. CRITERIA FOR SELECTION OF THE WOMEN   137
APPENDIX B. GROUP PROFILE AND INDIVIDUAL
              BIOGRAPHIES   142
APPENDIX C. SUMMARY OF BIOGRAPHICAL MATERIAL   156
MANUSCRIPT COLLECTIONS CITED   158
NOTES   160
INDEX   197

Beyond Suffrage

INTRODUCTION

The depression decade of the 1930s continues to fascinate successive generations of Americans. For historians, the period provides an opportunity to analyze the collective response of American society to the social and economic trauma of the Great Depression, and to trace the depression's impact on individuals and institutions. Not all parts of the society felt the devastation of the depression equally, but none escaped contact with the changes it worked on American life.

Though historians have chronicled the human suffering and courage of the decade, their particular interest has been to examine the federal government's response to the depression. Practically every aspect of the New Deal has been studied extensively—economic policy, agriculture, labor, foreign affairs, politics, relief and social security, and conservation, to name a few. Detailed descriptions of the world of President Franklin D. Roosevelt abound: his day-to-day activities, his circle of advisers, his friends and enemies in Congress and on the Supreme Court, even speculations about his health and extramarital affairs.

Yet there is a significant gap in our knowledge of the New Deal. In the conventional histories of the period, women are hardly mentioned. This omission is misleading, because the New Deal offered greatly expanded roles for women in public life in the 1930s, a record not matched until the 1960s. As this study brings to light, women made important contributions to the planning and administration of the New Deal's social welfare programs. Women also took on larger roles within the Democratic party. No longer can the New Deal be portrayed as strictly a male affair.

The experiences of women who achieved prominence in politics and government in the 1930s add to our understanding of the New Deal. Their story is important to women's history as well. Until recently, the

1

1930s have been described as a bleak period for women. Because of the absence of an organized women's movement in the decade, historians have often skipped straight from the winning of suffrage in 1920 to the revival of feminism in the 1960s. The decade of the 1930s rarely receives more than a passing glance.[1] The few general descriptions of women's experiences during the period usually concentrate on job discrimination against women workers during the depression. A 1936 Gallup poll, in which four-fifths of those questioned thought that a wife should not work if her husband had a job, reflected the strong public sentiment against married women working. Such restrictive attitudes extended to the federal government itself, which dismissed 1,600 married women from the government service between 1932 and 1937.[2]

Although these images of women's experiences in the 1930s contain some validity, new research is broadening our understanding of how women actually fared during the decade. Work by Ruth Milkman and Alice Kessler-Harris suggests that despite the prejudice against women working, women as a group often had an easier time than men in obtaining employment during the depression.[3] As women's participation in the New Deal suggests, old attitudes about the lack of feminist activity in the 1930s also require reconsideration. The forms that these initiatives took add to our understanding of women's goals in public life in the years after the passage of the woman suffrage amendment in 1920.[4]

The story of women in the New Deal has a further significance. The outstanding characteristic of women's participation in the New Deal was the development of a "network" of friendship and cooperation among the women, which maximized their influence in politics and government. This network, which had its roots in a generation's common experiences in the woman suffrage campaign, Progressive reform movements, and political and social welfare activities in the 1920s, flourished within the experimental climate of the New Deal.

This New Deal network is one of a number of women's networks brought to light by the recent interest in women's history. Yet while the term has been loosely applied to a variety of familial, social, and political ties,[5] few definitions or guidelines have emerged. This study attempts to provide a model for future undertakings. Why a network developed among this remarkable group of women in public life, how their network influenced politics and social welfare initiatives in the 1930s, and how these developments related to the broader context of the New Deal will be the major themes of this book.

1

THE WOMEN'S NETWORK

In May 1940, Democratic women from every state in the nation came to Washington for a three-day National Institute of Government sponsored by the Women's Division of the Democratic National Committee. Since about one hundred women were expected to attend, Franklin Roosevelt followed his wife's suggestion and invited the delegates to drop by his Executive Office for an informal chat. When preregistration reached five hundred, White House officials switched the reception to the East Room. When five thousand women actually registered for the conference, President Roosevelt decided to address the group on the White House lawn.

No one had dreamed that this Institute of Government, the first in the history of women's political activity, would generate such enthusiasm. Mary ("Molly") Dewson, ex-director of the Women's Division and herself a moving force behind the new recognition of women in politics, exclaimed in a magazine interview, "And they didn't think my . . . program would work. Oh, gee!" According to *Time*, the success of the conference confirmed women's progress in political life since passage of the suffrage amendment in 1920.[1]

The National Institute of Government allowed women interested in the social and economic problems of the country to meet with the New Deal administrators responsible for attacking those problems through government action. The women could observe government at work on the national level, educate themselves about current affairs in Washington, and report back to their local communities. The Institute served a further purpose as well. Since 1940 was an election year, the conference encouraged local Democratic women to begin organizing for victory in November.[2] The Institute of Government's dual emphasis on education and politics characterized women's approach to government in the 1930s.

The high point of the National Institute of Government came at a final dinner honoring important women in the New Deal administration. Molly Dewson, "toastmistress" for this gala evening, took great pride in introducing the prominent women at the Speakers' table, including the featured speaker, Eleanor Roosevelt. The group at the Speakers' table was a virtual *Who's Who* of high-ranking women in politics and government. Molly Dewson spoke for them all when she said: "My heart filled with pride at that long line of intelligent, competent, well-balanced women . . . who represented Roosevelt's confidence in our ability."[3]

Molly Dewson had good reason to be proud of the recognition women had received in the politics and government of the New Deal in the 1930s. Seventy women sat at the Speakers' table at the 1940 banquet, all holding important positions in the federal bureaucracy or the Democratic party. "The opportunities given women by Roosevelt in the thirties changed our status," Dewson declared.[4]

The significance of women's accomplishments in the 1930s was not lost on women who had been active in the woman suffrage movement twenty years earlier. Carrie Chapman Catt, president of the National American Woman Suffrage Association during the final years of the suffrage campaign, wrote to Eleanor Roosevelt early in the New Deal:

> For some time I have had a collection of statesmen hanging upon my wall, but, under the new administration, I have been obliged to start a new collection and that is one of stateswomen. Now it is ready and you are at the center of it all . . . You, Miss Perkins, Mrs. Owen, Miss Woolley, Miss Abbott, Miss Anderson, and some others, make a fine looking group—the beginning of the grand display of stateswomen we are going to have after a time.[5]

Carrie Chapman Catt and other former suffragists were especially pleased with women's progress during the 1930s because it demonstrated the continued vitality of the women's movement in the postsuffrage era. The 1920s had been a hard time for women in public life, as American society grew increasingly hostile to their social welfare and feminist ideals. During the 1930s, however, women found an administration and a national mood more sympathetic to their goals. It is in the 1930s that many of women's expectations beyond suffrage finally found fulfillment.

The woman suffrage campaign captured the imagination and support of several million American women in the early twentieth century. By 1914 the suffrage movement had built a broad coalition of women's organizations united for the purpose of winning the vote. Women viewed suffrage as the first step toward a wide range of social reforms: once they got the vote, women would purify the cities, abolish child labor, clean up politics, end all wars. Such exaggerated claims set the stage for an inevitable letdown once the vote finally was won. In 1919, Anna Howard Shaw, prominent suffrage leader, had predicted difficulties in the years after passage of the suffrage amendment to a member of the next generation, Emily Newell Blair: "I am sorry for you young women who have to carry on the work for the next ten years, for suffrage was a symbol, and now you have lost your symbol."[6]

Feminism did not die in the 1920s, but much of the energy that had gone into winning the vote dissipated. One Connecticut suffragist recalled, "After we got the vote, the crusade was over. It was peacetime and we went back to a hundred different causes and tasks that we'd been putting off all those years. We just demobilized."[7] Lacking its unifying symbol, the women's movement splintered into a variety of smaller groups.

Some women turned to pacifism, which they saw as a natural outgrowth of their feminism. During the 1920s Carrie Chapman Catt founded the National Conference on the Cause and Cure of War. The Women's International League for Peace and Freedom, which had been founded in 1915, widened its activities in the 1920s; Jane Addams gave her strong public support to the League in its efforts to organize women in pursuit of peace. Other women, many of them from the now-defunct National American Woman Suffrage Association, founded the National League of Women Voters, a nonpartisan group dedicated to educating women in citizenship and responsible democracy. Another offshoot of the suffrage movement, the more militant National Women's Party, concentrated its energies after 1923 on a new symbol, the Equal Rights Amendment. Yet the Women's Party's single-minded devotion to the ERA split the women's movement, since most women in public life believed that protective legislation for working women was more important than a general statement of equality under the law. This rift, and the bitterness it engendered on both sides, further weakened the women's movement in the 1920s.[8]

But the main problem confronting reform-minded women in the decade was that they found themselves increasingly out of step with American society. The 1920s proved far more hostile to women's goals than the Progressive period had been. What success women did achieve came early in the decade, when politicians still feared that organized womanhood might vote as a bloc. For example, in 1921 women were instrumental in the passage of the Sheppard-Towner Federal Maternity and Infancy Act, one of the first federally funded health-care programs. This bill, which called for an annual appropriation of $1,250,000, provided match-ing federal funds to set up maternity and pediatric clinics for instruction in the health care of mothers and babies. The Women's Joint Congres-sional Committee, a lobbying group representing ten prominent national women's organizations, mobilized much of the support for this bill and overcame objections that the bill was a harbinger of socialized medicine.[9]

By the mid-1920s, however, women's political clout was on the de-cline. Politicians had discovered that they had little to fear from female voters: women tended to vote just like their husbands, if they voted at all. Symbolic of women's loss of political power was their failure to secure renewal of the Sheppard-Towner Act in 1929. They employed the same arguments and tactics that had succeeded in 1921, but this time to no avail. The mood of the country had shifted perceptibly.[10]

The stock market crash in 1929, the deepening depression, the election of Franklin D. Roosevelt in 1932, and the unfolding of the New Deal in 1933 and 1934 changed all this. As the New Deal acted to revitalize and preserve the capitalist system, it fostered a new relationship among the federal government, society, and the individual. In the 1930s the federal government took on new responsibilities for managing the national econ-omy, providing work relief and social security for its citizens and pro-tecting the rights of consumers, labor, and blacks.[11]

These developments also led to broadened opportunities for women. Agitation for women's rights traditionally has found its greatest success in times of widespread social reform. The relationship between the anti-slavery crusade and the early women's rights movement in the 1840s, the link between woman suffrage and Progressive reform in the early twen-tieth century, and the strong connection between the civil rights and anti-war movements of the 1960s and the reemergence of feminism in that decade suggest the complementary nature of women's issues and social reform.[12] A similar, though less comprehensive, interaction was at work in the 1930s. The New Deal, although it did not produce a radical re-structuring of the American system, represented a period of important social and economic change. The experimental, reformist atmosphere of the New Deal encouraged and facilitated progress for women, particu-larly those interested in pursuing careers in public life.

The New Deal brought to Washington a remarkable group of women who would rise to positions of power and prominence in many of the new government agencies. These were the "intelligent, competent, well-balanced women" whom Dewson honored at the 1940 National Institute of Government.[13] As a group, these women had much in common. The similarities of their backgrounds and career patterns formed the basis for shared attitudes toward feminism, social reform, and the role of government. Many of these women had known each other from social welfare and reform activities during the Progressive period and the woman suffrage campaign. To these old friendships were added new ones as other talented women gathered in Washington and worked together to institutionalize reforms they had been promoting over the past thirty years. The interaction of these women, on both the personal and the professional level, led to what can be described as a "network" of women within the New Deal.[14]

This network among women in politics and government in the 1930s became an important force in enlarging women's influence in the New Deal. Women in the New Deal network took an active interest in furthering the progress of their sex. They recruited women for prominent government positions, demanded increased political patronage, and generally fostered an awareness of women as a special interest group with a substantial role to play in the New Deal. Their network provided them with the means to mobilize in pursuit of these objectives.

Though promoting the advancement of women always remained a central concern of the network, the women ultimately identified themselves as social reformers rather than as feminists. Since most of these women followed careers in social welfare administration in the federal government, the network emerged as an important influence on New Deal policy in this area. Yet as these women pursued social welfare goals benefiting both men and women in the society at large, they also advanced the cause of women by taking on new and unprecedented roles in the public sphere. The story of the women's network adds a chapter to the history both of the New Deal and of feminism in the postsuffrage era.

Eleanor Roosevelt was the foremost member of the women's network in the 1930s (figure 1). Her institutional role as First Lady, her willingness to use her public position to push for reform, and her ability to inspire loyalty in friends and colleagues placed her "at the center of this growing New Deal political sisterhood."[15] It is difficult to imagine the progress that occurred for women in the 1930s without Eleanor Roosevelt in the White House.

Eleanor Roosevelt occupied a strategic position in the Washington community. As First Lady, she was highly visible in all her activities. (Molly Dewson once wrote her, "Eleanor dear as you live in a glass bowl I know all about you.") Roosevelt commanded attention in her own right through her daily column "My Day" and her weekly press conferences with women journalists in Washington. Because she was not tied down to an official government position, she enjoyed a flexibility denied to the President.[16]

Figure 1.   Members of the network and their positions in the New Deal.

Grace Abbott	Chief of the Children's Bureau, U.S. Department of Labor, 1921-1934
Mary Anderson	Chief of the Women's Bureau, U.S. Department of Labor, 1920-1944
Marion Glass Banister	Assistant Treasurer of the United States, 1933-1951
Clara M. Beyer	Associate Director, Division of Labor Standards, U.S. Department of Labor, 1934-1957
Emily Newell Blair	Consumers' Advisory Board, National Recovery Administration (NRA), 1933-1934
Jo Coffin	Assistant to the Public Printer, Government Printing Office, 1934-1941
Mary W. Dewson	Director of the Women's Division, Democratic National Committee, 1932-1934; Chairman of the Women's Division Advisory Committee, 1934-1937; Member of the Social Security Board, 1937-1938
Florence Jaffray Harriman	U.S. Minister to Norway, 1937-1941
Jane Hoey	Director of the Bureau of Public Assistance, Social Security Administration, 1936-1953
Lucy Somerville Howorth	Member of the Board of Appeals, Veterans Administration, 1934-1950
Mary LaDame	Associate Director of the U.S. Employment Service, 1934-1938; Special Assistant to the Secretary of Labor, 1938-1945

Figure 1 (*continued*).

Katharine Lenroot	Chief of the Children's Bureau, U.S. Department of Labor, 1934-1949
Dorothy McAlister	Director of the Women's Division, Democratic National Committee, 1936-1940
Lucille Foster McMillin	Civil Service Commissioner, 1933-1949
Emma Guffey Miller	Democratic National Committee-woman, Pennsylvania, 1932-1970
Mary T. Norton	Democratic Congresswoman, New Jersey, 1925-1950
Caroline O'Day	Democratic Congresswoman-at-large, New York, 1935-1942
Ruth Bryan Owen	U.S. Minister to Denmark, 1933-1936
Frances Perkins	Secretary of Labor, 1933-1945
Josephine Aspinwall Roche	Assistant Secretary of the Treasury, 1934-1937; Chairman of the Government Interdepartmental Health Committee, 1936-1940s
Eleanor Roosevelt	The First Lady, 1933-1945
Nellie Tayloe Ross	Director of the U.S. Mint, 1933-1952
Mary Harriman Rumsey	Chairman of the Consumers' Advisory Board, NRA, 1933-1934; adviser on consumer affairs for the National Emergency Council, 1933-1934
Rose Schneiderman	Labor Advisory Board, NRA, 1933-1934
Hilda Worthington Smith	Director of the Workers' Service Program, Federal Emergency Relief Administration (FERA) and Works Progress Administration (WPA), 1933-1943

Figure 1 (*continued*).

Sue Shelton White	Assistant Chairman of the Consumers' Advisory Board, NRA, 1934-1935; legal staff of the Social Security Administration, 1935-1943
Carolyn Wolfe	Director of the Women's Division, Democratic National Committee, 1934-1936
Ellen Sullivan Woodward	Director of the Women's Division, FERA, 1933-1936; Director of Women's and Professional Projects, WPA, 1936-1938; Member of the Social Security Board, 1938-1946

One of Eleanor Roosevelt's main contributions to the network was the access she provided to the President for her friends. Molly Dewson remembered, "When I wanted help on some definite point, Mrs. Roosevelt gave me the opportunity to sit by the President at dinner and the matter was settled before we finished our soup." Many women in Washington contacted Eleanor if they had a problem they wanted brought to the President's attention. As Mary Anderson of the Women's Bureau recalled, "She always knew what we were doing and understood what our problems were. I felt that working women everywhere could turn to her for help and support, and through her could get the kind of sympathetic interest from the President that would be very useful."[17] Women in Washington knew they had a friend in the White House.

Eleanor Roosevelt inspired women in public life everywhere, but she had an especially large impact on those women working in the Washington community. Women in the network thought of Eleanor Roosevelt as their own spiritual leader, equally important as the President: "I am sure, Eleanor dear, that millions of people voted with you in their minds also," Rose Schneiderman wrote in 1936. Molly Dewson referred to Eleanor Roosevelt as "my wonder woman," and said, "You are sort of my Mother Earth that I need to touch once in a while." Ellen Woodward summarized this debt succinctly: "You do such wonderful things for us there seems nothing we can ever do to show appreciation except—to strive harder and harder to measure up to the responsibilities of the positions that the President and you have given us."[18]

Besides Eleanor Roosevelt, three other women in particular shaped developments for women in the New Deal through active roles in the network. The first was Molly Dewson, who served as head of the Women's Division of the Democratic party from 1932 to 1937. Dewson was perhaps the most self-conscious activist in women's behalf in the 1930s. An 1897 graduate of Wellesley College, Dewson had spent her early career working in various social welfare organizations, but by 1928 had switched her attention to political activism. A close personal friend of the Roosevelts from New York, Dewson became their trusted deputy for women's activities in the Democratic party. In addition to running the Women's Division, Dewson also served as a member of the Social Security Board from 1937 to 1938.[19]

An equally important member of the network was Frances Perkins, Secretary of Labor from 1933 to 1945. Like Dewson, Perkins was a graduate of a women's college (Mount Holyoke, 1902) and active in New York reform circles. Her pathbreaking appointment to the Cabinet opened the way for more women to enter government service, and she herself brought other talented women to Washington to join the Labor Department. Much of the social welfare legislation during the New Deal came about as a result of her leadership. Although Perkins has sometimes been portrayed as unsympathetic to women's issues, she played an important symbolic and substantive role within the network.

Finally, Ellen Sullivan Woodward, one of the most powerful women in official Washington during the 1930s, moved quickly to the forefront of the network. Unlike Dewson and Perkins, Woodward was not a personal friend of the Roosevelts. A native of Mississippi, she gained her political and social welfare experience in that state. Woodward came to Washington in 1933 to set up relief programs for women under the auspices of the Federal Emergency Relief Administration, and eventually became head of Women's and Professional Projects for the Works Progress Administration. In addition, she served for six years on the Social Security Board.

In all, twenty-eight women belonged to the network. The remaining network members were scattered among various New Deal agencies and the Democratic party apparatus (figure 2). Many were concentrated in the Labor Department, particularly in the Women's Bureau and Children's Bureau. Others found jobs in the new relief agencies established to meet the crisis of the depression, such as the Works Progress Administration, the National Recovery Administration, and the Social Security Administration. Several found positions within the Democratic party structure, and two women were members of Congress.

Figure 2.   Distribution of members of the network in federal government and Democratic party positions.

White House:
  Eleanor Roosevelt

Congress:
  Mary T. Norton
  Caroline O'Day

Women's Division,
Democratic National Committee:
  Mary W. Dewson
  Dorothy McAlister
  Emma Guffey Miller
  Carolyn Wolfe

Cabinet Departments
  Labor: Grace Abbott
        Mary Anderson
        Clara M. Beyer
        Mary LaDame
        Katharine Lenroot
        Frances Perkins
  State: Florence Jaffray Harriman
        Ruth Bryan Owen
  Treasury:
        Marion Glass Banister
        Josephine Roche
        Nellie Tayloe Ross

Independent Agencies
  FERA-WPA:
        Hilda Worthington Smith
        Ellen Sullivan Woodward
  NRA: Emily Newell Blair
        Mary Harriman Rumsey
        Rose Schneiderman
        Sue Shelton White
  Social Security:
        Jane Hoey
        (Mary W. Dewson)
        (Sue Shelton White)
        (Ellen Sullivan Woodward)
  Veterans Administration:
        Lucy Somerville Howorth
  Government Printing Office:
        Jo Coffin
  Civil Service Commission:
        Lucille Foster McMillin

The network encompassed virtually all of the women in top federal jobs in Washington in the 1930s, as well as several women who did not hold government positions but were important figures in Washington nonetheless.[20] The only major omission was prominent black educator Mary McLeod Bethune, head of the Office of Minority Affairs in the National Youth Administration from 1936 to 1944. Although Bethune held a job more important than that of many other women in the administration, she was rarely mentioned as an important "woman" in the New Deal. Instead she was seen, and she saw herself, as a representative of black people. For example, Bethune was the unofficial leader of the Black Cabinet, which pushed for equal treatment for blacks in New Deal agencies. That Bethune was not considered part of the women's network is both a sad and provocative commentary on the 1930s and the attitudes the other women brought to their government jobs.[21]

What drew certain women into the network, and excluded Mary McLeod Bethune, was something more than just their sex. The women in the network were united by close personal friendship and loyalty, such as Frances Perkins expressed to Molly Dewson: "I cannot tell you how much that luncheon which you arranged for me has meant in my life and I want you to know not only that I am grateful for all that you did to make it a success but that it has given me new insight into the beauty and loyalty and chivalry between women. How fine it is to play the game together all these years, isn't it?"[22] Molly Dewson noted that she and Perkins had never been intimate personal friends ("Between us two cooperation has been of the head, not the heart"), but she clearly reciprocated Perkins's strong feelings: "Personally we two were on excellent terms. For thirty years we have worked for a common interest without misunderstanding."[23]

Working together over the years led to strong and lasting relationships among the women and formed the basis for much of the collaboration in the network throughout the 1930s. Network members frequently wrote to each other as one friend to another, offering support and congratulations on their various endeavors. Frances Perkins wrote to Daisy Harriman in Oslo in 1937, "I can't tell you how much I miss you and the opportunity to have a good heart-to-heart talk with you once in a while. You are doing a grand job and everyone here thinks you are perfectly splendid." Mary Harriman Rumsey penned warm notes to her co-worker Sue Shelton White: "This is just a line of love before leaving to tell you how grateful and appreciative I am of all you have been and done for me these past extraordinary months. As I said, just to know you were there was a help and a security."[24]

Molly Dewson's letters, short but affectionate, full of wit and humor, kept her in contact with women friends in Washington. Dewson started one letter to Ellen Woodward, "Keep at it, Sister Woodward"; another addressed to Josephine Roche in 1936 began, "You old ten-striker." Dewson prodded Clara Beyer about a pending appointment, "Put your left hand on the Bible and write. Is she the best there is in sight or good? . . . Step on the gas Clara and get me any helpful data . . . you can." And Dewson wrote to Woodward in 1935, "I like your little Lucy Howorth. I knew I should. I was prejudiced in her favor." Dewson called on her friends so often that she had to demur to Josephine Roche, "I hope you will not get to feel as Mrs. Roosevelt does that I never open my mouth except to ask her to go somewhere. Everyone seems to think that I can command her time and yours and Frances'."[25]

Women in the network demonstrated the importance of these friendships in other ways as well. Frances Perkins seconded Josephine Roche's nomination for the Cosmopolitan Club. Rose Schneiderman and Jo Coffin sent gloves and roses to Eleanor Roosevelt every year on her birthday. Frances Perkins shared homes with Daisy Harriman and Mary Harriman Rumsey in 1933 and 1934. Ellen Woodward gave autographed copies of Eleanor Roosevelt's *This Is My Story* to her sisters at Christmas.[26] These small gestures are reflections of the strong bonds that developed among women in the network in the 1930s.

Equally important to the successful operation of the network was the sharing of attitudes concerning social reform and the role of women in politics and government. This common ideology held by the members of the network helped to define the group and enabled it to pursue agreed-upon and clearly articulated goals. Except for minor dissension concerning the Equal Rights Amendment (which only two members of the network supported),[27] the network spoke with one voice.

The most important tenet shared by women in the network was that women had special roles to play in society. Eleanor Roosevelt spoke for them all when she concluded, "When all is said and done, women *are* different from men. They are equals in many ways, but they cannot refuse to acknowledge the differences." Certainly the women viewed the differences between men and women in a very positive light. Eleanor Roosevelt hoped for a social order built not only "by the ability and brains of our men," but with "the understanding heart of the women." Daisy Harriman remarked in the early 1930s, "I feel, as do most women, that the government should adjust its policies to the demands of human need." Frances Perkins noted, "It is a generally recognized fact that because women on the whole have a humanitarian viewpoint they excel rather strikingly in service work where the factor of monetary projects is not the objective." Ellen Woodward believed that women's activities in the public sphere were fundamentally influenced by their domestic and family concerns: "Whether we are actively engaged in homemaking or not, we are family conscious."[28] The network's concentration within the field of social welfare shows how strongly the women took their own advice.

Similar high ideals and expectations applied to women's role in the political arena. Molly Dewson believed that women's interests in politics were fundamentally different from men's. Men focused on power and personalities, while women were more interested in social issues and programs. Emily Newell Blair came to the same conclusion after interviewing Molly Dewson in 1934. Blair noted that women politicians measured their success not by how it had benefited them personally, but rather by what it had accomplished in improving social conditions—" . . . talking not at all as politicians but as if they had never quitted their social service work." Eleanor Roosevelt even claimed that women deserved credit for the government's increasing attention to humanitarian concerns in the years since women had won the vote.[29]

By focusing on women's special gifts, women in the network developed a strong consciousness of themselves as women. Eleanor Roosevelt was once asked whether she had ever wanted to be a man, and she replied no. She said she had often wanted to be more effective as a woman, but never felt that trousers would do the trick. Women in the network were proud of their sex and worked hard to expand opportunities for other women in the public sphere. Marion Glass Banister said, "Every time a woman achieves public recognition, I feel that the way is being made easier for her successors . . . In such victory, as it came, I have rejoiced. At each setback, as it came, I have grieved." Congresswoman Mary T. Norton proclaimed: "To prove that women are neither brainless or useless is the job of every woman in America." And Frances Perkins, writing about her decision to accept the position of Secretary of Labor, explained: "I had more sense of obligation to do it for the sake of other women than I did for any other thing. It might be that the door would close on them and that weaker women wouldn't have the chance."[30]

At the same time, the women in the network were acutely conscious of humanitarian concerns, concerns that transcended and ultimately overshadowed their commitment to women. Frances Perkins probably spoke for most of the network when she said, "But so far as I personally was concerned, woman's rights and woman suffrage even were not matters of primary importance. I was much more deeply touched by the problems of poverty, the sorrows of the world, the neglected individuals, the neglected groups and the people who didn't get on well in this great and good civilization."[31]

Very often the women in the network pointedly referred to themselves not just as women, but as human beings. Mary Anderson did not believe that women should have a say only in "women's problems": "I do not know of any matter that is not of interest to women, who are, after all, people and citizens." Congresswoman Mary T. Norton was pleased that the 1938 Fair Labor Standards Act, which set maximum hour and minimum wage standards for all industries involved in interstate commerce, put men and women on an equal footing. And when Eleanor Roosevelt was once asked about sex solidarity, she replied, "It is the person and not the sex which counts."[32]

Friends and allies of women in the network stressed similar themes. Geno Herrick of the National Consumers' League disliked being asked what the New Deal had done for women: "It's done the same thing for them that it has for men. There's nothing feminist or anti-feminist about it." Writing about the participation of women in government in the post-suffrage era, United States Court of Appeals Judge Florence Allen said, "No longer need the achievements of women be viewed from a feminine angle alone. Now that the vote is won, the work of men and women is blended, as it should be, into a human whole."[33] These ideas were widespread among women in public life in the 1930s.

In emphasizing their commitment to social change without regard to sex, the women were sometimes ambivalent about their attitude toward women's issues. In an article she wrote on women in politics for *Good Housekeeping*, Eleanor Roosevelt made an admittedly paradoxical suggestion: "Women must become more conscious of themselves as women and of their ability to function as a group. At the same time they must try to wipe from men's consciousness the need to consider them as a group or as women in their everyday activities, especially as workers in industry or the professions." She concluded that women should unite only for fundamental causes, such as peace or protection of the home, while performing the day-to-day work of the world as individuals.[34]

Molly Dewson echoed this ambivalence. Though she believed that women's interests in politics were fundamentally different from men's, Molly Dewson never subscribed to a "woman's angle" in politics. According to her, there was no political or social issue in which a woman did not have as legitimate an interest as a man. In the 1936 campaign, Dewson wanted Franklin Roosevelt to treat women voters as "people without special feminine interests," and she was pleased that the 1936 Democratic platform did not specifically mention women. "We are now persons," Dewson wrote to a friend.[35]

The women in the network were not the first to face this dilemma of women's divided loyalties, nor the last to face confusion over their own priorities. Today we would call the women in the network "feminists" because of their crusading efforts on behalf of women, but the women in the network consciously shied away from that label. They generally reserved the term for members of the National Women's Party and supporters of the Equal Rights Amendment, using it in a fairly narrow (and slightly pejorative) sense. After spending an entire year mobilizing to get women appointed to the Platform Committee of the Democratic party for the first time, Molly Dewson said in an interview with journalist Ruby Black, "Don't you think that, *for one not a feminist*, I get in some pretty good licks for the girls?" (emphasis added).[36]

Even though Molly Dewson did not consciously consider herself a feminist, her campaigning efforts on behalf of women fit the definition of feminism that she and other members of the network shared. Eleanor Roosevelt said in 1935, "The fundamental purpose of feminism is that women should have equal opportunity and equal rights with every other citizen." Frances Perkins described the "so-called feminist movement" in slightly broader terms: ". . . the movement of women to participate in service to society through politics, through economic security, through social organization." And Emily Newell Blair, in a 1931 article entitled "Putting Women into Politics," remarked, "By feminist here I mean the woman, who, whether she calls herself a feminist or not, wants to make it easier for women to contend with men in politics without disability because they are women."[37]

Mary Anderson hinted at how women in the network resolved this dilemma of definitions and loyalties. In a eulogy to settlement leader Jane Addams, who died in 1935, Anderson wrote: "She was not one of those feminists who are for women alone. Her heart and brilliant mind recognized that as long as one group could be exploited society as a whole must suffer."[38] Anderson's description suggests a wider conception of feminism, one in which the commitment to broader social concerns subsumes the narrower commitment to women's issues.

Historians have followed Mary Anderson's line of thought and coined the term "social feminist" to describe social reformers like Jane Addams who made important contributions to their sex and to society at large, but for whom social reforms ultimately took priority over women's issues.[39] Clearly this definition of social feminism applies to all the women in the network. Within the network, the relative importance of women's issues and social welfare concerns naturally varied among individual women—Emma Guffey Miller, for example, was more concerned with feminism than was Frances Perkins, who identified herself primarily as a social reformer. But all the women in the network shared this dual outlook. These women truly were, to paraphrase Mary Anderson, feminists who were not for women alone.

The social feminism of the women in the network helped to resolve their simultaneous commitments to women's issues and social reform. This shared belief system united the women on an ideological level, just as they were linked on a personal level by patterns of friendship and sisterhood. As Frances Perkins wrote to Molly Dewson in 1953, "Those of us who worked to put together the New Deal are bound together by spiritual ties no one else can understand."[40] These ties, dating back to the Progressive era and greatly strengthened in the 1930s, remained with the women for the rest of their lives.

2

A GENERATIONAL APPROACH

Although there were ample opportunities for the network of women in politics and government to expand and grow within the fertile climate of the early New Deal, it is hard to imagine such an extensive network simply springing into existence in March of 1933. In fact, its roots date to the late nineteenth century, specifically to a generation of women born around 1880. The experiences shared by these women, especially during the decade of the 1920s, played an important part in shaping the development of the network.

Women in the network consciously identified themselves as members of a single generation. When Molly Dewson donated her papers to the Schlesinger Library at Radcliffe College in 1952, she enclosed a short statement on why her records might be useful to later generations of women. Dewson described the "slow and steady development" of women that she had seen during her lifetime, and her own part in it: "Yet I expect now and then some young woman might care to contemplate women's slow emergence from family and domestic affairs alone to public concerns as shown step by step in one person's life. Of course no one life touches more than a tiny part of the social, economic and political field but it is somewhat indicative of the way the generation after the great pioneers applied their principles."[1]

An awareness by participants that they indeed belong to a special generational unit is an important element in defining a generation. Elements that "locate" an individual within a generation include date of birth, socioeconomic class, gender, socialization process in childhood, and access to education. Equally important is the specific historical setting within which these factors are operating. Members of a generation need not be personally acquainted, nor will every individual of similar age and background necessarily share these feelings of belonging to a special group. Rather, the unity of a generation comes from the common experiences of its members within the society as a whole: "Groups of coevals are stamped by some collective experience that permanently distinguishes them from other age groups as they move through time."[2]

Molly Dewson's description of her own generation as "the generation after the great pioneers" identified a continuing tradition of women in public life in the late nineteenth and early twentieth centuries, in which she herself participated. The "great pioneers" Molly Dewson referred to were the first generation of American women to enter the public sphere. For the most part, these women were also the first generation of American women to have access to higher education. Women like Jane Addams (1860-1935), Florence Kelley (1859-1932), M. Carey Thomas (1857-1935), and Julia Lathrop (1858-1932) were prominent leaders of this pioneering generation. To find fulfillment beyond the traditional route of marriage and children, and to make use of their newly acquired education, these women chose careers in the public sector, especially in the fields of social welfare and settlement work. Their pathbreaking struggles to ensure women access to education and the professions made it easier for women of the next generation to expand women's participation in the public sphere.[3]

Women like Molly Dewson (1874-1962) and Frances Perkins (1880-1965) saw themselves as part of this next generation of women, as did most of the women prominent in the New Deal. This second generation of women reformers shared the sense of mission that had characterized their predecessors, and they were determined to consolidate and expand the gains already won. Hilda Worthington Smith thanked Jane Addams's generation for laying "foundations for younger women, like myself, who were trying to follow their leadership, and learn from their experience." Sue Shelton White added: "We should be a bit ashamed to stand on ground won by women in the past without making some effort to honor them by winning a higher and wider field for the future. It is our business. It is a debt we owe."[4]

This second generation of women social reformers made important contributions to the tradition of women in public life. These women participated in the social justice wing of the Progressive coalition and built national reputations as leaders of the emerging settlement house movement. This generation revitalized the suffrage campaign and propelled it to victory in 1920. They also led the crusade for federal legislation such as minimum wage laws, regulation of hours for women workers, and the passage of the Child Labor Amendment.

What of the next generation of women, those born around 1900? Were they ready to take up the concerns of their elders and become the third generation of female social reformers? This next generation of women is harder to categorize than the previous two. In the 1920s many observers complained that young college women were spending their time smoking in public, bobbing their hair, discarding their corsets, and even openly discussing sex, instead of worrying about conditions of workers in sweat-shops.[5] But it is too simplistic to claim that the next generation of women abandoned social reform in favor of private and personal concerns. Women have continued to enter public life in ever-increasing numbers throughout the twentieth century.

As the 1920s and 1930s progressed, however, younger women turned to concerns different from those that had engaged earlier generations of women. These shifting priorities opened a gap between women coming of age in the 1920s and previous generations of women social reformers. The playwright and author Lillian Hellman (who was born in 1905) captured her generation's spirit of change in a description of the New York literary world in the 1920s:

> By the time I grew up the fight for the emancipation of women, their rights under the law, in the office, in bed, was stale stuff. My generation didn't think much about the place or the problems of women, were not conscious that the designs we saw around us had so recently been formed that we were still part of the formation. (Five or ten years' difference in age was a greater separation between people in the 1920's, perhaps because the older generation had gone through the war.) . . . I was too young to be grateful for how much I owed them in the battle of something-or-other in the war for equality.[6]

The conditions that had shaped and influenced Molly Dewson's and Frances Perkins's generation in the Progressive period were no longer operating in the 1920s.

What happened to the generations of American women who came of age after 1920 is beyond the scope of this study. It is women of the generation born in the 1870s and 1880s who engage our attention. These women became active in social reform during the Progressive period, kept alive the Progressive faith in the hostile 1920s, and capped their careers with participation in the New Deal. A particular set of circumstances influenced the patterns of their lives: date of birth, access to education, common choices to combine marriage and career, participation in the woman suffrage campaign, involvement in social welfare activities and political activities in the 1920s. A generational approach embracing these factors suggests the complex historical setting out of which the New Deal network developed.

In tracing the collective experiences of a generation of women, date of birth is an obvious initial consideration. As table 1 shows, most of the women in the network were approximately the same age.[7] The average date of birth was late 1881, and the median lay between 1881 and 1882. Translated into personal terms, Frances Perkins (born in 1880) and Eleanor Roosevelt (1884) were close to the average. Molly Dewson (1874), Grace Abbott (1878), and Caroline O'Day (1869) were among the older members of the group; Ellen Woodward (1887), Clara Beyer (1892), and Hilda Worthington Smith (1888) were among the younger. The youngest, Dorothy McAlister, was born in 1900, but her education, social welfare orientation, and political work placed her squarely within this generation.[8] By the time of the New Deal (1933), the average woman in the network was fifty-two years old. This, of course, differs from the stereotype of eager young (male) workers flocking to the government in the 1930s, but conforms to the pattern that women in positions of power are generally older and more experienced than their male counterparts.[9]

A formative experience shared by many women in the New Deal network, one that set them apart from the general population (both male and female), was their access to higher education. More than 70 percent of these women attended college; almost half of the college graduates went on to graduate school. Table 2 shows college enrollments for men and women in this period. In 1890 only one of every fifty women attended college; in that year, less than 3,000 women actually received degrees. (The comparable figure for men was 13,000.) Between 1890 and 1910, female college enrollment almost tripled.[10] The educational backgrounds of the women in the network reflected this widening of women's

Table 1. Date of birth by decade.

Decade of birth	Number of women
1865-1874	6
1875-1884	10
1885-1894	10
1895-1904	2

Source: Appendix C.

Table 2. Women enrolled in institutions of higher learning, regular session, 1870-1958.

Year	Number of women enrolled (thousands)	Percent of all women aged 18-21	Percent of all students enrolled
1870	11	0.7	21.0
1880	40	1.9	33.4
1890	56	2.2	35.9
1900	85	2.8	36.8
1910	140	3.8	39.6
1920	283	7.6	47.3
1930	481	10.5	43.7
1940	601	12.2	40.2
1950	806	17.9	30.2
1958	1148	23.0	35.2

Source: Mabel Newcomer, A Century of Higher Education for American Women (New York: Harper Brothers, 1959), 46. Copyright 1959 by Mabel Newcomer. Reprinted by permission of Harper & Row, Publishers, Inc.

opportunities for a college education: all of the women in the network born after 1885 went to college, while substantial numbers of those born in the 1870s did not.

The expansion of higher education was a far-reaching development for women in the late nineteenth and early twentieth centuries. Demands for education for women (and by extension, access to the male realm of knowledge and public affairs) have been an important element in the emergence of feminism from Mary Wollstonecraft's time through the present. During the first half of the nineteenth century, women won the right to education on the secondary level, either in public schools or in the more famous female seminaries such as Emma Willard's school in Troy, New York. But if a young woman wanted to go beyond the secondary level prior to the Civil War, only Oberlin and Antioch were open to her.

In the years after the Civil War, much progress was made. Women's colleges like Vassar (1865), Smith (1875), and Wellesley (1875) were founded. Although women's colleges in the East received much attention, these single-sex colleges accounted for only a minority of female college students. In fact, 70 percent of all college women in the late nineteenth century attended coeducational institutions. Major universities such as Boston University, Cornell, and the Universities of Wisconsin and Michigan began admitting women in the late 1860s and 1870s. In addition, late nineteenth century coordinate colleges like the Radcliffe Annex to Harvard allowed women to attend college with men. Such advances, while impressive, were not universal: this expansion of higher education was strictly limited to small numbers of women of the middle class.[11]

The colleges attended by the women in the network fit these general patterns. One-fourth of the women attended Seven Sisters colleges. Bryn Mawr led with three alumnae: Emma Guffey Miller, Hilda Worthington Smith, and Dorothy McAlister. Other Seven Sisters colleges were represented by Molly Dewson (Wellesley), Frances Perkins (Mount Holyoke), Josephine Roche (Vassar), and Mary Harriman Rumsey (Barnard). The majority of women in the network attended institutions other than Eastern women's colleges. Grace Abbott graduated from Grand Island College in Nebraska, Ellen Woodward from Sans Souci Women's College in South Carolina, Clara Beyer from the University of California, and Katharine Lenroot from the University of Wisconsin.

Although higher education was important for many members of the network, some of the most prominent of the women never attended college. Eleanor Roosevelt's education ended after the years she spent at the Allenswood School in England during her teens; Mary Anderson, Daisy Harriman, Rose Schneiderman, Jo Coffin, Marion Glass Banister, Lucille Foster McMillin, and Nellie Tayloe Ross likewise never had the chance to attend college. With the exception of Mary Harriman Rumsey, who was the first woman in her family to attend college, women from families of the upper classes (like Eleanor Roosevelt or Daisy Harriman) and the working classes (Mary Anderson, Jo Coffin, and Rose Schneiderman) generally did not go to college in this period.

The diversity in the college backgrounds of the women in the network is not found with respect to their graduate education. Of the nine who did graduate work, an astonishing six were at Columbia between 1910 and 1920: Jane Hoey, Lucy Somerville Howorth, Mary LaDame, Frances Perkins, Josephine Roche, and Hilda Worthington Smith. They concentrated in the fields of economics, sociology, political science, and social work. Perkins and Roche met in Professor E. R. A. Seligman's graduate seminar in economics at Columbia in 1910, the same year when Frances Perkins first met Franklin Roosevelt.[12] Convergence within certain professional schools supports a prior study of New Deal intelligentsia (male and female) which found similar patterns in educational backgrounds.[13] Women in the network also did graduate work at the University of Chicago, the New York School of Social Work, Harvard University, New York University, the University of California, Bryn Mawr College, the University of Nebraska, and two law schools in the South.

At a time when so few men and women went on to higher education, those who did, especially women, must have felt like a class apart. Molly

Dewson had told her family she "ached" to go to college, even though she had never met a female college graduate. What were women like Dewson to do with the educations they had fought so hard to secure? The answer was not obvious. Jane Addams candidly described the "identity crisis" that followed her graduation from Rockford College in 1881. It was eight years before she finally embarked on her career at Hull House in Chicago.[14]

Many women of the second generation of college graduates experienced similar periods of indecision and self-doubt: Molly Dewson and Frances Perkins are two ready examples.[15] Hilda Worthington Smith, a 1910 graduate of Bryn Mawr, described the sense of drift: "I did not know what I wanted to do. Never had I felt so restless and unhappy. I tried to reconcile myself to the traditional idea of being a daughter at home, a companion to my mother . . . In casting about for a future field of interest, it was a relief to realize that some of my friends were as confused as I, in regard to the work they wanted to do." Seven years later she remained uncertain about her future: "I was twenty-eight, I remembered, and still drifting, undecided."[16]

Hilda Worthington Smith ended her indecision by becoming a specialist in workers' education. In choosing this path, she joined a small but growing number of educated middle-class women who were taking advantage of new opportunities for professional work outside the home. During the early twentieth century, young, single, and poor women predominated in the female work force; they worked out of economic necessity, not for personal fulfillment. These women worked for wages only until they married, when they returned to the home as full-time housewives. After 1900, however, these temporary women workers were joined by small numbers of middle-class, educated women who hoped to pursue careers. Some of these educated women entered the fields of law and medicine; others continued their education at the graduate level, often returning to the women's colleges to teach. For the most part, women entered professions that were already dominated by women: teaching, social work, library science, and nursing (table 3).

Even choices of traditional women's fields such as social work and teaching often met resistance from families unaccustomed to daughters who planned to earn their living. Hilda Worthington Smith's mother had strong objections to her daughter's pursuing any career at all. In the 1910s it was still bold for a middle-class daughter to choose full-time employment rather than remaining a "daughter at home."[17]

Another major dilemma for women of this generation was reconciling marriage and career. For the select group of women who pursued profes-

A GENERATIONAL APPROACH

Table 3.   Women in selected professional occupations.

Occupation	Percentage of all workers						
	1900	1910	1920	1930	1940	1950	1960
Lawyers	—	1.0	1.4	2.1	2.4	3.5	3.5
College presidents, professors	—	19.0	30.0	32.0	27.0	23.0	19.0
Clergy	4.4	1.0	2.6	4.3	2.2	8.5	5.8
Doctors	—	6.0	5.0	4.0	4.6	6.1	6.8
Engineers	—	—	—	—	0.3	1.2	0.8
Dentists	—	3.1	3.2	1.8	1.5	2.7	2.1
Biologists	—	—	—	—	—	27.0	28.0
Mathematicians	—	—	—	—	—	38.0	26.4
Physicists	—	—	—	—	—	6.5	4.2
Librarians	—	79.0	88.0	91.0	89.0	89.0	85.0
Nurses	94.0	93.0	96.0	98.0	98.0	98.0	97.0
Social workers	—	52.0	62.0	68.0	67.0	66.0	57.0

Source: Cynthia Fuchs Epstein, *Woman's Place: Options and Limits in Professional Careers* (Berkeley: University of California Press, 1971), 7.

sional careers in the early twentieth century, many made the decision not to marry. This was not an uncommon choice for early women college graduates: in 1915 only 39 percent of all living alumnae from the eight major women's colleges and Cornell had married.[18]

Of the twenty-eight women in the network, ten never married. The women who remained single gave a variety of reasons for their decisions. Hilda Worthington Smith wrote, "Every year I watched the men I knew marry other women, and found that I did not care."[19] As a young girl, Mary Anderson had assumed she would marry, "but somewhere I lost myself in my work and never felt that marriage would give me the security I wanted. I thought that through the trade union movement we working women could get better conditions and security of mind."[20]

Sue Shelton White showed more ambivalence about marriage. In a revealing essay in *The Nation* in 1927, written anonymously and only recently attributed to White, she discussed the formative influences on her personal development. White ended with her thoughts on marriage: "I have not married. I have had my chances—one of the first being a station agent who insisted on 'giving me a home.' I suspected that he needed assistance in checking freight bills at the depot. I have also had my disappointments—one especially. He is still singing in the choir and is president of a Kiwanis Club. Without regard to my register of eligibles, I believe I could not now be induced to enter into the present legal status of marriage." White concluded, "Marriage is too much of a compromise; it lops off a woman's life as an individual. Yet renunciation too is a lopping off. We choose between the frying-pan and the fire—both very uncomfortable."[21]

The decision not to marry did not necessarily preclude a satisfying personal life. Single professional women of this generation often shared their homes and their lives with other like-minded women on a fairly permanent basis. Two sisters sometimes lived together, as Grace and Edith Abbott did after Grace returned to the University of Chicago in 1934. At times during her tenure in Washington, Mary Anderson lived with her sister Anna and various government colleagues. Sue Shelton White shared a similar arrangement with Florence Armstrong, a government economist.[22]

Sometimes the bonds were even stronger. Molly Dewson maintained a lifelong relationship with a friend and companion, Mary ("Polly") Porter. These two women met while running a home for delinquent girls in the 1910s and spent the rest of their lives together, some fifty years, sharing homes in Connecticut, New York City, and a summer place in Castine, Maine. Molly Dewson's primary emotional fulfillment came from her long and devoted association with Polly Porter.[23]

In many ways it was easier for a woman of Dewson's generation to spend her life living with another woman than it would be for later generations of women. Throughout the nineteenth century and into the early twentieth, women looked to other women for their closest and most intimate friendships. Many of the settlement houses were predominantly all-female communities. Moreover, living with another woman was a common and respectable life-style, especially for upper-middle-class professional and educated women. There was even a phrase to describe such arrangements—"Boston marriages."[24]

After the popularization of Freudian ideas during the 1920s, however, young women were encouraged to find emotional fulfillment and satisfaction primarily in relationships with men rather than women; unmarried women were seen as neurotic, sex-starved spinsters in the popular mind.[25] This did not bother Molly Dewson, who wrote jokingly to Sue Shelton White, "After all us old maids have been repaid in our secret hearts for what we sacrificed to some principles and standards thro' which I suppose we sublimated the sex instinct." Dewson and White had made their own choices and were not troubled by conventional expectations, Freudian or otherwise, for women. Dewson wrote with some spirit in her thirtieth-reunion classbook for Wellesley: "Yes I have no children. And I hope it will not be considered sour grapes as it undoubtedly is, for me to plaintively hope that at our reunion all '97s will think of themselves as human individuals rather than as proud progenitors or as part of some human conglomeration."[26]

For most American women, however, marriage would be a significant part of the female life cycle. Two-thirds of the women in the network were married at some point during their adult lives, a figure much higher than the usual estimates of women who combined marriage and career in the early twentieth century. By the 1930s, the number of women in the network who were still married had been cut in half. Two marriages had ended in divorce: Josephine Roche's to Edward Hale Bierstadt after two years, and Ruth Bryan Owen's first marriage to Homer Leavitt. Many more marriages had been ended by death than by divorce: by the time of the New Deal, the network counted nine widows.

Often it was the death of a spouse that propelled these women into full-time careers: economic necessity, rather than feminism, forced women to break out of traditional patterns and expectations for their sex. For example, Ellen Sullivan Woodward at first had a fairly conventional marriage, giving piano lessons to earn pin money while raising a child. She did manage her husband's campaign for a local judgeship, but her life revolved primarily around home and family. Only when Woodward was widowed at age thirty-eight with a teenage son to raise did she turn to a career in politics and social welfare administration to support herself. Similarly, Daisy Harriman, Nellie Tayloe Ross, Lucille Foster McMillin, and Ruth Bryan Owen expanded their professional activities for economic and personal reasons after the deaths of their husbands.[27]

Women in the network also demonstrated a generally low fertility rate; as a group, they had significantly fewer children than the national average. Here women in the network reflected a well-established pattern: from 1800 to 1900 the birth rate for white women in America fell 40 percent.[28] Of the eighteen women who married, sixteen had children, and the average number of children per married woman was 2.2. More than one-third of the women in the network who had children had only one child, and most of the rest spaced the births of their children. This suggests that many women of their generation consciously limited family size through birth control, probably to give the women more time to pursue outside activities.[29] Moreover, by the time the women became most active in their professional careers (in the 1920s and 1930s), their children were already full grown. Both factors—having fewer children and delaying full-time professional activity until children were older—made the conflict between home duties and professional activities less acute for these women.

Frances Perkins spoke for many members of her generation in her attitudes toward marriage and career. She remembered, "The women that I knew of my generation who had a career and a family were practically all of them accidents and had no deliberate purpose at all. That was true of me—it was pure accident." (Perkins was speaking of careers, not children, as unplanned accidents.) Perkins had been reluctant to marry ("I liked life better in a single harness") but felt it was something she should do sooner or later.[30] When she married at age thirty-three, she had never heard the word "career" and did not know that she had one. She kept her given name, and continued to work after her daughter was born: "I suppose I had been somewhat touched by feminist ideas and that was one of the reasons I kept my maiden name. My whole generation was, I suppose, the first generation that openly and actively asserted—at least some of us did—the separateness of women and their personal independence in the family relationship."[31]

At a testimonial luncheon given in her honor in 1929, Frances Perkins gave a spontaneous speech about what her marriage had meant to her career. Perkins's remarks provide a rare statement on the relation between marriage and career for a woman of her generation:

> Above all, as a background and a contribution to my work, I have had that greatest blessing anyone can have, man or woman. I have had a happy personal life. I have the friendship of a husband who has put a brilliant mind to work on some of my knotty problems, and let me have the praise. I have had a good daughter, who has grown to girlhood without being a troublesome child. And I am thankful indeed for my good fortune in the women who have helped me bring up my child and take care of my home, for I am one of those who believe that, after all, some one must look well into the ways of the household. There is no coin in which I can repay those fine and loyal helpers who have worked for me and with me in that intimate way. No one succeeds in a career without the help of many people, and I have had my satisfaction of achievement through the cooperation and the good-will of those who have made it possible.[32]

The omissions from Perkins's description of married life were perhaps as significant as the inclusions. After 1918 her husband became seriously ill and spent the rest of his life in and out of mental institutions. Out of necessity, Perkins became the main family breadwinner.[33] Clearly many considerations were involved in juggling marriage and career for the women in the network.

Marriage appeared in a different light in correspondence between Molly Dewson and Clara Beyer. Dewson and Beyer had worked together in the New York Consumers' League on minimum wage legislation and other social welfare causes. When Beyer married in 1920, Dewson asked her whether she planned to keep up her career: "Spare time from your wedding journey to tell me that you are modern and plan to return to it." When Beyer took several years off to raise three children, Dewson bombarded her with letters like, "Yet it is grand to bring up such swell lads but you know even in Soviet Russia it is not *all*." Beyer responded somewhat acidly: "I was patting myself on the back for participating, as I thought, in the world's work by bringing up three future leaders and here you come along and destroy all my illusions. We poor married women have a hard time measuring up to standards set by our unencumbered sisters and when we think we have succeeded we are brought to earth with a bang."[34]

The story had a happy ending for both women. In 1928, when her children were in school, Clara Beyer returned to work at the Children's Bureau, prompting Dewson to write, "Well one woman whom we thought was lost to domesticity has been salvaged for the world's work." Beyer believed that once children were in school, mothers could return to work. Even though neighbors gossiped about Beyer's decision, Beyer herself noted she was "second to none" in taking care of her children while she was working. Parenthetically, Beyer's friends noted that she had enough energy for at least three full-time jobs.[35]

In general, the personal lives of women in the network, married or unmarried, seem to have provided these women with the strength and emotional support to pursue their active careers. Yet the evidence remains sketchy, suggesting that these women consciously separated their personal from their professional lives. Perhaps women of this generation felt that women had too often been judged solely on their accomplishments as wives, mothers, and dutiful daughters, rather than on their public achievements. Alternatively, these women might not have foreseen that future generations would be interested in their personal lives. Just as likely, the women consciously chose not to share the tensions and rewards of this side of their lives with posterity.

Whether to marry or have children, how to balance personal and professional commitments are dilemmas faced by every generation of women. Two historical developments affected this generation of women in particular: the woman suffrage campaign and World War I. Their experiences in these events further defined this group of women as a generational unit.

By the early twentieth century, the woman suffrage movement had mobilized more women than any other reform in American history. Women's demand for the vote was first enunciated at the Seneca Falls Convention in 1848. During the rest of the century, activists such as Elizabeth Cady Stanton, Susan B. Anthony, and Lucy Stone worked tirelessly to promote the cause of woman suffrage, but their pleas were deemed far too radical to be taken seriously by the society as a whole. Factionalism in the women's movement further weakened the cause. As late as 1910, only four states had given women the vote.

The Progressive period provided a more supportive climate for women's reform than had the nineteenth century, and the suffrage movement steadily gained strength after 1900. Several factors contributed to this new success. A younger generation of suffrage leaders, armed with fresh ideas for suffrage parades and open-air meetings, revitalized the movement. Women also argued for the vote in a new, more effective manner: instead of stressing women's absolute right to the vote, women emphasized what they would do with the vote. Such an argument was persuasive in a period of generalized reform. Finally, as public-minded women realized it would be easier to accomplish their broad reform goals if they had the vote, a broad coalition of women's organizations, ranging from the General Federation of Women's Clubs to the Socialist Party, made winning the vote their number one priority after 1914. By that year, the National American Woman Suffrage Association (NAWSA), the largest of the suffrage organizations, claimed more than two million members.[36]

Suffrage as a mass movement influenced several generations of American women, but it had especially large implications for the women who were to serve in the New Deal. More than half held leadership positions in the suffrage movement, and actual participation was probably even higher. Some women in the network came late to the suffrage cause (Eleanor Roosevelt did not convert until World War I), but none of the network was involved in the organized antisuffrage campaign. The only split in the network came over the tactics necessary to win the vote. Foreshadowing the later breakdown on the Equal Rights Amendment, most women were members of the moderate NAWSA headed by Carrie Chapman Catt, but two (Emma Guffey Miller and Sue Shelton White) belonged to the National Women's Party, the militant wing of the suffrage movement.

Many years later Molly Dewson looked back fondly on "the old suffrage days when all we asked was an opportunity to serve." Dewson was active in the Massachusetts Woman Suffrage Association. While attending the 1914 NAWSA convention, she met Emily Newell Blair, Florence Allen (appointed to the United States Court of Appeals in 1934 at Dewson's suggestion), and the noted Southern suffragist Nellie Nugent Somerville (mother of Lucy Somerville Howorth, whose appointment to the Veterans' Administration Board of Appeals Dewson later arranged). Grace Abbott belonged to the second generation of women in her family to participate in the suffrage movement: her mother was an early suffragist, and Susan B. Anthony stayed in the Abbott home when Grace was a child. Daisy Harriman led a woman suffrage parade down Fifth Avenue in New York in 1912. Emma Guffey Miller was active in the Rhode Island fight, and Rose Schneiderman was the chairman of the Industrial Section of the Woman Suffrage party in New York City. Sue Shelton White led the final stages of the state suffrage campaign in Tennessee in 1920.[37]

Frances Perkins and Hilda Worthington Smith both left recollections of what the suffrage movement meant to them personally and to their generation. Frances Perkins emphasized the importance of suffrage to women who were part of the campaign: "The friendships that were formed among women who were in that suffrage movement have been the most lasting and enduring friendships—solid, substantial, loyal—that I have ever seen anywhere. The women learned to like each other in that suffrage movement." As proof of this, Perkins asserted, these same women stood by her when she was under political attack in the late 1930s.[38] Perkins also noticed that many techniques first used in the suffrage movement were later employed successfully by the Women's Division of the Democratic party.[39]

Hilda Worthington Smith remembered the suffrage movement from a slightly different perspective. Smith's recollections of the movement were influenced by her own indecision regarding a career at the time, but they nonetheless illustrate the wider implications of suffrage:

> The suffrage seemed like an opening door to the world of women's professional work, and to wider recognition for useful community service. I was eager to go through this door myself, and had had enough trouble to gain individual freedom to know what the wider movement meant for women. In later years, as I was associated with younger women who stepped blithely from college into well-recognized professional work, I saw that suffrage, with all its long struggle, meant little to them, and that they regarded a strong feminist attitude, typical of my generation, as ludicrous. They never had to fight for their freedom, I knew, and therefore took their good fortune for granted.[40]

In this way did the suffrage campaign set one generation apart from another.

Another experience shared by many women in this generation was participation in patriotic activities during World War I. Half of the women in the network were active in the war effort. Historians have noted the New Deal's institutional debt to the country's experiences in World War I;[41] many women in the network gained important training and experience during the war as well. Eleanor Roosevelt's work during World War I reoriented her life toward humanitarian and social service.[42] For others, war work was equally important. Molly Dewson, Daisy Harriman, and Ruth Bryan Owen served with the Red Cross in France, England, and Egypt, respectively; Jane Hoey, Lucy Somerville Howorth, and Mary T. Norton were active in the Red Cross in this country. Mary Anderson got her start in government service with the wartime Women in Industry Committee from 1918 to 1919. Mary LaDame, Marion Glass Banister, Clara Beyer, Emily Newell Blair, Mary Harriman Rumsey, and Josephine Roche all served on various relief committees and projects. Many of these women, if they were still alive and active, would serve in World War II as well.[43]

World War I also gave the final push to the drive for woman suffrage. The inconsistency of fighting to make the world safe for democracy while half of the domestic population remained disfranchised became clearer to the American people. In part, the vote was token recognition of women's contributions to the war effort. Equally important was a shift to militant tactics by one wing of the suffrage movement after 1917. Activities such as round-the-clock picketing, burning Woodrow Wilson's speeches, and women chaining themselves to the White House fence led to the arrests and imprisonment of prominent women leaders. Once in jail, the women promptly went on a hunger strike, imitating their sisters in the militant English suffragist movement. Prison officials responded by force-feeding the militants, a physically harmful and humiliating experience for the women. Public outcry over the treatment these women received, combined with respect for the strength of their convictions in the face of such terrible prison conditions, gave a final push to the suffrage cause. Women in public life throughout the country rejoiced when the Nineteenth Amendment finally was ratified on August 26, 1920.[44]

Historians no longer believe that the organized women's movement fell apart after women won the vote, nor do they claim that the reform spirit completely disappeared during the 1920s. Progressivism was generally in eclipse during the period between the World War and the New Deal, but women in the network were among those who struggled to keep the Progressive spirit alive in the hostile climate of the 1920s. Although their social welfare activity had little immediate impact, it did lay the groundwork for many programs later enacted by the New Deal.[45] As part of this small band of social reformers, women in the network gained experience and made contacts they would later use in the New Deal. It was in the 1920s, therefore, that the network itself began to take shape.

New York was the center for the emergence of the network in the 1920s: ten women, more than one-third of the New Deal network, were active in social welfare circles there. National leadership for the social welfare movement was firmly centered in New York in the 1920s. Except for the National Women's Trade Union of Chicago, major voluntary associations such as the National Consumers' League, the National Child Labor Committee, Paul Kellogg's Survey Associates, and the American Association for Labor Legislation had their headquarters in New York or Washington. New York predominated, as historian Clarke Chambers observed: "It was in New York that day-to-day direction was asserted, and this by a relative handful of leaders all of whom knew each other intimately, if not always with affection."[46]

Frances Perkins described New York in the 1920s as "a small world": "The people who did anything were few in number, so that no matter what they did, whether it was art, music, the drama, social work, religion, they all touched each other sooner or later." Molly Dewson is a case in point. Grace Abbott asked Dewson to leave the Consumers' League and come to Washington as her assistant at the Children's Bureau in 1922 ("Do come—I'll do everything I can to make you happy and comfortable and can promise to keep you hard at work"), but Dewson decided to stay in New York where all her friends and contacts were.[47]

As Civic Secretary of the Women's City Club and Research Secretary of the National Consumers' League in the 1920s, Dewson had remarkable access to women. She regularly worked with women from the Women's Trade Union League, the League of Women Voters, the Industrial Board of the Young Women's Christian Association, the American Association for Labor Legislation, the Women's Christian Temperance Union, the New York Child Labor Committee, and women's clubs like the Business and Professional Women and the Federation of Women's Clubs. In this manner, Dewson met all the leading women in the community—access she would take advantage of in the 1930s.[48]

Friendship and trust developed among the women who worked together in New York in the 1920s. These women thought of themselves as part of a large family bound together by an almost mystical commitment to social reform. At a testimonial luncheon in her honor in 1929, Frances Perkins elaborated on this sense of community and solidarity:

I take it that we are gathered not so much to celebrate Frances Perkins, the person, as we are to celebrate Frances Perkins as the symbol of an idea. It is an idea that has been at work among us for many years—the idea that social justice is possible in a great industrial community . . . How can I express what I owe the loyalty, the intelligence, and the wisdom of the women of this state, both organized and unorganized? There is, a little above the rest, that group who, stealing the phrase from dear Mary Dreier's Christmas card, have called ourselves—humorously, I hope—The Children of Light. That cordial, interlocking group of minds has meant much to all of us who have been welcomed to the inner conference of those who were trying to decide the best thing to do this year, and next year, and the year after, for the cause of industrial reform.[49]

Two principal components of this "cordial, interlocking group of minds" were the Women's Trade Union League (WTUL) and the National Consumers' League (NCL). The WTUL was founded in 1903 to improve industrial conditions for women workers, and to encourage the organization of women workers into trade unions as affiliates of the American Federation of Labor. The WTUL was the only national organization dedicated to the unionization of women workers in the early twentieth century, a monumental task far beyond the capabilities of one group. The WTUL did what it could on the local and national levels—it hired full-time organizers to work in various trades, lobbied for protective legislation for women workers, and set up educational classes for working-class women at the WTUL clubhouse on Lexington Avenue in New York. Some of the League's strongest action came in support of women workers on strike. During the 1909-1910 strike of shirtwaist workers in the New York garment industry, the WTUL provided crucial support by organizing picket lines, raising money for strike funds, and recruiting workers for the union. The WTUL's participation in the 1909-1910 strike was probably its most important contribution to the cause of working women in the Progressive era.

While the WTUL pursued trade union organization as a primary function, the organization also stressed political action to secure equal industrial rights for women. In many ways this dual emphasis reflected the membership of the WTUL, which was composed equally of working women and wealthy women (called "Allies") who were interested in labor issues. Not surprisingly, conflicts over priorities occurred. The women workers usually wanted the League to concentrate its limited resources on union membership drives and support for striking women. The Allies, led by WTUL president Margaret Dreier Robins, were often more interested in securing protective legislation as the League's main goal. Since these wealthy women contributed most of the money for the budget and had more time to volunteer to the group, a gradual shift in WTUL philosophy toward legislation and education over union organizing occurred after 1913.[50]

The WTUL also had an important influence on the development of the network. Mary Anderson and Rose Schneiderman, who worked together closely in the New Deal, first met through the WTUL. Mary Anderson became active in the League while she was working in the garment industry in Chicago. For her, and many others, WTUL activities meant more than just union organizing: "We began to feel that we were part of something that was more important than just our own problems." Cap-maker Rose Schneiderman joined the WTUL in New York around 1907 and represented the New York League at a memorial rally for the 143 women workers killed in the Triangle Shirtwaist fire in 1911, one of the worst industrial accidents of the early twentieth century. There Schneiderman first met Frances Perkins, who was representing the Consumers' League. Perkins later remembered, "But it was little Rose Schneiderman [she was only four and a half feet tall] who, I think, impressed on most of us the tragedy of this and the fact that it was imperative to do something."[51] Schneiderman and Anderson retained their WTUL outlook throughout their careers, just as Molly Dewson and Frances Perkins always approached problems from the Consumers' League point of view.

Eleanor Roosevelt was also quite active in the WTUL in the 1920s, both with the national organization and the New York League. She invited the WTUL to hold its twenty-fifth anniversary picnic in 1929 at Hyde Park and made sure that the women workers had a chance to meet Governor Roosevelt. In the winter of 1932-33, Eleanor Roosevelt worked closely with Jo Coffin to set up centers for unemployed women in New York under WTUL auspices. Eleanor Roosevelt's association with the WTUL marked a significant broadening of her outlook, since she had never before worked with women outside her social class. As a result of her work with the WTUL, Eleanor Roosevelt soon considered women like Mary Anderson, Rose Schneiderman, Maud Swartz, and Jo Coffin her friends. Many of these women became her associates in the New Deal as well.[52]

The National Consumers' League (NCL) played an even greater role in the development of the network in the 1920s. Founded in 1899, the NCL was profoundly influenced by Florence Kelley, its general secretary from 1899 until her death in 1932. The slogan of the NCL, "investigate, agitate, legislate," reflected its philosophy that if people were educated to social ills, they would work to cure them. Its orientation was toward working on behalf of labor rather than banding together to fight high prices or industrial concentration.

Early activities of the Consumers' League included publishing a "white list" of employers whose establishments met minimum standards of hygiene and fairness, helping Louis Brandeis prepare the brief in support of limiting hours for women workers in *Muller* v. *Oregon* in 1907, and working for the establishment of the Children's Bureau in 1912. In the 1920s the NCL lobbied for passage of the Child Labor Amendment and minimum wage-maximum hours legislation for women workers.[53] Another important, though unintentional, by-product of Consumers' League activity was the training of future government administrators. A number of NCL alumnae joined government service in the 1920s and 1930s.[54] For many of them, like Frances Perkins, their commitment to the Consumers' League stayed with them throughout their careers. In 1939 Frances Perkins remarked that she did not feel that she personally had been appointed as Secretary of Labor, "but that it was the Consumers' League who was appointed, and that I was merely the symbol who happened to be at hand, able and willing to serve at the moment."[55]

Florence Kelley strongly influenced the next generation of women reformers, especially women in the network. Kelley was the daughter of a liberal Pennsylvania Congressman and a strong Quaker mother. She received a bachelor's degree from Cornell in 1882, and then went on to the University of Zurich for graduate studies. A marriage to a Russian medical student produced three children but ended in divorce. In 1891 Kelley became a resident at Hull House and was hired as an investigator for the Illinois Bureau of Labor Statistics; she played a large role in pushing through the 1893 Illinois law limiting hours of work for women. In 1899 she left Chicago and Hull House to become National Secretary of the NCL. Keeping up her contacts with the settlement movement, Florence Kelley moved into Lillian Wald's Henry Street Settlement in New York. She remained with the Consumers' League until her death in 1932.[56]

It is easy to see how women like Molly Dewson and Clara Beyer looked upon Kelley as their spiritual foremother, and drew inspiration from her courage and dedication. Frances Perkins referred to Florence Kelley as "that mother of us all" and "the head of the family in this enterprise which binds us all together." Perkins had first decided on a career in social reform after she heard Florence Kelley speak at Mount Holyoke in 1902. For the next thirty years, Perkins received encouragement and prodding from her first mentor: "Countless times Mrs. Kelley's steely look and steady, 'Frances, you've got to do it!' have meant the difference between doing it that year and not doing it at all."[57]

In addition to the training and friendships they gained from voluntary associations like the National Consumers' League and the Women's Trade Union League, women in the network also shared the experience of entering social work at a time when the profession was in its infancy. Frances Perkins remembered what social work was like then:

> It seems odd to people today who regard the social worker as a queer kind of profession which would be out of everything of any interest. But in those days social work was new and rare and we were very interesting people to the rest of the world. Other people were fascinated by the experiences of a social worker and would ask people to meet you because you were a social worker and knew such interesting things about the poor. We were not ostracized. We were very much desired. There weren't many of them. They were few and far between. So we knew everybody.[58]

Perkins started in social work without any special training: "The truth is that social work was so new, so undefined, that almost any energetic young person of good will could pitch in and do what seemed best." As Frances Perkins did, most women in the network came to social work after having done graduate work in political science or economics, or through organizations like the Russell Sage Foundation or the Consumers' League. Only two women in the network, Jane Hoey and Hilda Worthington Smith, had professional training in social work.[59]

The outlook these women brought to social work reflected the Progressive spirit which dominated American reform in the early twentieth century. Hilda Worthington Smith recalled her perspective on social work in 1913: "By this time I began to think of the city as a great social laboratory—to have a sense of New York's submerged population . . . The task of social work seemed overwhelming." In searching for the causes of poverty, social workers like Smith stressed the social and economic environment: the fault lay not with the individual, but with conditions that could be ameliorated by legislation and social action. This early group of social workers felt a strong impulse toward reform which stayed with them for the rest of their professional careers.[60]

By the 1920s, however, social work was undergoing fundamental changes. The profession began to concentrate less on improving the social environment through reform, and more on curing the problems of individuals. This shift was the result of several factors. The 1920s saw more hostility to reform than had the Progressive era. The development of the social casework method focused attention on the individual rather than on society, as did the growth of psychiatric social work in the 1920s. The new emphasis on formal graduate training reflected the increasing preoccupation with professionalism. A group professional identity, maintained through professional associations like the National Conference of Social Work, began to emerge in the 1920s.[61]

In many ways, the changes occurring in social work in the 1920s paralleled the emerging differences between generations of American women: in both cases individual, specific concerns came to predominate over broader social issues. Most women in the network, however, were unaffected by the professionalization and changing priorities of social work in the 1920s. Just as the women in the network continued agitation for social reform in the 1920s while the younger generation of women turned their attention elsewhere, so did they keep alive the traditional reformist approach to social work.[62]

Activities in the political sphere were equally important to the development of the network. The decade of the 1920s was a testing time for women in political life—what would their postsuffrage roles be? Many women in the network helped to answer that question in the 1920s, and beyond.[63]

Often the women in the network were predisposed to politics because they had grown up in or married into families where politics was an important part of day-to-day life. Ellen Sullivan Woodward and Katharine Lenroot were daughters of United States senators. Woodward's father had served briefly as the senator from Mississippi, and she spent several years of her childhood in Washington; Katharine Lenroot was the daughter of the prominent Wisconsin Republican leader, Irving Lenroot. Emma Guffey Miller and Marion Glass Banister were the sisters of Senator Joseph Guffey of Pennsylvania and Senator Carter Glass of Virginia, respectively. Ruth Bryan Owen was the daughter of William Jennings Bryan, and Lucille Foster McMillin had been married to a Tennessee congressman. Carolyn Wolfe and Dorothy McAlister were both wives of elected state supreme court justices. Grace Abbott's father had been the first lieutenant governor of Nebraska, and Lucy Somerville Howorth was the daughter of Nellie Nugent Somerville, noted suffragist and first woman member of the Mississippi legislature. Nellie Tayloe Ross was the wife of the governor of Wyoming before she succeeded him when he died. And Jane Hoey's brother was a Tammany political leader in New York City.[64]

Such familiarity with politics set women in the network off from the general population and probably made it easier for them to become involved in politics in the first place. Their political backgrounds also highlight what an exceptional group of women they were—daughters and sisters of United States senators, the daughter of a presidential candidate and Cabinet member, wives of congressmen and governors. These women were not starting at the bottom in their efforts to win a place for women in politics; they enjoyed considerable advantages and access to begin with.

Since the suffrage amendment was not ratified until August of 1920, women were not an organized factor in the 1920 election. Eleanor Roosevelt's role as wife of the Democratic vice-presidential nominee was small. For Eleanor and many others, active political work began in 1921. Although the Republicans were the majority party in the 1920s, most women in the network were Democrats. The national Democratic party was rather weak in the 1920s, but it attracted the old suffragists because the party's general tenor was more sympathetic to the reformist attitudes these women brought to politics.[65] Only two women in the network, Katharine Lenroot and Mary Anderson, were registered Republicans, and Anderson often voted for Democratic candidates.

Emily Newell Blair was one of the first to gain a position of influence within the Democratic party, rising to vice-chairman of the Democratic National Committee by 1924. She was in charge of women's activities, and two of her close assistants were Sue Shelton White and Marion Glass Banister. All three of these women would later work together in the New Deal. Here in Democratic politics were the beginnings of the political side of the network.[66]

The 1924 Democratic convention gave women in the network important experience in the ways of politics. Of the 180 women delegates and 293 alternates, one of the most prominent was Emma Guffey Miller, who formally addressed the convention. The 1924 platform announced prominently, "We welcome the women of the nation to their rightful place by the side of men in the control of the government whose burden they have always shared." But the women found it difficult to make the men live up to their promises. Cordell Hull, the chairman of the Democratic National Committee, appointed Eleanor Roosevelt head of a subcommittee to canvass various women's organizations for planks on social welfare. Unfortunately, the women's recommendations were not taken seriously by the male politicians. Eleanor Roosevelt remembered: "They [women] stood outside the door of all important meetings and waited."[67] The women never forgot the experience.

In 1928 Eleanor Roosevelt and Governor Nellie Tayloe Ross headed the women's effort for Democratic presidential nominee Al Smith. Eleanor handled the work at the Democratic National Committee headquarters, while Ross, much in demand as a speaker, toured the country. Among the women who played prominent roles in the national campaign were Congresswoman Mary T. Norton as head of the Speakers' Bureau, and Molly Dewson, making her debut in regular Democratic party work. Daisy Harriman, Emily Newell Blair, Mary Harriman Rumsey, Sue Shelton White, and Caroline O'Day played lesser roles.[68]

Eleanor Roosevelt was clearly emerging as a leader of women in public life by 1928. In the early 1920s, she had moved quickly into positions of leadership in the New York League of Women Voters, the New York Consumers' League, the New York Women's Trade Union League, and the Women's Democratic Committee of New York State. Later in the decade she expanded her influence to the national level, foreshadowing many of her activities as First Lady in the 1930s.[69]

By the late 1920s, Eleanor Roosevelt was already serving as an intermediary between her friends and her husband, then governor of New York. Frances Perkins took advantage of Eleanor's hospitality during a trip to Hyde Park in 1928: "It was awfully nice to see you on Saturday and I enjoyed tremendously my glimpse of your lovely place. I thank you so much for asking me out. I had a very satisfactory talk with Mr. Roosevelt and under conditions which couldn't possibly have occurred elsewhere." Molly Dewson did the same thing later that year: "Since Mrs. Roosevelt seemed satisfied with my campaign efforts, like a good social worker I decided to cash in on them and asked her advice on how to interest Governor-elect Roosevelt in the legislative program of the New York Consumers' League of which at that time I was President. She said, 'Go to Warm Springs to see Franklin before others talk to him.' " Women in public life were delighted to have Eleanor there at Franklin's side. As Emily Newell Blair wrote to Eleanor Roosevelt after the 1928 election, "What a First Lady you will make! And how splendid it is to have one in that place with the political acumen and feeling for women you have! I really believe that is about the greatest victory yet that women in public life have attained."[70] That is, until 1933.

Several other political developments for women in the 1920s influenced the emergence of the network. The Women's Division of the New York State Democratic Committee, under Caroline O'Day, Nancy Cook, and Marion Dickerman, pioneered new roles for women in New York politics that later were used successfully on a national level during the New Deal.[71] The Women's National Democratic Club was founded in Washington in 1924, with Emily Newell Blair, Marion Glass Banister, and Daisy Harriman as important backers of this venture. This club, a meeting place for Democratic women in the nation's capital, served social and political purposes at the same time. The club provided a haven where Democratic women could find the sympathy and support so often lacking in the regular party machinery.[72]

Women also made gains in elective office. Mary Norton was first elected to Congress in 1924, and sixteen Democratic and Republican women served for shorter periods in the House, including Ruth Bryan Owen from 1928 to 1932. Hattie Caraway was appointed to the Senate in 1931. Florence Allen won election to the Ohio Supreme Court in 1922, and made a well-publicized but unsuccessful try at the Democratic nomination for the Senate in 1926. Two women served as governors in the 1920s—"Ma" Ferguson in Texas and Nellie Tayloe Ross in Wyoming—but both were standing in for their husbands. Ross's attempt to win election in her own right after her husband's death was unsuccessful. Women also served in state legislatures, including Ellen Woodward and Lucy Somerville Howorth in Mississippi. The gains were not enormous, but they did mark progress toward larger political roles for women.[73]

Strong friendships developed among the women in politics that paralleled those among women in social welfare circles in New York. In 1923 Ruth Bryan Owen wrote her new acquaintance Emma Guffey Miller, "I hope that our paths will cross again before long." In 1924 Emily Newell Blair wrote to Sue Shelton White, "I am truly grateful for all of your efforts in my behalf and shall strive in the future—as I have in the past—to merit the faith reposed in me by you." Mary T. Norton told Emma Guffey Miller in 1926 of the "very lasting and splendid impression upon all of the women who have the great privilege of listening to you. You surely have the gift, and I know will always be ready to use it for the benefit of the party we both love."[74]

By the late 1920s, female social workers and more politically inclined women had begun to join forces in Democratic politics. Molly Dewson, for example, switched to political work to push for her social reform goals. This caused temporary perplexity on the part of old-timers like Mary Norton, according to Dewson: "I think Mrs. Norton at first may have been a little dubious about me, a social worker, being in politics, but she was a woman of independent judgment and could adapt herself to changed conditions."[75] In the 1930s, the strands of social welfare and politics became inextricably interwoven—only then was the network complete. This development was well under way by the 1920s.

In 1932 much of the network mobilized for Franklin D. Roosevelt's presidential campaign. Molly Dewson began organizing support among Democratic women in New York for Roosevelt as early as 1931. Dewson served as Roosevelt's informal floor manager for women at the 1932 Chicago convention and became director of the Women's Division for the campaign itself.[76] Sue Shelton White served as Dewson's executive assistant, Emily Newell Blair as Director of the Bureau of Women's Clubs, and Jo Coffin as Director of the Bureau of Labor. Nellie Tayloe Ross, Ruth Bryan Owen, Mary Norton, Frances Perkins, Daisy Harriman, and Emily Newell Blair actively participated in the Women's Speakers' Bureau. Eleanor Roosevelt was not an official part of the organization, but she had a desk at headquarters and helped out behind the scenes. Molly Dewson remembered, "Having through Mrs. Roosevelt a direct line to the Governor, to Louis [Howe], and to Jim [Farley], and having such a sympathetic operator, was an incalculable time saver."[77]

Women in the network took pride in the 1932 election results. They also deserve credit for their activities during the 1920s. The social reformers and political activists among them had kept alive the Progressive faith until the appearance of the New Deal in the 1930s. Frances Perkins recognized the continuities: "I think there was a direct line from the progressivism of Theodore Roosevelt, through Mayor Mitchel, to Governor Smith, to Governor Roosevelt, to President Roosevelt to the national scene. That is an historic episode. It's all one episode. It grew as times grew. It's always been clear in my mind."[78]

The women in the network had been part of this historic progression. The experiences of their generation—access to higher education for women, participation in the woman suffrage campaign and World War I, widening activities in the 1920s, growing friendships from social work and politics—provided the foundation for their cooperation in the New Deal. Molly Dewson expressed their collective sense of delight early in the New Deal: "I cannot believe I have lived to see this day. It's the culmination of what us girls and some of you boys have been working for for so long it's just dazzling."[79]

3

THE CRITICAL YEAR, 1933-1934

Between Franklin D. Roosevelt's election in November of 1932 and his inauguration in March 1933, the country sank to the low point of the depression. Thirteen million were unemployed, almost a quarter of the work force. Industrial output hit its nadir in the winter of 1932-33; the 1929 levels would not be reached again until 1941. Agriculture was especially hard hit, pushing farm leaders like Milo Reno to strikes and violence to protest deteriorating farm conditions. Bonus marchers, veterans from World War I, camped out in Washington to demand early payment of their bonuses, only to be repulsed with violence by government troops called out by President Herbert Hoover. On the eve of Roosevelt's inauguration, thirty-eight states had closed their banks. The outlook for America seemed bleak.

Against this backdrop, Franklin Roosevelt ascended to the Presidency on March 4, 1933. In his inaugural address, Roosevelt rekindled hope and courage in the minds of disheartened Americans by pledging bold action to get the country moving again. Roosevelt may not have stimulated immediate economic recovery, but his vision caught the imagination of the American people.

Roosevelt's first priority as President was to deal with the problem of the banks. On his second day in office, Roosevelt declared a national bank holiday and submitted an emergency banking bill to the Congress. Several days later Roosevelt gave his first fireside chat, explaining the banking situation in simple terms and assuring Americans that it was now safe to take money out of the banks. As testimony to people's trust in the new system, deposits outnumbered withdrawals on the Monday morning the banks reopened.

Beyond the banking crisis, Franklin Roosevelt and his advisers saw three areas in which government help was most urgently needed: agriculture, unemployment, and industrial recovery. The farm program, embodied in the Agricultural Adjustment Act, pledged federal price supports for agricultural products. To meet the needs of the unemployed, Roosevelt proposed the imaginative and immensely popular Civilian Conservation Corps, which eventually placed millions of young men in reforestation and conservation work. Roosevelt also proposed direct federal grants to the states for relief. To get industrial output moving again, in May Roosevelt proposed the National Industrial Recovery Act, which established the National Recovery Administration (NRA). Like all the other New Deal measures of the frantic first hundred days of the administration, the NRA quickly passed the Congress. The NRA program of government-business cooperation allowed businesses to draft code agreements for individual industries, set production output levels, and fix prices on an industry-wide level. As a concession to labor, all codes mandated the right of collective bargaining and set minimum wage and maximum hour provisions. The National Industrial Recovery Act also contained a public works program.

Roosevelt set the bold, experimental tone of the emerging New Deal in other ways as well. Prohibition was lifted, and beer became legal in the spring of 1933. In April, the United States went off the gold standard. The federal government took on new responsibility for guaranteeing home and farm mortgages. And the government embarked on an experiment in regional planning with the Tennessee Valley Authority. The TVA built dams to provide flood control and to generate cheap hydro-electric power. In addition, the TVA worked imaginatively to improve the quality of rural life through education and regional cooperation.[1]

All these measures, and more, were accomplished in the hundred days after Roosevelt's inauguration. By mid-June, the federal government had committed itself to managing the economy and guaranteeing the welfare of ordinary citizens on a scale unprecedented in twentieth century American history. Whether these measures attacked the root causes of the depression is debatable, but the New Deal was dramatically under way.

The early days of the New Deal were an exciting time for the women in Washington as well. Molly Dewson later described herself as "so all fired excited and pleased I was beside myself."[2] Roosevelt's preliminary steps raised hopes that the government would seize the opportunity to enact even more far-reaching reforms. With a sense of change in the air, women in public life sought to ensure that women shared in the progress. In the areas of politics and government, they were not disappointed.

In retrospect Molly Dewson could describe the growth in recognition for women as "unbelievable," but in 1933 and 1934, she was considerably less optimistic about the outcome of her efforts. As head of the Women's Division of the Democratic National Committee, Dewson was responsible for patronage for women in the early New Deal. Her job was a difficult one, as she confided to her successor at the Women's Division: "Yes patronage is a nut. I had plenty of headaches over it and so has every man and woman." She once described herself as "like the Jewish Wailing Wall and the wails come thicker and closer as the Forgotten Women see their chances lessen and press closer to the wall."³ Molly Dewson found that she had to fight long and hard for every appointment.

Molly Dewson pursued twin objectives in seeking patronage for women in the early New Deal. First, she wanted to arrange jobs for women who shared her own social justice outlook and who could help the country during the emergency of the depression. As a corollary to this goal, Dewson hoped that placing talented women in prominent government positions would demonstrate the value of women's contributions to the public sphere: "I am a firm believer in progress for women coming through appointments here and there and a first class job by the women who are the lucky ones chosen to demonstrate."⁴ The appointments of most of the women who made up the network fit this objective.

Dewson's second goal was equally important: she hoped to use patronage to reward women political leaders, and thereby build up the women's side of the Democratic party. Early in 1933, Molly Dewson wrote Eleanor Roosevelt, "I feel that the women's vote is going to be important four years from now and that we must look after our able *organization* women." Dewson further explained to presidential aide Marvin McIntyre, "Mac, I am not a feminist. I am a practical politician out to build up the Democratic party where it sorely needs it." To this end, Dewson spent as many hours getting positions for faithful Democratic women as Regional Directors of the Subsistence Homestead Board, District of Columbia Principal Assistant Purchasing Officer, or Division Chief of the Aeronautics Board as she did obtaining many of the jobs for women in the network.⁵

Dewson succeeded in both objectives in her campaign for Frances Perkins's nomination as the Secretary of Labor. Realistically Dewson knew that not all deserving Democratic women party workers would receive recognition. Dewson hoped that appointments like Perkins's to the Cabinet would demonstrate that the Roosevelt administration sincerely believed in women's approach to social welfare—vicarious satisfaction at least for those women who did not get jobs. Perkins's appointment was particularly significant for Molly Dewson, for it represented her baptism into the ways of patronage and politics, foreshadowing many of the tactics she later relied on to obtain government positions for other women.

Nineteen thirty-three looked like a promising year for the appointment of a woman to the previously all-male Cabinet. Speculation about that possibility had circulated in every presidential campaign since women won the vote in 1920. In 1928 Mabel Walker Willebrandt was mentioned for Attorney General, and in 1930 Grace Abbott was widely discussed as Hoover's next Secretary of Labor. Grace Abbott's candidacy had the support of prominent social workers like Julia Lathrop, Pauline Goldmark, Jane Addams, Lillian Wald, Clara Beyer, and Mary Anderson, but was opposed by the American Federation of Labor. Despite the AFL's opposition, Clara Beyer was optimistic about Abbott's chances: "It is very interesting to me to see the way the idea of having Miss Abbott in the Cabinet takes hold. Every person to whom I have mentioned it has become enthusiastic at once. It would be a master stroke politically if only Hoover could see it."[6]

Franklin Roosevelt, on the other hand, had decided by 1933 that he wanted to be the first President to appoint a woman to the Cabinet. The drama of breaking precedent appealed to him, and he recognized the major roles women were now playing in the Democratic party. Ruth Bryan Owen was a candidate for the Labor position and Nellie Tayloe Ross for Interior, but Frances Perkins was the definite front-runner. Roosevelt had been pleased with Perkins's work as Industrial Commissioner of New York, and he believed that her appointment had been popular with women.[7] The same considerations influenced Roosevelt's 1932 decision, Perkins remembered: "It was easy. I was right there and I was trustworthy."[8]

Molly Dewson, however, took nothing for granted. In 1931 she began gathering support for Perkins should Roosevelt be nominated and elected. Frances Perkins's appointment was to be Dewson's own reward for her political and social welfare work. "This was not an act of friendship on my part. Frances and I were never personal friends. I just believed that here was the golden opportunity for pushing ahead the labor legislation program for which I had worked for so many years." In December 1932, Dewson wrote to Perkins directly: "I am glad you appreciate how much I want you at the head of the Labor Department—but you don't have to go a bit further than that for it's very selfish on my part."[9]

Although many people later assumed Eleanor Roosevelt had convinced her husband to appoint Frances Perkins, Molly Dewson deserved most of the credit. Dewson was the architect of the nationwide campaign mounted in support of Perkins's appointment. Dewson arranged with Grace Abbott for Perkins to speak at an important Washington conference, a plan, Frances Perkins realized, "to get me into the public eye at the Washington level." In December 1932, Daisy Harriman held one of her Sunday night suppers (a Washington institution from the 1920s when

Democrats were out of power) in honor of Perkins at Dewson's and Clara Beyer's suggestion. Articles supporting Perkins's candidacy, planted by Molly Dewson, appeared in various newspapers. In case Roosevelt might have missed the stories, Dewson sent him the clippings with notations like, "F. D. R. Interesting Editorials M. W. Dewson."[10]

The main thrust of the drive for Perkins, however, was a letter-writing campaign. "Make it an endless chain," Dewson wrote to Clara Beyer. Letters came to the President-elect from social workers and academics throughout the country. The list of Perkins's supporters was impressive: Jane Addams, Florence Allen, Margaret Dreier Robins, Paul Douglas, Alice Hamilton, Katherine Edson, Lillian Wald, Elizabeth Brandeis, Susan Kingsbury, Sophonisba Breckinridge, Graham Taylor, Owen Lovejoy, and Felix Frankfurter, to name a few. Perkins also received strong support from the women she would later work with in the New Deal. Josephine Roche wrote Roosevelt that she had known and worked with Frances Perkins for years, and that Perkins's appointment would meet with "extensive and hearty approval." Emily Newell Blair stressed how pleased Democratic women would be with the appointment.[11] Such letters probably confirmed the desirability of an appointment that President-elect Roosevelt was leaning toward already.

No matter how much support Dewson could generate among social workers, or how sympathetic Franklin Roosevelt was to the request, the matter finally rested with Perkins herself. Perkins had been hesitant from the beginning. The disadvantages of the job (moving to Washington and leaving her friends, subjecting her family to publicity, being conspicuous as a woman public official, and leaving what she considered a perfect job in New York) seemed to outweigh the boost to her professional pride. The move would also cause financial hardship.[12] But Molly Dewson kept after her: "After all, you owe it to the women. You probably will have this chance and you must step forward and do it." And less subtly: "Don't be such a baby, Frances. You do the right thing. I'll murder you if you don't."[13]

Perkins finally found such arguments persuasive. In late February 1933, after she received Roosevelt's assurance that he agreed with her basic goals for the Labor Department, she accepted the position.[14] Molly Dewson's arguments were crucial in the end, as Perkins later admitted to Carrie Chapman Catt: "The overwhelming argument and thought which made me do it in the end in spite of personal difficulties was the realization that the door might not be opened to a woman again for a long, long time, and that I had a kind of duty to other women to walk in and sit down on the chair that was offered, and so establish the right of others long hence and far-distant in geography to sit in the high seats." Even in

1933 Perkins saw her appointment in a broader context: "I have always felt that it was not I alone who was appointed to the Cabinet, but that it was all the women of America; and I have been happy that so many women have shared with me the sense of gratification that this time has come."[15]

Frances Perkins's pathbreaking appointment as Secretary of Labor in late February was followed in early April by Ruth Bryan Owen's nomination as Minister to Denmark—a first for women in the diplomatic field. Owen's appointment was so popular (she had spent four years in the House as a representative from Florida) that she was confirmed by the Senate the same day it received her nomination.[16] These appointments had high symbolic value for women in public life and seemed to augur well for expanded roles for women in the Roosevelt administration.

But then the momentum slowed. Molly Dewson wrote plaintively to Louis Howe that when the appointments of Perkins and Owens had been announced, "Women believed that it was a 'New Deal' for our sex but since then nothing has happened more than a few routine appointments."[17]

Women were not alone in facing delays and disappointments on patronage. The Roosevelt administration shelved important and not so important jobs for men from early 1933 until late in the summer for political reasons. Dewson did not see why the delay should affect jobs for women as well. Even small positions seemed large to women who had previously gone unrecognized. In addition, women did not have to be held in line through promises of a job. Dewson was upset because she believed that women approached the issues of patronage and politics quite differently from men: "If the men wrangle over prestige and patronage, we cannot change their attitudes, but we certainly do not need to copy it." Dewson also feared that women's chances would diminish if they had to wait too long. It was much easier to find a job for a male lawyer or banker than for a woman whose experience came in less traditional areas.[18]

In this context, Democratic women in the network began to mobilize early in the New Deal on the patronage issue. In April of 1933, Nellie Tayloe Ross suggested a meeting among Ross, Dewson, Eleanor Roosevelt, and Sue Shelton White to "get our heads together over the numerous applications women have sent in for federal appointments and try to arrive at an intelligent conclusion as to the merits or lack of merits of the aspirants." Ross added, "Mrs. Roosevelt thinks our recommendations will be treated with respect." Since the women realized "how much more clamorous the men are" about patronage matters, they kept the list deliberately short (around one hundred names). Once these important leaders had been recognized, Dewson and Ross hoped that many more women would be appointed.[19] To get the process started, Dewson arranged a meeting with James ("Jim") Farley, head of the Democratic National Committee.

Molly Dewson touched on Jim Farley's reaction to this list of women in an April 27, 1933 letter to Eleanor Roosevelt which she called "about the most important letter I ever wrote you!"[20] The letter read in part: "I want to give you the up-shot of my conference with Jim and Mr. O'Mahoney. I think they are '100%' friendly toward recognizing the work of the women and that they will probably do it. I do think, on the other hand, that because so much pressure is being brought on them from the men that continuous pressure will have to be brought on Mr. Farley on behalf of one woman today and another woman another day."[21] This seven-page letter showed the remarkable attention Dewson paid to the smallest details of patronage where women were concerned. It also demonstrated Eleanor Roosevelt's pervasive role in patronage. Often Eleanor Roosevelt's intercession made the difference between a request's being taken seriously and its being ignored.

Molly Dewson felt optimistic about women's chances after this meeting: "As I look over the ten women whom it is absolutely imperative to give recognition to and the thirteen who are hardly second to this first group in the importance of their work to the Party, it seems to me that both lists could be taken care of in a morning by Mr. Farley in consultation with the Senators and Cabinet officers who would have to be consulted." It took considerably more than a morning, however, for the women's appeals to be acted on. In June Dewson complained to Eleanor Roosevelt that only seven women on the Women's Division list had been appointed, and only six other appointments were pending. In July Dewson wrote to Jim Farley about a particular appointment, "Heads you win, Tails I lose," while adding in a postscript to Eleanor Roosevelt, "Heavens but the nicest of men are slippery as eels."[22]

Then in July of 1933, several newspapers reported Emily Newell Blair's complaint that the one outstanding female appointment of the Roosevelt administration (Frances Perkins) had been a woman without political experience. Molly Dewson was upset that her friend and colleague Blair aired her grievances so publicly. Dewson quickly pointed out that Frances Perkins had had twenty years of practical political experience in New York State, but that did not really answer Blair's criticism. Blair was concerned about the delay in finding jobs for women who had worked hard in the campaign and who would be the backbone of the women's side of the Democratic party in the future.[23] In this area, Molly Dewson's frustrations were just as real as Emily Newell Blair's in the summer of 1933. As late as January 1934, Dewson was still complaining to the President through his secretary Missy LeHand, "I do not like to seem ungrateful for the few nice positions that have been given the women but if anyone asked me to be frank, I certainly could not say that they were getting anywhere near what seems to me their due, or, in fact, what it would be good politics to give them."[24]

Dewson had grounds for complaint, but her expressions of frustration at the time concealed the success she achieved in obtaining positions for women in the New Deal. In her autobiography Molly Dewson compiled a list of more than one hundred women she placed in New Deal positions, ranging from three women who marked airstrips for the Aeronautics Board up to the Secretary of Labor.[25] Not all of the women in the network owed their jobs directly to Molly Dewson, but in many cases Dewson, with the strong support of Eleanor Roosevelt and Frances Perkins, played a crucial role in bringing these women into government and politics.

As head of the Women's Division, one of Molly Dewson's first tasks was to take care of those women who were "important personalities in the party and who reflect a great deal of credit to it."[26] Women like Marion Glass Banister, Emily Newell Blair, Daisy Harriman, Sue Shelton White, and Nellie Tayloe Ross had been prominent in the Democratic party in the 1920s, often serving without pay on party committees. These women continued to volunteer their services to the Democratic party in the 1930s, but usually their political work was supplemented with an official position in the administration.

Nellie Tayloe Ross, head of the Women's Division in the 1928 campaign and active there in 1932 as well, was mentioned for a Cabinet position, either Labor or Interior, but instead was appointed Director of the Mint.[27] Marion Glass Banister's appointment as Assistant Treasurer of the United States was based primarily on her past services to the Democratic party, not on the fact that she was the half-sister of Senator Carter Glass of Virginia. When Dewson met Banister in Washington, she described her as "one of our ablest Democratic politicians." Noting that Banister was a widow finding it hard to get by in the depression, Dewson added, " . . . and she certainly is almost destitute." Senator Glass, who was an important (if not always friendly) member of the Democratic coalition, was not even consulted about the appointment.[28] Daisy Harriman's position as Minister to Norway during the second term supplemented her service as National Committeewoman from Washington, D.C. Molly Dewson pleaded Harriman's case to Eleanor Roosevelt: "They say her Sunday night suppers have been really quite valuable to the Democratic party when it was a minority party. Of course she has always been terribly hard up and I suppose she is worse off than ever today."[29]

Dewson sometimes rewarded both the women and their husbands as repayment for past services to the party. Emily Newell Blair's job at the National Recovery Administration allowed her to continue her work in consumer affairs, but the position was not a permanent one. Emily Newell Blair knew, as did most of Washington, that her main reward was the appointment of her husband, Harry Blair, as an Assistant Attorney General. Lucille Foster McMillin was appointed to the Civil Service Commission, according to Eleanor Roosevelt, "first because she was not so definitely identified with the national party office as to be considered too partisan, and secondly because her husband has been the outstanding person who had backed my husband." Finally, Emma Guffey Miller, who served the Democratic party throughout the New Deal as National Committeewoman from Pennsylvania, held only a minor official position—chairman of the National Youth Administration advisory board for Pennsylvania from 1935 to 1943. Her principal reward was the appointment of her husband, Carroll Miller, to the Interstate Commerce Commission.[30]

Several women in the network found official jobs within the Democratic party. Besides Dewson herself, both Carolyn Wolfe (1934-1936) and Dorothy McAlister (1936-1940) became full-time paid directors of the Women's Division. But Sue Shelton White, the assistant director of the Women's Division from 1932 to 1933, grew tired of working for the Democratic party. White wanted a job using her skills as a lawyer, and Molly Dewson maneuvered extensively to obtain a suitable position for her.

Dewson wrote first to Franklin Roosevelt: "When you have settled the dollar you may be ready to take care of Sue S. White. I ought to begin to organize my division and I can't announce my assistant until Sue is placed as counsel for the T.V.A. Jim says no one can arrange with Mr. Morgan but you." Dewson then wrote to Eleanor: "Louis Howe says Franklin has been too busy to do anything about the 15 women. Inevitably. But Sue White can't get placed except on F's request to Morgan of the T.V.A. Mrs. Fickle can't come until Sue is fixed."[31] Dewson's appeal to Eleanor Roosevelt was much less optimistic and certainly less deferential—she showed her frustrations ("inevitably") about the delays in securing patronage for women. Dewson was completely candid with Eleanor Roosevelt about her problems with the President and his political advisers, and she felt no hesitancy in asking for Eleanor's help. The final resolution placed Sue Shelton White on the staff of the Consumers' Advisory Board of the National Recovery Administration; White then joined the Social Security Administration in 1935.

Eleanor Roosevelt also assisted in the appointment of Jo Coffin as Assistant Public Printer. Coffin and Roosevelt had worked together during the winter of 1932-33 setting up a clubhouse for unemployed women under New York Women's Trade Union League auspices. Eleanor Roosevelt's pressure on Farley and Howe on behalf of Jo Coffin was strong and unremitting:

April, 1933.   I am anxious to see that Jo Coffin gets a job. Will you tell me what can be done.

May, 1933.   I think I have written to you before about Jo Coffin. I really am anxious to have her get some kind of a job, and if she cannot get what she wants, I do wish you would try to find something else for her.

October, 1933.   He [Farley] promised me that he would not forget to take care of Jo Coffin and I have jogged his memory almost every time I have seen him.

February, 1934.   I haven't reminded you for a long time, but I am still hoping you will find something in the Government Printing Office for Jo Coffin. She has a temporary job, but is really hoping to be made one of the assistants.[32]

Even when Eleanor Roosevelt personally backed a candidate, Molly Dewson found that "continuous pressure . . . in behalf of the women" was necessary.[33]

Although Molly Dewson and Eleanor Roosevelt frequently badgered the men about patronage requests, the women under consideration were often reticent about pushing their candidacies. Lucy Somerville Howorth's approach was typical: "Probably from my own standpoint, unless something really good is developed in Washington, it would be more to my own interest to have some less important position in Mississippi which would not break up my entire business, social and political connection." Howorth told Dewson she was interested in the Veterans' Board of Appeals but would not flood Washington with letters of endorsement. Molly Dewson believed this attitude on the part of women seeking jobs distinguished them from men. Dewson always remained suspicious of women who descended on Washington with piles of letters and endorsements. Quoting Shakespeare, Dewson would remark, "good wine needs no bush." But Dewson still had to fight like a "bag of Cats" to get Lucy Somerville Howorth a position on the Veterans' Board.[34]

In addition to Dewson's and Eleanor Roosevelt's efforts, Frances Perkins helped to bring other women into the government, especially in the Labor Department and some of the new government agencies. Perkins urged Mary Harriman Rumsey, with whom she shared a house in 1933 and 1934, to accept the offer of their mutual friend General Hugh Johnson to head the Consumers' Advisory Board of the National Recovery Administration. Perkins also named her old friend from New York reform days, Rose Schneiderman, to the Labor Advisory Board of the NRA. Perkins personally tapped Josephine Roche for the Consumers' Advisory Board of the NRA and probably pushed Roche's appointment as Assistant Secretary of the Treasury in late 1934 after Roche's unsuccessful Senate primary campaign in Colorado. Finally, Frances Perkins recruited Mary LaDame from New York to work in the United States Employment Service and then promoted her to special assistant to the Secretary of Labor in 1938.[35]

Clara Beyer also owed her new job to the combined efforts of Frances Perkins and Molly Dewson. When Grace Abbott resigned as head of the Children's Bureau in 1934, there was quite a scramble for the job. One of Molly Dewson's old friends wrote her, "But darling, count yourself lucky that you are out of Washington as I understand that nearly fifty of your girls are after it."[36] Clara Beyer, then head of the Child Labor section of the Children's Bureau, was prominently mentioned for the position. In this context Molly Dewson and Frances Perkins put their heads together to solve the dual problem of who should head the Children's Bureau and what to do with Clara Beyer:

Dear Frances,

I have been thinking a lot about Grace Abbott's successor. I *know* Clara Beyer thinks why she should not be chosen "considering what is available." Really Clara is miles ahead of practically any possibility. She is rare. She has brains, judgment, common sense, sense of values, balance, energy, and friendliness. *And she cares.*

There is so little superior human material I want to see it utilized to the limit. Clara and Frieda [Miller] are the two hopes in the labor field. I should like to see Clara stay there. But to my mind it is not quite fair to pass her over and choose an outsider for Grace Abbott's place unless you promote Clara at the same time. It would give Clara a black eye.

Would not Clara be quite ideal to head your new standards department? She has the brains and the practical experience . . .

Then if you wanted to put say Harriet Elliott in for Grace Abbott and Elizabeth Magee in place of Clara in the Child Labor Department it would be an immensely strong set up. You are a peach to ask my opinion Frances for of course nothing interests me more. Heaven give you wisdom.

Faithfully yours,
Molly Dewson[37]

The final outcome reflected Molly Dewson's advice. Katharine Lenroot, another Children's Bureau member, became its new head, and Beyer was named to set up the Labor Standards Division in the Department of Labor. Beyer was delighted with her new job and the chance to work closely with Perkins: "The Secretary considers it her New Deal in the department. It will be rather fun starting from scratch and building up an organization."[38]

Frances Perkins could only go so far in making the Labor Department a female enclave. As the first woman Secretary of Labor, Perkins did not feel she could appoint another woman as head of one of Labor's main divisions. Consequently, although Clara Beyer did most of the planning for a new Division of Labor Standards, Perkins named Verne Zimmer as director. Zimmer worked mainly on compensation; Beyer became associate director with equivalent power and prestige. Molly Dewson confronted this same problem when she approached Eleanor Roosevelt about a job for herself in the Labor Department: "That would interest me enormously but with a woman as Secretary probably a woman assistant would be too much."[39]

Molly Dewson also had a hand in Ellen Sullivan Woodward's 1933 appointment as head of the Women's Section of the Federal Emergency Relief Administration (FERA). Based in part on Woodward's strong contributions in Mississippi during the 1932 campaign, Dewson highly recommended Woodward to FERA head Harry Hopkins, who then offered a position to Woodward. Dewson and Woodward had already developed an easy working relationship through Democratic women's politics, and this expanded once Woodward came to Washington. In June of 1933, Woodward (in her role as National Committeewoman from Mississippi) wrote Molly Dewson bemoaning the lack of patronage for women in her home state. A scant four months later, the tables were turned and Dewson was writing Ellen Woodward at FERA suggesting five women with social work and political experience for supervisory jobs on the new work relief programs. Dewson then contacted leading Democratic women all over the country soliciting suggestions of Democratic women qualified to be assistant administrators or to develop new work projects.[40] Dewson rarely missed an opportunity to push for more jobs for women.

Molly Dewson was less involved in filling positions that required specific professional skills. Many governmental positions created in response to the depression required expertise in social welfare and public assistance, not political connections. Hilda Worthington Smith did not even apply for her job directing Workers' Education at FERA. When Smith went to Washington to lobby for funds for schools for industrial workers, the FERA people took one look at her qualifications and offered her a job on the spot.[41]

Slightly different considerations applied to the case of Jane Hoey. The President and Harry Hopkins had approached Hoey about several possible jobs, but Hoey waited until she was offered a job that best utilized her skills as a professional social worker. Although she was a close friend of the Roosevelts, Dewson, and Frances Perkins, that was not the primary reason for her obtaining a job in the Bureau of Public Assistance: "I had known the Roosevelts a great much of my life, but it wasn't on that basis that I came in. I came in as an experienced person, to head up the assistance program."[42] Jane Hoey was correct in stressing her professional qualifications for the job, although her friendship with the Roosevelts, Dewson, and Perkins undoubtedly did make a difference. When qualified social workers were needed in Washington, it was natural to turn to colleagues from New York.

In the cases of some prominent positions for women, no action was necessary. The Roosevelt administration did not intend to disturb prominent career women already in government, such as Mary Anderson at the Women's Bureau and Grace Abbott at the Children's Bureau. But even here Dewson played a small role. In 1933 Mary Anderson began to inquire about the new Democratic administration's attitude toward her and the Women's Bureau. One day she met Molly Dewson at the National Consumers' League offices in New York City, and Dewson called out to Anderson that she was completely in favor of keeping the Women's Bureau intact. Dewson remembered later, "Mary has a poker face but she registered that was what she came to hear about."[43]

One final appointment that Dewson arranged was that of Florence Allen, then of the Ohio Supreme Court, to the United States Court of Appeals for the Sixth Circuit in 1934. Both in its importance (a "first" for women, and the highest women had risen in the federal judiciary) and in its timing and tactics, the campaign for Allen bore a remarkable similarity to that behind Frances Perkins for Secretary of Labor. Emily Newell Blair had written to Molly Dewson as early as 1933 suggesting Allen for the position, adding, "I do not know how well you know Judge Allen but I consider her a very fine woman indeed—one in the tradition of Mrs. Catt if you get what I mean." Dewson needed no introduction to Allen, however, for they had first met at a national suffrage convention in Washington in 1914. Dewson and Blair, together with Franklin Roosevelt, Eleanor Roosevelt, Louis Howe, Mary Anderson, and many other women associated with the network, gathered support for Allen's nomination. Continuous pressure, both in Washington and in Ohio, finally paid off and the appointment went through.[44]

Florence Allen would have been an important member of the network if her nomination to the Sixth Circuit had not kept her in Ohio. She was sorely missed. Dewson once wrote her, "I was awfully sorry to miss you in Washington. How does it seem to be a cloistered nun?" The women in the network mobilized again in the late 1930s to promote Florence Allen for the United States Supreme Court, but their efforts were unsuccessful.[45]

Occasionally women in the network had to mobilize to keep the wrong kind of women from being appointed. Molly Dewson told Jim Farley that *after* the women who had done organizational work in the campaign, and *after* the women who were prominent in the party had been taken care of, then "I have no objection to the most pressing importunities of the boys for their girl friends . . . being taken care of in modest numbers." Dewson did not want to alienate the men by turning down their requests unequivocally, but she still intended to oppose such appointments until her solid Democratic workers had been taken care of. In another case, Eleanor Roosevelt wrote to Jim Farley how "horrified" she was by the appointment of a certain woman from California. She asked Farley, "Must we have terrible women who are opposed to us, just because McAdoo [the California senator] wishes it?" Although Farley had pledged to clear all female appointments with Dewson and Eleanor Roosevelt, occasional oversights occurred.[46]

Molly Dewson did not handle patronage for stenographers, clerks, elevator operators, and the like. Emma Guffey Miller later criticized Dewson for neglecting this aspect of the women's organization, but Dewson wanted to win the allegiance of Democratic women through the programs of the New Deal, not through minor secretarial jobs. In any event, such small-scale patronage was usually the province of the state's National Committeeman (theoretically to be shared jointly with the National Committeewoman, but this was rarely the case). Dewson let the Democratic National Committee staff handle the distribution of minor jobs in consultation with state leaders, while leaving the much smaller staff of the Women's Division to build up the women's side of the Democratic party.[47]

In addition, since Dewson realistically concluded that not all of her original patronage requests would be honored, she learned to compromise. Anna Dickie Olesen's appointment as a state director of the Emergency Council of the Department of Agriculture (the one woman out of forty-eight state directors) was one such compromise. Dewson remarked, "The thing that makes it hard for us was that if Mrs. Olesen had been a man she would have been offered an ambassadorship." Another compromise strategy was to secure positions for the husbands of faithful women Democratic leaders. Part-time jobs as regional directors for the Women's Division sometimes took the places of federal positions, as Eleanor Roosevelt explained: "Miss Dewson was afraid that you would think this work not as worth while as some administrative post so she asked me to write you what I think myself and that is that we cannot draft all of our most able women into administrative positions but must keep some of the most able to build up the women's organization." Dewson also tried to get as many women as possible named to honorary positions (such as delegates to international conferences), appointments that carried some status but no remuneration. As Dewson said of one appointment, "Hope she takes it. No pay but a good chance."[48]

Even if Molly Dewson could not offer Democratic women federal positions in Washington or in the Democratic party, she devised ways of showing Democratic women that their opinions were well respected. In one case, she told Jim Farley it would be very "handsome" if he asked a certain woman if she had any recommendations for federal positions in her state. Dewson did not think the woman would have any suggestions, but knew she would greatly appreciate the compliment. In another instance, Molly Dewson suggested that Lavinia Engle be invited to a luncheon party that Frances Perkins was giving at the Department of Labor. Molly Dewson described Engle (who, like Florence Allen, would have belonged to the network if her job had brought her to Washington) as "the whole cheese in Maryland and not rewarded as she would have liked to be and in my humble opinion should have been, so please ask her." And if all else failed, Molly Dewson had friends in Washington newspaper circles who gave out-of-town Democratic women leaders good publicity when they visited Washington—"sort of compensation in many cases for jobs."[49]

Dewson's success in securing patronage for women was a result of a number of factors. The Democrats were returning to power after twelve years, and—in 1933 at least—they had many positions at their disposal. Women expected their fair share of patronage because they had played large roles in the 1932 election campaign. Molly Dewson told Frances Perkins after the campaign, "The Women's Division has something to say about these things. We did a lot to elect him. I know I did, and he knows I did." Dewson persistently reminded the White House of that debt. "Molly Dewson is back on my neck," presidential aide Marvin McIntyre wrote in a confidential memo to Jim Farley.[50]

Franklin Roosevelt's attitude about women in public service was another important factor in winning new roles for women in politics and government in the 1930s. If Roosevelt had failed to appreciate women's abilities or had felt uncomfortable working with women, no amount of pressure from his wife or Molly Dewson could have changed his mind. Two considerations contributed to Roosevelt's positive attitude. First, he was accustomed to dealing with talented women in political and governmental circles in New York, many of whom he had met through Eleanor. Moreover, Franklin Roosevelt appreciated women's importance to the future of the Democratic party. As Molly Dewson said, "Roosevelt had understood our potential value and had backed us to the limits and his programs had made political work a recreation. It was like picking quinces on a crisp sunny day in the fall."[51]

Molly Dewson thought that Franklin Roosevelt appreciated women's native ability more than any other man she had ever known, and she sincerely believed that if he had not been so busy with plans for economic recovery, he would have appointed even more women. Frances Perkins agreed with Dewson about Roosevelt's appreciation of women's talents, and she too stressed the large role women played in the Roosevelt administration and Democratic politics. Both Dewson and Perkins acknowledged Eleanor Roosevelt's influence in shaping Franklin's opinions.[52]

Franklin Roosevelt's attitudes about women were also influenced by Eleanor's friends. Women like Nancy Cook, Marion Dickerman, Caroline O'Day, and Frances Perkins, as well as Eleanor herself, were from social backgrounds similar to Franklin's. For example, Roosevelt had first met Frances Perkins at a tea dance in 1910.[53] From this limited circle of female acquaintances, Roosevelt formed his opinions about women's capabilities. When Roosevelt appointed Perkins as Industrial Commissioner of New York in 1928, she raised the question of whether her appointment would be popular with other women. "He said, 'Oh yes, it will. I asked Eleanor and she thinks it would. I asked Nancy Cook and she thinks so, and Caroline O'Day.' " Perkins continued, "These were women he saw all the time. He didn't have to go out on the highways and byways. He saw them personally all the time."[54] Roosevelt's contact with this small group of New Yorkers had a positive effect on his attitudes about women.

Even though Franklin Roosevelt admired and respected women, his ability to work with them did have limits. For one thing, FDR was rather a "ladies' man" and was partial to pretty women who flattered and played up to him. Several of his key advisers, such as Marvin McIntyre and Stephen Early, were Southerners who held rather conservative views on women's place; they did not have Roosevelt's experience working with women in government and politics in New York.[55] As a consequence, women were never part of Franklin Roosevelt's inner circle of political advisers. Eleanor Roosevelt never became his close political adviser the way Belle Moskowitz had been to Al Smith. Frances Perkins later remembered, "He never did rely on her. He liked her as a reporter . . . Liberal-minded as he was toward women he tended to think that a wife should keep out of those things." But Frances Perkins was not a member of his inner circle of advisers either, nor were Molly Dewson or any other women in the network. Dewson said, "I was not one of his brain trust."[56]

Franklin Roosevelt was just as capable of giving women the runaround as he was men. He could write Molly Dewson with charming ambiguity: "I am sure many of your letters to me went unanswered but please be assured that they did not go unread." And Roosevelt was only willing to go so far in entrusting major responsibilities to women. When Daisy Harriman was mentioned for a diplomatic post in 1937, Roosevelt replied that the foreign situation was so complicated that he could not put a woman in charge anywhere except a country unlikely to get involved in European hostilities. When by 1940 the international situation had changed dramatically, Molly Dewson reminded Roosevelt of his lack of faith in women's capabilities: "Daisy Harriman in Norway and doing all right has been my only chuckle these days."[57]

Franklin Roosevelt was not the only male politician whose attitudes affected the success of Molly Dewson's plans for women in the New Deal. As head of the Democratic National Committee, James Farley also had a large impact. Although Dewson and Farley did not always agree on patronage matters, they developed a fairly effective working relationship. Farley may not have completely understood Dewson's plans for women in the party,[58] but he respected her and granted her requests whenever possible: "Molly was a doggone persistent woman and hard to manage. If I said 'yes' to one of her big ideas, she ran off in a hurry for fear I would change my mind. If I said 'no' she stayed around a while until I said 'yes.' " Male politicians like Jim Farley felt at ease with Molly Dewson, which she attributed to her age: "Fortunately, I was old enough to be their aunt, and men are at their best with their mothers and favorite aunts." Frances Perkins thought that Farley was so taken with Dewson's forthrightness and candor that he sent his daughter to Wellesley because it was Dewson's alma mater.[59] Dewson took advantage of Farley's respect to win more positions for women in the administration.

Another dependable male ally was Louis Howe. In the 1920s Howe contributed significantly to Eleanor Roosevelt's education as a politician, and he respected the work done by women in the 1928 and 1932 campaigns. In a 1935 article entitled "Women's Ways in Politics," Howe noted, "I would rather have a half dozen women field workers than a hundred men every day." Howe even speculated that a woman might be elected President if the federal government continued to focus its attention on humanitarian questions. Until his death in 1936, Louis Howe could always be counted on where women's requests were concerned. Molly Dewson remarked to Eleanor Roosevelt, "And, after all, what Louis says goes and he does not forget."[60]

But the women's real ally in the White House was not Franklin Roosevelt or Louis Howe; it was Eleanor Roosevelt. In the same way that Eleanor Roosevelt served as the center of the network among women in government in the 1930s, so was she a vital link in women's political advancement in the early New Deal. "What would the Democratic women of America do without you there on the spot," Molly Dewson exclaimed to Eleanor Roosevelt in 1933. Although Molly Dewson appeared as the main dispenser of patronage for women in the Roosevelt administration, in reality often she and Eleanor worked together behind the scenes. In addition, Dewson found it profitable to use Eleanor Roosevelt's name as leverage. Dewson approached General Hugh Johnson about jobs for women in state NRA agencies by saying, "You will remember Mrs. Roosevelt gave me the opportunity of speaking to you about this." Molly Dewson did not always rely on Eleanor Roosevelt's name to get jobs for women, but Dewson's position as "practically a member of the President's family" undoubtedly helped her to press her claims. Dewson, in turn, always felt "primarily responsible" to Eleanor Roosevelt for whatever she accomplished for women in the New Deal.[61]

Molly Dewson's efforts to win increased roles for women in the New Deal were aided by long-term trends toward greater participation of women in government and politics. Women's political involvement in the twentieth century steadily increased, particularly after the passage of the nineteenth amendment in 1920. Women also experienced a slow but steady expansion of their roles at all levels of the federal government during the twentieth century. Much of this progress was concentrated in the growing clerical field, where women predominated; but upper-level gains also occurred. Appointments such as that of Julia Lathrop to the Children's Bureau in 1912, Grace Abbott as her successor in 1921, Mary Anderson to the Women's Bureau in 1920, Louise Stanley to the Bureau of Home Economics of the Department of Agriculture in 1923, and Helen Hamilton Gardener and Jessie Dell to the Civil Service Commission showed growing opportunities for women in the upper echelons of government. In addition, by the mid-1920s all Civil Service examinations were officially opened to men and women alike.[62]

Within these broader trends several predictable variations worked to women's benefit during the depression of the 1930s. As figure 3 demonstrates, during wars or other emergencies the percentage of appointments given to women rose dramatically, whereas the percentage tended to decrease at the beginning of economic recessions. After a marked increase in women's appointments during World War I and a subsequent decrease in the early 1920s (probably linked more with the demobilization after the war than with the recession of 1922), the next significant downward turn for women occurred from 1930 to 1932 at the onset of the depression. After 1932 the percentage of appointments for women rose substantially with the inauguration of the New Deal and its expansion of government functions. The peak was reached in 1934. Beginning in 1935, as fewer new programs were established, the percentage of women appointees declined. Were this chart to continue into the 1940s, it would show a dramatic increase during World War II and a sharp drop-off after the war.

These figures support the general proposition that in times of expansion or emergency, the usual inhibitions against hiring women are dropped, and women as a group make important, albeit temporary, progress. Women generally do better in the formative periods of organizations when there typically is less prejudice against using female talent. Conversely, when the sense of emergency or newness recedes and the bureaucratic structure stabilizes or tightens, the situation for women deteriorates.[63] In broad outline, this is what happened to women in the New Deal.

Predictably, conditions for women in the New Deal varied in different sectors of the government. Women formed a significantly larger proportion of the work force in the independent government agencies than in the executive departments: more than one-third of the employees in independent agencies were women, compared to one-sixth in the executive departments. The newest independent agencies had the strongest records in hiring women (table 4). Between 1923 and 1939, of the total government employees, the percentage of women increased from 15.8 to 18.8 percent—a numerical increase of 90,000 jobs for women. The growth in women's employment was proportionally greater in independent establishments than in executive departments, and the Works Progress Administration alone accounted for 18 percent of the increase. Since executive departments employed twice as many women as did the independent agencies, however, this progress benefited only a minority of female government employees (table 5).[64]

Figure 3. Women's percentage of appointments to government positions, 1883-1937. (From Lucille Foster McMillin, *Women in the Federal Service* [Washington, D.C., 1938], 13.)

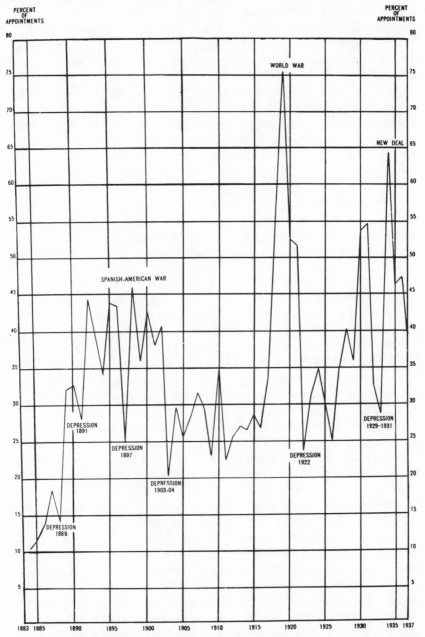

During war or other emergencies, the proportion of appointments given women tends to increase. During depressions a sharp decrease may be seen.

This chart, which shows the percent of the total appointments received by women to the departmental service at Washington, is based on the Annual Reports of the United States Civil Service Commission.

Table 4.   Distribution of women employees in executive departments
and independent establishments, 1939.

Executive departments and independent establishments	Percent of women among total employees
All executive departments and independent establishments	18.8
10 executive departments	15.2
49 independent establishments	34.2
7 newest independent establishments	44.4

Source: "Employment of Women in the Federal Government, 1923-1939," Women's Bureau Bulletin, no. 182 (Washington, D.C., 1941), 25.

The Women's Bureau attributed the expansion to the concern of the newer agencies with problems of social welfare, an area in which women traditionally have predominated. The Women's Bureau also noted that such agencies were less likely to have prejudices against hiring women because they had only recently been established.[65]

Frances Perkins recognized that the expansion of government welfare services in the 1930s provided an ideal opportunity for women, especially those trained as social workers, to move quickly into positions of responsibility: "Undoubtedly in many of the New Deal agencies women have had greater opportunity to occupy positions of real importance than in the old-line agencies. Obviously, women with high academic qualifications have encountered less prejudice in the new than in many of the older permanent bureaus, and have thus been able to forge ahead more rapidly—if not to the position of direction, at least to high administrative posts."[66] This factor certainly aided in the efforts to win places for women in the government structure.

The experiences of the women in the network fit these general patterns quite closely. The Departments of State, Treasury, and Labor, which had the highest percentage of women employees among the executive departments (see table 5), also provided important opportunities for women in the network. Ruth Bryan Owen and Daisy Harriman held ministerial positions in the State Department. Nellie Tayloe Ross, Marion Glass Banister, and Josephine Roche served in the Treasury Department; Roche's position as Assistant Secretary of the Treasury was especially significant. The Labor Department likewise had a strong concentration of women in high-level positions—Frances Perkins, Clara Beyer, Mary LaDame, Mary Anderson, Grace Abbott, and Katharine Lenroot. The large number of women in the Labor Department reflected the depart-

Table 5.   Total number of civil employees, number and percent
distribution of women, and percent women constitute of total,
June 30, 1939, by department or establishment.

| Department or establishment | Total employees | Women Employees | | |
		Number	Percent distribution	Percent of total employees
ALL AGENCIES	920,310	172,773	100.0	18.9
Executive departments	748,403	113,990	66.0	15.2
Post Office	288,979	29,358	17.0	10.2
War	109,886	14,042	8.1	12.8
Agriculture	107,712	21,575	12.5	20.0
Navy	85,400	4,662	2.7	5.5
Treasury	68,002	24,661	14.3	36.3
Interior	51,923	10,920	6.3	21.0
Commerce	14,491	2,160	1.3	14.9
Justice	9,605	2,237	1.3	24.3
Labor	6,646	2,211	1.3	33.3
State	5,759	2,074	1.2	36.0
Independent establishments	171,798[a]	58,724	34.0	34.2
Civil Aeronautics Board	4,214	440	.3	10.4
Civil Service Commission	1,768	997	.6	56.4
Farm Credit Administration	3,176	1,361	.8	42.9
Fed. Communications Commission	616	220	.1	35.7
FDIC	1,396	497	.3	35.6
Fed. Emerg. Admin. Public Works	10,305	2,575	1.5	25.0
Fed. Housing Administration	4,707	1,697	1.0	36.1
Federal Power Commission	721	231	.1	32.0
Federal Trade Commission	687	255	.1	37.1
General Accounting Office	4,915	1,747	1.0	35.5
Government Printing Office	5,534	1,060	.6	19.2
Home Owners' Loan Corp.	10,950	5,495	3.2	50.2
Interstate Commerce Commission	2,621	794	.5	30.3
Maritime Commission	1,471	387	.2	26.3
Nat. Labor Relations Board	841	343	.2	40.8
Panama Canal	11,604	513	.3	4.4
Railroad Retirement Board	2,598	778	.5	29.9
Reconstruction Finance Corp.	4,073	1,718	1.0	42.2
Rural Electrification Admin.	778	315	.2	40.5
Securities & Exchange Comm.	1,576	538	.3	34.1

Table 5 (*continued*).

Department or establishment	Total employees	Women Employees		
		Number	Percent distribution	Percent of total employees
Social Security Board	9,661	4,634	2.7	48.0
Tennessee Valley Authority	12,149	987	.6	8.1
Veterans' Administration	36,787	12,867	7.4	35.0
Works Progress Admin.	33,972	16,614	9.6	48.9
Office of the President	109	19	—	17.4

Source: *Women's Bureau Bulletin*, no. 182 (Washington, D.C., 1941), 50.
a. Excluded in list are those with less than 600 total employees.

ment's social welfare functions as well as Frances Perkins's active recruitment of other women to work in her department.[67]

None of the women in the network held a position in an executive department other than Labor, Treasury, or State. Perhaps the only surprising omission was the Department of Agriculture, often the center for experimentation and social change in the New Deal. Other than the Division of Home Economics, headed by career civil servant Dr. Louise Stanley, no prominent women served in Agriculture.

The rest of the women in the network were concentrated in the newer independent agencies of the government. Hilda Worthington Smith and Ellen Sullivan Woodward held positions in the Federal Emergency Relief Administration and the Works Progress Administration, the federal relief agencies. Mary Harriman Rumsey, Molly Dewson, Emily Newell Blair, Sue Shelton White, and Rose Schneiderman served in the National Recovery Administration. Jane Hoey, White, Dewson, and Woodward worked in the Social Security Administration. Two women in the New Deal were appointed to independent commissions—Lucy Somerville Howorth to the United States Veterans' Board of Appeals and Lucille Foster McMillin to the Civil Service Commission. Jo Coffin worked in the Government Printing Office, an older independent government agency.

Women in the network shared two further characteristics that affected their participation in government. In the first place, many women in the network brought the "woman's angle" or the "woman's viewpoint" to their jobs. The appointments of Ruth Bryan Owen and Daisy Harriman in the diplomatic field were designed in part to recognize women's interest in international affairs. Rose Schneiderman represented the interests of women workers in her tenure on the Labor Advisory Board of the NRA. Ellen Sullivan Woodward had special responsibility for women in the relief programs, and Hilda Worthington Smith oversaw the camps for unemployed women under the Federal Emergency Relief Administration and the National Youth Administration. Lucille Foster McMillin of the Civil Service Commission took a special interest in the problems of women in the federal service. Lucy Somerville Howorth's appointment to the Veterans' Board, according to Molly Dewson, fit the President's general desire to use the "judgment of able, judicial, and socially-minded women" to decide borderline cases of compensation and benefits. Jo Coffin took special responsibility for the needs of women personnel in the Government Printing Office.[68]

Another common characteristic of most of the women in the network was their continued association with the various reform groups in which they had been active throughout their careers. That Eleanor Roosevelt, Mary Anderson, Clara Beyer, Frances Perkins, and Molly Dewson would maintain their contacts with organizations like the National Consumers' League and the Women's Trade Union League could have been predicted from the patterns of cooperation developing among these women since the 1920s. During the New Deal, women in government turned to their friends in voluntary associations for expert technical help and to obtain broader public support for specific proposals. By the same token, their friends in reform groups used the women in government as intermediaries to hasten federal action on social welfare proposals. "The lines of influence, in these cases, worked both ways, from voluntary associations to public service and back," one historian noted.[69]

The similarities of these women's experiences in government and politics help explain the development of the network. Because of their concentration in social welfare and women's activities, the women naturally found themselves working together within particular departments or agencies. Molly Dewson hinted at this phenomenon when she said of her working relationship with Mary Anderson, "We were always there in the same committee rooms."[70] An observer of Washington political life in 1939 described the institutional framework in which such interaction occurred:

One cannot live in Washington for long without being conscious that it has these whirlpools or centers of activity focusing on particular problems . . . These people in their various permutations and combinations are continually meeting in each other's offices, at various clubs, lunching together, and participating in legislative hearings or serving on important but obscure committees set up within the departments. Among such human beings are bound to emerge—ideas for programs, ideas for strategy.[71]

This description fits the women's network perfectly. Building on common friendships and shared concerns, the women began working together in the day-to-day operation of the government. Soon the network of women was functioning as an influential group in Washington life, especially in the development of the New Deal's social welfare policies and in Democratic party politics.

Molly Dewson never used the term "network" to describe the cooperation among women in government and politics that she was part of, but a remarkably similar concept was on her mind in the early New Deal. In November of 1933, Dewson participated in an all-day White House Conference on the Emergency Needs of Women. Most of the members of the network who were already on the job in Washington also attended.[72] Perhaps influenced by this impressive array of female talent, Dewson speculated to her friend Lavinia Engle later that same day on the implications of women's strategic placement in positions of power throughout the government:

> I am with you on wishing that there were a few women in the policy making group. I think this is a position that we have to earn. I am proud that we have Frances Perkins in a most prominent place in the policy making group, and Mrs. Rumsey, Emily [Newell Blair], Belle Sherwin, Mrs. Poole, and Yours Truly on the Consumers' Committee and Rose Schneiderman on the Labor Committee. Unofficially, Mrs. Roosevelt is on the spot and Mrs. Woodward is near the top of the FERA which is a policy making group of a kind.[73]

Dewson's list was not comprehensive, nor did she offer any predictions as to what this "policy making group of a kind" might undertake. But her musings to Lavinia Engle suggest that Dewson was intrigued by the possibilities of cross-departmental cooperation among women in politics and government. Perhaps Molly Dewson was more a conscious architect of the women's network in the New Deal than she let on.

4

WOMEN AND DEMOCRATIC POLITICS

During the early New Deal, the network turned its attention to the roles women would play in the Roosevelt administration, both in the implementation of its social welfare policies and in the Democratic party itself. Given the network's attitudes about women in public life, its members naturally gravitated toward politics. Women's involvement in Democratic party politics in the 1930s took several forms. Women in the network worked to increase patronage for loyal Democratic women workers; they supported and participated in Molly Dewson's plans for the Women's Division of the Democratic National Committee; they played important roles in the election campaigns of 1932 and 1936. As a result, the network emerged as the major influence on women's experiences in Democratic politics in the 1930s.

Molly Dewson directed many of these initiatives. Her primary political goal was promotion of a clear and widespread understanding of New Deal policies among the public at large, but especially among women. Educating the country about the social and economic programs of the New Deal, Dewson later admitted, became an "obsession" with her. Emily Newell Blair once observed that for women to succeed in politics, they would have to build a following so that men would be forced to listen to them.[1] This is precisely what Dewson did, but with one significant difference: instead of assembling a personal following for herself, she gathered a group of women who promoted public support for the programs of the New Deal.

Molly Dewson doubted that Democratic women would devote their considerable talents to advancing the New Deal unless the Roosevelt administration demonstrated that it took women seriously: "The sine qua non of my ideas was that women competent to be leaders in politics must be given responsibility and power in their party's organization." Unfortunately, Dewson realized, women's recognition within the Democratic party in 1933 was "pathetically small," often "given on the basis of their looks, their money, or their late husband's service to the party, not on their ability."[2] Increased patronage would be a gesture of good faith toward Democratic women.

For Molly Dewson, getting jobs for women in the Roosevelt administration became her own full-time job in 1933 and 1934: "Until January 1, 1934, I did no work but press the claims of the women who deserved good appointments." Dewson did not enjoy badgering men in the Democratic party about jobs for women, but she thought it was necessary before she could move on to her broader educational and political goals. Dewson wrote to Emily Newell Blair in the summer of 1933, "Anyhow I am going to paddle right ahead and wring as many jobs out of the men for the women who will help build up the party, as I can."[3]

The jobs that Dewson arranged for women in the network, as well as those for other Democratic women, were testimony to her perseverance and skill at securing patronage for women. By early 1934, the end was finally in sight. Molly Dewson continued to handle patronage requests throughout the 1930s (in fact, she played a role in her own appointment to the Social Security Board in 1937), but patronage ceased to be her primary concern. Dewson wrote Lavinia Engle in May, 1934, "Pretty near all the leaders who wished for appointments have been taken care of. A few wait on final developments but I consider the patronage issue closed except for casual happenings. The government has settled down to its stride."[4]

Molly Dewson gladly relinquished the burden of patronage, as she confided to Eleanor Roosevelt: "The real joy will be that I will not have to pester you and Franklin about these dashed jobs. I have set my jaw and gone through with it but I was not born to nag and I hate it. . . . I shall be able to call it a day on patronage and be free to give my attention to building up the women's side of the party organization."[5] Enlarging women's roles in the political system had always been one of Molly Dewson's primary concerns. In 1934 she finally had time to implement her innovative ideas. Once again, she had the strong support of other women in the network.

The cornerstone of Molly Dewson's approach to politics in the 1930s was promotion of widespread public understanding of the programs of Franklin Roosevelt's New Deal. When she became the first full-time director of the Women's Division of the Democratic National Committee in October of 1933, Dewson was not sure that her issue-oriented approach would appeal to the older style of Democratic women—women, as Dewson once described them in jest, whose idea of organization was handing out cookies in the shape of donkeys at Democratic teas. But, Dewson wrote Ellen Woodward in 1935, every day she received confirmation that women were more interested in the broad objectives of government than in mere party politics.[6] In fact, the issue-oriented style of women's politics that Molly Dewson pioneered has remained the norm for both Democratic and Republican women ever since. Begun during the woman suffrage campaign, this approach saw its widest application in the politics of the New Deal.

Molly Dewson unveiled her education scheme, which she dubbed the "Reporter Plan" (to the lasting confusion of journalists covering the project), at Eleanor Roosevelt's press conference on January 15, 1934. Dewson said later, "Things were marching so fast and everyone was so busy that even Mrs. Roosevelt had never heard of it or anyone else before it was presented." Dewson had not cleared the Reporter Plan with President Roosevelt either, but she acted with his implicit support: "In the early days Roosevelt was too busy to consult about my plans. I knew what I wanted to do and I was sure it would suit him."[7]

The original description of the Reporter Plan showed Dewson's broad goals:

Every woman may become informed and aid in the recovery program of her government.

How?

By continuous work in the following way:
Every county organization of Democratic women appoints women in every community to serve as Reporters of each Federal agency.
Each Reporter writes to the Washington agency for all available information on her particular agency . . .
She pastes newspaper and magazine clippings on her agency in note book, and fortifies herself with accessible facts.
She reads the critics and is prepared to answer criticism.
Reporters tell their neighbors what they have learned.
Reporters and other interested women should meet frequently for round-table discussions.
The Reporter whose agency is under discussion acts as a leader.

Result: Reporters are prepared to speak before civic groups - clubs - and at local Institutes of Government.
Reporters help elect Democratic candidates.
Reporters become a real force in helping shape the trend of government.[8]

Emma Bugbee of the New York *Herald Tribune* said, "Just another paper plan," but Molly Dewson replied, "Wait and see." Dewson had the last word. The 1940 Institute of Government, where five thousand "intelligent, informed, alert and enthusiastic women . . . astounded government officials by the sagacity of their questions," effectively rebutted predictions that the Reporter Plan would never get off the ground.[9]

Dewson geared the Reporter Plan to the "extraordinary opportunity" presented by the depression to encourage wider public appreciation of the workings of government and the policies of the New Deal. The Reporter Plan might not have worked so well without the excitement generated by the new directions of Roosevelt's programs. Women were not just to study these new programs—they were to perpetuate the mood of social reform. Signing on as a Reporter became a woman's patriotic duty. "Any woman who studies the New Deal is helping her country," proclaimed the *Democratic Digest* in June 1934. Dewson further explained: "We are in the midst of a great movement of national forces which often lie dormant or are controlled by finance. I hope that big things will be accomplished before everything settles down again . . . That is where we [Democratic women] come in."[10]

In addition to educating women about the New Deal, the Reporter Plan gave women in the Democratic party something interesting and useful to do, especially between elections. According to Dewson, it really put "ginger" into the women's Democratic organization. The Reporter Plan served less lofty purposes as well. Since many newspapers were hostile to Franklin Roosevelt and the New Deal, the Reporter Plan generated pro-New Deal publicity in communities throughout the country.[11]

With her emphasis on education and policy issues, Molly Dewson was pursuing objectives quite different from those that interested Jim Farley and the Democratic National Committee. Dewson saw their two roles as quite distinct: Farley kept the party bosses and faithful stalwarts in line, while Dewson concentrated on wooing independent voters, especially women, to Roosevelt.[12] Dewson gladly abdicated responsibility for areas already solidly Democratic. Voters there, about 40 percent of the electorate, voted Democratic no matter what—all one had to do was get them to the polls. But Dewson thought that a national party needed more than just party faithful:

The men's organizations do not know what to do about foot loose voters—the twenty per cent that decided elections. They put their trust in conventional old fashioned methods, big meetings, spellbinding, dull "literature," newspaper publicity, bill board advertising, sunflowers and what not and let it go at that. All these things are grand for Party enthusiasm, but leave the independent voter cold even if they ever reach him.[13]

It was this independent voter, especially of the female variety, that Molly Dewson was trying to snare.

A corollary to Dewson's belief that the Democratic party could not stay in power without appealing to the independent voter was her conviction that Democratic strength in large Eastern industrial cities was not sufficient to elect national Democratic candidates. The party also had to court small towns and rural areas for support, and Dewson did just that in the 1930s. Dewson's concentration on smaller communities helps to explain, at least in part, why so few black women were prominent in the Women's Division. Most black women lived in the cities, where Dewson did little work, or in the South, where they were not registered voters. Dewson's program had the greatest success in small towns in the Midwest and West, areas lacking large blocs of black voters.[14]

Jim Farley was willing to let Dewson go her own way as long as she did not interfere with his activities. But conflict developed over financial support for the Women's Division's plans, especially between elections. Farley had been schooled in New York politics, where politicians believed that the best campaigns were the shortest. With the party faithful safely in line between elections, why waste time and money courting their support? Dewson, on the other hand, saw the months and years between elections as the ideal time to cultivate new voters and build up the women's organization. Campaigns were too frenzied for converting undecided voters with facts and figures, or for intelligent discussion of the issues.[15]

Matters came to a head in April of 1934, when Dewson asked the National Committee for a budget of $50,000. (By way of comparison, the Women's Division budget had been $42,000 for the 1932 campaign.) Jim Farley turned her down. Dewson suggested they let the President ("The Boss," as she called him) make the final decision. After meeting with both Farley and Dewson, Franklin Roosevelt asked Dewson to accept a budget of $36,000. Dewson agreed. Claiming victory, Dewson interpreted Franklin Roosevelt's decision as a pledge of confidence in the women's work: "Obviously the President thinks it is worth our effort for even though the Democratic National Committee is in debt he is willing to have us go ahead for such an end and we are to have the money."[16]

After 1934, with the financial dispute settled to the women's satisfaction, the Women's Division expanded its activities. Although Molly Dewson resigned as director of the Women's Division to head its Advisory Committee, she still retained control over most Division activities. Dewson was assisted by two able directors of the Women's Division,

Carolyn Wolfe of Utah and Dorothy McAlister of Michigan. They, along with the rest of the Women's Division staff, handled the day-to-day work in the office. The Reporter Plan continued as the keystone of the Women's Division program. By November 1935, there were 15,000 active Reporters operating in every state except Louisiana.[17]

The Reporters were usually local women who volunteered their time to Democratic women's organizations in their communities. Occasionally such women rose through the ranks to state or regional Reporter Chairmen, or state National Committeewomen, but this was fairly rare. None of the women in the network was a Reporter—their contributions to Democratic politics came much further up the ladder. Women in the network concentrated on politics at the national level, not on grass-roots organizing at the state and local levels.

Women in the network assisted Dewson and the Women's Division in many ways. For instance, women volunteered to speak at Regional Conferences for Democratic women throughout the country. These conferences, initiated by the Women's Division in late 1934, were designed to stimulate interest and morale among Democratic women between elections. The programs offered by the Regional Conferences foreshadowed the 1940 Institute of Government in Washington. Surveys of Women's Division activities, discussions of party organization (male and female), pep talks about the Reporter Plan, and speeches concerning current government programs of interest to women were typically featured. These conferences encouraged local and state Democratic women leaders to think of the party as an organization concerned with national issues, thereby (in Molly Dewson's words) expanding women's perspective "beyond the saddle galls of local politics."[18]

An impressive array of women in the network participated in these Regional Conferences. At a Regional Conference in Georgia in January 1935, Ellen Sullivan Woodward spoke on the Works Progress Administration, Emily Newell Blair discussed consumer affairs under the NRA, Carolyn Wolfe of the Women's Division spoke on the farm program, Assistant U.S. Treasurer Marion Glass Banister talked about taxation, and Mary LaDame discussed her work in the U.S. Employment Service.[19]

Women in the network also cooperated with the Women's Division through the *Democratic Digest*. This magazine, begun in the mid-1920s by the Washington-based Women's National Democratic Club, was taken over by the Women's Division in March 1935, with a circulation of only 1,600. The magazine's format was revised and expanded, with a corresponding growth in subscriptions: 13,000 by 1936, and a peak of 26,500 in 1938.[20]

The *Democratic Digest* covered both politics and government, being "devoted to giving facts about the accomplishments of the departments and agencies in the Federal government as well as the activities of our Party leaders."[21] Although many of its features were geared to the Reporter Plan, the magazine appealed to all women in the Democratic party. Regular features covered recent legislation and Supreme Court actions, and an ongoing series described specific agencies and Cabinet departments. These articles often were written by network women prominent in these areas.[22] Reading the *Democratic Digest* was an excellent way to keep up with the work of women friends in various areas of government and politics, similar to reading Eleanor Roosevelt's syndicated column, "My Day." In effect, "My Day" served as a daily network newsletter, and the *Democratic Digest* was its monthly counterpart.

The Women's National Democratic Club served as a center for many women in politics and government in the network. The club had been founded in the 1920s at a time when women were not very welcome in regular party organizations. Daisy Harriman, Emily Newell Blair, Marion Glass Banister, and Lucy Somerville Howorth were early backers who continued their association with the Women's National Democratic Club into the 1930s. Its clubhouse on New Hampshire Avenue served as a meeting place for prominent Democratic women throughout the country when they came to Washington.[23]

The club also provided numerous opportunities for women in the network to keep in touch through the teas and receptions it sponsored. Carolyn Wolfe described one such gathering: "No new gossip here, but I have not yet seen Ellen Woodward. She always has more news than anyone else I know. Saturday the club entertained at Tea for all the women campaigners and I saw most of the stars. Frances Perkins was there and I had a short visit with her. She really is a grand person!"[24]

A Women's National Democratic Club banquet in March of 1935 honoring women in the New Deal served a similar purpose. Anticipating the National Institute of Government dinner five years later, the guest list of this banquet read like a *Who's Who* of prominent women in government. Speakers at the dinner included Frances Perkins, Congresswomen Mary T. Norton and Caroline O'Day, Marion Glass Banister, Lucille Foster McMillin, Ellen Sullivan Woodward, and Dorothy McAlister. Emily Newell Blair, Clara Beyer, Jo Coffin, Lucy Somerville Howorth, Jane Hoey, Mary LaDame, and Katharine Lenroot were honored guests. Molly Dewson and Eleanor Roosevelt were among the few absentees in. an otherwise complete representation of the network. Having dinner together at a political gathering, whether a banquet, a Regional Conference, or a local fund-raiser, was one more way for women in the network to communicate and collaborate on common goals.[25]

The women in the network also participated in Democratic political activities in other ways. All of these women helped Molly Dewson with her work at the Women's Division on occasion. Emily Newell Blair wrote Dewson in 1935 with ideas and suggestions for the Women's Division, adding, "Think your plans splendid. Want to co-operate as you think best—but do acknowledge to an ache sometimes to be 'in the know.'"[26] Many women in the network went beyond just offering advice—they were active and trusted confidantes in Dewson's maneuvers to increase women's roles in the Democratic party.

Ellen Sullivan Woodward, for example, could not work openly on political matters because of her official positions at the Federal Emergency Relief Administration and the Social Security Board, but she confessed that she often helped out behind the scenes. Ellen Woodward and other Southern women like Lucy Somerville Howorth worked closely with Molly Dewson to increase the participation of Southern women in national Democratic politics. The National Consumers' League even got involved occasionally. Before Molly Dewson left on an organizing trip among Democratic women in the South, she asked the NCL for lists of their Southern supporters from their files. Since the Consumers' League had devoted considerable effort in the 1930s to work in the South, especially in textile regions, it had developed strong contacts with the more progressive elements there. When Dewson went South she sent notices of the Democratic women's regional meetings to those already sympathetic to NCL aims, and no doubt she picked up some new recruits.[27]

Eleanor Roosevelt was also active in Democratic politics in the 1930s, both publicly and behind the scenes. Apart from her role in securing patronage for loyal Democratic women, Roosevelt's most important contribution to politics was probably her intermediary role between Dewson and the men at the Democratic National Committee. For example, a White House dinner party given in December 1935 included President Roosevelt, Eleanor Roosevelt, Molly Dewson, Ellen Woodward, and James Farley of the Democratic National Committee to discuss women's roles in the upcoming campaign. (To show who was behind the meeting, the invitation to Farley read, "Molly Dewson and I think it would be a very good idea to have a discussion with the President about various things of political interest.")[28] Jim Farley admired Eleanor Roosevelt tremendously, and he gave close attention to her suggestions.

For the most part, Eleanor Roosevelt did not participate directly in the Women's Division organization, nor did she usually take part in political campaigns. Yet she felt so strongly about the need for more women in Congress that she broke this rule to campaign for her friend and fellow New Yorker Caroline O'Day when O'Day ran for Congress in 1934. Her public endorsement of a close friend for political office definitely raised some eyebrows, but Eleanor Roosevelt replied that since Caroline O'Day was working toward the same goals that she and the President supported, it was perfectly proper for the First Lady to speak on her behalf. Many other women in the network, especially those long active in New York State politics, assisted in O'Day's successful campaign.[29]

Caroline O'Day occupied an interesting place in the network because she and Mary T. Norton were the most prominent Democratic women holding elected office in the 1930s. Unlike Mary T. Norton, who worked quite well with Dewson and the Women's Division, O'Day's experience with the New York State Women's Democratic Committee (quite a strong organization in its own right) occasionally put her at odds with Molly Dewson's national organization. Because of concern over conflicting priorities and overlapping initiatives on the national and state levels, the Women's Division basically allowed the New York women to run their state organization on their own. New Yorkers Caroline O'Day, Nancy Cook, Florence Casper Whitney, and Elinor Morgenthau wielded more influence as a consequence of the Women's Division decision.[30]

By the late 1930s, and possibly earlier, many felt that Caroline O'Day was trying to do too much. She had two full-time jobs: Congresswoman-at-large from New York, and head of the Women's Division of the Democratic party in New York State. Since Eleanor Roosevelt was well acquainted with both the policies and personalities of the New York women's organization from the 1920s, she volunteered to act as an intermediary. Eleanor wrote to Eddie Flynn, prominent New York and New Deal Democratic leader, about O'Day: "I think it is quite obvious that she can not be in session in Congress, campaign for herself, and run the state committee office, but I wonder if this should not be said to her by Jim [Farley] rather than by me. I am perfectly willing to do it but I think she might take it with better grace from him."[31] O'Day retained her position, but delegated some of her responsibilities to other members of the New York Women's Division staff.

Despite such tensions, Caroline O'Day remained an important member of the team. She and Mary T. Norton, representatives of the few Democratic congresswomen in the 1930s, reflected credit on the women's side of the party and contributed an important dimension to the network of women in the New Deal.

While women in the network were involved in some of the more mundane aspects of political life, such as obtaining patronage, fighting for larger budgets, and mediating between rival state and national organizations, they were also very concerned with political issues of importance to women in public life. During the 1930s, the two major political issues around which women in the network mobilized were the Equal Rights Amendment and Section 213 of the National Economy Act.

The Equal Rights Amendment was a highly emotional issue for women in public life. It had first been proposed by the National Women's Party in 1923 as the next step toward winning full equality for women under the law after the passage of the nineteenth amendment. Unlike today when most feminists agree on the need for the ERA, the amendment proved a divisive issue for the women's movement in the 1920s and 1930s. The main bone of contention was the effect of the ERA on protective legislation. Members of the National Women's Party (NWP), the main backer of the ERA in the 1930s, claimed that laws limiting night work or setting minimum wage levels for women workers did more harm than good by restricting opportunities for women workers. Women whose backgrounds included work in organizations such as the National Consumers' League and the Women's Trade Union League (that is, most of the women in the network) disagreed. As Molly Dewson said to National Women's Party member Sue Shelton White: "You could not expect me not to be sour about the NWP considering their attitude toward my life's endeavor to prevent employers from using women's dire need to force their wages below the subsistence level."[32]

Another ERA supporter, Emma Guffey Miller, had lobbied for protective legislation during the suffrage campaign but afterward changed her mind: "I found that the so-called protective legislation for which I had so ardently worked was not protective but restrictive and prohibitive." Miller wrote to Dorothy McAlister of the Women's Division that working women should be allowed to stand on their own feet, adding that "the day for paternalistic legislation had gone by and that working women would advance much faster and further if they were given equal treatment with men." Molly Dewson wanted nothing to do with such a philosophy: "I respectfully submit that those of us who are professional and business women should not be permitted to write a principle in the law which will sacrifice women in industry. These latter women are not vocal like their more fortunate, but not overly sympathetic sisters." Frances Perkins seconded this view, writing sarcastically: "There is one whole group of women who is always greatly excited about the word 'equality.' You make them equal and that suits them splendidly."[33]

Clearly the Equal Rights Amendment evoked strong emotions from women in the network. At base were conflicting conceptions of women's equality. Supporters of the ERA in the 1920s and 1930s believed that men and women were alike, and that women could never be free until laws and custom eliminated sex-based distinctions. Opponents of the ERA believed that men and women were fundamentally different when it came to physical strength and emotional makeup, thereby concluding that women in the work force needed the protection of special legislation. Differences over tactics and emphasis existed as well. Opponents of the ERA recognized that legal discrimination against women still existed after the passage of the nineteenth amendment, but they were unwilling to sacrifice the positive good that protective legislation had provided for women workers in order to strike down other legal discrimination. This strong clash over priorities affected all women active in public life in the 1920s, 1930s, and beyond.

In the end, only two members of the network, Emma Guffey Miller and Sue Shelton White, belonged to the National Women's Party, and only Miller was a vocal advocate of the amendment in the 1930s. Yet women in the network still found it necessary to be on their guard where the ERA was concerned, especially at international conferences where the National Women's Party several times attempted to put the ERA question on the formal agenda. The tactics of the National Women's Party at the 1936 Inter-American Peace Conference held at Buenos Aires, and the network's response, illustrate one such confrontation.

As a matter of course, women in the network suggested suitable women for delegations to conferences or international commissions. Before the conference at Buenos Aires, Molly Dewson had sent the names of several women to the State Department. Florence Casper Whitney, a prominent Democratic woman in New York State who was a social reformer and a friend of the Roosevelts, was Dewson's first choice. But Whitney was passed over, even though she was also Frances Perkins's first choice. The State Department told the Women's Division that of the five delegates, only one could be a woman, and she must be fluent in Spanish. Dewson exclaimed in exasperation to Frances Perkins, "Getting near my limit."[34] Elise Musser, an active Democratic woman from the Midwest and Dewson's second choice, was ultimately chosen for the delegation.

Women in the network were generally pleased with the choice of Musser, but they wanted to make sure that she was ready for possible trouble over the ERA in Buenos Aires. Frances Perkins reminded Frieda Miller of the Women's Bureau that although Musser spoke Spanish fluently, "she does not, however, know the details which she will require to deal with the Women's Party, nor the general principles of social and labor laws, and other important factors."[35] Several women in the network gave Musser a crash course in these areas.

The advance preparations paid off, because the Women's Party did attempt to put the ERA question onto the conference agenda. Molly Dewson learned of the plan from a friendly member of the United States delegation, probably Musser or Sumner Welles, and Dewson immediately contacted Josephine Roche. Roche then urged Frances Perkins to use her influence with the State Department to keep the ERA off the agenda. Roche also asked Emily Newell Blair and Belle Sherwin, former president of the National League of Women Voters, to rally their friends in government. The Inter-American Conference never took up the question of the Equal Rights Amendment.[36]

Women in the network were quite successful in preventing the Equal Rights Amendment from becoming national (or international) policy. Franklin Roosevelt showed no inclination to support the measure, and it was not yet a matter of serious discussion in the Democratic party, although it would be in the 1940s. Though other factors were at work (such as the amendment's limited support among women's groups during the decade), the pressure and support women mobilized through the network was certainly decisive in forestalling action on the ERA in the 1930s.

Women in the network were less successful in mobilizing against Section 213 of the 1932 National Economy Act. This law prohibited both husband and wife from working for the federal government at the same time. While not discriminatory against women on its face, the law usually forced women to resign because they made less money than their husbands. In all, 1,600 married female government employees were dismissed from government service between 1932 and 1937. Molly Dewson called this law "that dumb clause" and the "one black mark" against the Roosevelt administration's record on women. The Government Workers' Council, which included Marion Glass Banister, Ellen Sullivan Woodward, Emma Guffey Miller, Lavinia Engle, Sue Shelton White, and Carolyn Wolfe of the Women's Division, petitioned President Roosevelt for repeal of Section 213, but with no success.[37]

Molly Dewson viewed Section 213 as "a temporary expedient of the depression which I firmly believe will be sloughed off as we return to normalcy." She got herself into trouble in 1936 when she hinted that Section 213 would be repealed and then could not deliver on her promise. Dewson wrote to Eleanor Roosevelt, "Well F.D.R. did say it and poor harassed man he has let me down. It's embarrassing but not fatal." There was a collective sigh of relief when the act finally was repealed in 1937.[38]

Failure to bring about the repeal of Section 213 was not the only setback faced by Democratic women in the 1930s. While the Women's Division grew and expanded during the first term of the Roosevelt administration, some ongoing problems remained. The greatest disappointment for Dewson was the failure to make headway toward the goal of fifty-

fifty (equal) representation on all party committees. Only seventeen states had adopted this rule by 1937. Continued male resistance was part of the problem, but the existence of organizations outside the regular party structure, like the Women's National Democratic Club, contributed as well. Dewson wrote to Congresswoman Caroline O'Day, "Perhaps we may still be in the stage where we have to do our fighting by clubs formed of selected groups of women, but I think we should try to burst into the Party and count for something in the regular organization." An uneasy truce between such women's clubs as the Women's National Democratic Club and the Women's Division existed for the rest of the decade.[39]

Even the Reporter Plan had limitations. Ellen Woodward pointed out to Molly Dewson in 1935, "I think the Reporter Plan has worked out splendidly in many places among the more intelligent women, but we must do something more in order to reach the large groups a little further down the line." The Reporter Plan, Dewson admitted, had not caught on in the South.[40] Moreover, it kept women on the outside of the power structure of the Democratic party itself. Dorothy McAlister of the Women's Division praised women for learning about government policies, but acknowledged that the Reporter Plan had an unfortunate side effect: "The result is that in many states the women have the knowledge of issues but do not have the opportunity to use that knowledge for the benefit of the party, because of the fact that the men control the party machinery."[41]

Notwithstanding these problems, the Women's Division commanded a much stronger position approaching the 1936 election than it had in 1932. Molly Dewson noticed a change in Jim Farley's attitude since the 1932 campaign. As a matter of course, Dewson was invited to attend all DNC staff meetings, and out-of-town Democratic leaders who came to see Farley often stopped by Dewson's office as well. No doubt Dewson's political stature was enhanced by the 15,000 Reporters serving as a "nationwide force of New Deal saleswomen" for the upcoming election campaign. In addition, Dewson had at her disposal some 60,000 Democratic women precinct workers, as well as 10,000 state and county leaders.[42]

Molly Dewson and the Women's Division had begun looking ahead to the 1936 election almost as soon as Roosevelt was elected, but active planning commenced in late 1935. Much of the women's preconvention activity centered on the platform. Molly Dewson wrote to Eleanor Roosevelt in June 1936, "We don't ask for much in the way of patronage or power but we do think we should have a say in what the party stands for." Fifteen women chosen for the Women's Advisory Committee on the Platform formulated planks of special interest to women. Dewson sought prior agreement on most issues, as she lobbied to one woman on the committee: "For example, I hope you are for the ratification of the Child Labor Amendment." After the fifteen women forwarded their suggestions to Caroline O'Day, head of the group, O'Day and a subcommittee in Washington drafted the planks. This subcommittee was composed of O'Day, Harriet Elliott, Dorothy McAlister, Carolyn Wolfe, and Molly Dewson from the Women's Division; Emily Newell Blair; Jo Coffin; and Lavinia Engle, prominent Maryland Democrat.[43]

The final document summarized the ideology Democratic women brought to politics and government in the 1930s. The opening statement of the Advisory Committee reiterated their general views:

> During the past three years women have widened their interest from isolated individual laws to broader social and economic trends and are looking at America as a whole. They have come to realize that human welfare is inseparably integrated with economic conditions.
>
> Possessed of a broader social outlook, aware of the responsibility of the Federal Government—women commend this administration for taking the lead in solving these modern human problems. Such leadership, such government commands the respect and confidence of women and offers a challenge and a future opportunity to those whose zeal for service is strong.[44]

Among specific recommendations of the committee, the "chief and first" concerned peace, since war and its consequences destroyed the fundamental security of citizens and impeded programs for social and economic betterment. The proposed plank supporting ratification of the Child Labor Amendment was a close second in importance. Another suggested plank commended the Roosevelt administration for its recognition of "the intellectual and spiritual contributions of women to the welfare of our country," exemplified by the large number of women appointed to responsible positions in national affairs. The plank also urged repeal of laws that discriminated on the basis of marital or economic status, such as Section 213. Other planks endorsed by the Women's Advisory Committee covered consumers' rights, a strengthened Civil Service, an expanded federal housing program, federal support for education, and civil liberties.[45] There was no mention of the Equal Rights Amendment.

Molly Dewson's next step was to ensure that the women's suggestions would be considered by the Platform Committee. Dewson feared a repetition of women's experiences in 1924, when Eleanor Roosevelt and her colleagues waited in vain outside the door of the smoke-filled committee room in which the men were drafting the platform. Dewson confided to a member of the advisory committee, "I am not for staging any petty revolutions and if we were not to be heard, I, myself, would not be for having the committee. This would sound spineless to any feminist but I am practical and am concentrated on a Democratic victory this fall."[46]

Dewson first enlisted Eleanor Roosevelt herself, penciling "Can You Help?" on a letter stressing the importance of the platform to women. Dewson also turned to Mrs. Bennet Champ Clark, whose husband, the Democratic Senator from Missouri, was on the Committee on Resolutions and Platform. Dewson deputized Mrs. Clark to find out whether the women's suggestions would be considered, and to report back to her. Clark's report was positive.[47]

When the convention convened, therefore, Molly Dewson was reasonably sure that the women's recommendations would be heard by the Platform Committee. The actual breakthrough came when women were designated as alternates to the Platform Committee. (The actual wording was that alternates be of the opposite sex from the delegates, all of whom were male.) Since men often missed the platform meetings as a result of other convention business, the women alternates were able to present their planks and vote on them. The event rated a first-page story in the *New York Times*, which read in part, "What is called the biggest coup in years so far as women in politics are concerned materialized at the Democratic convention this afternoon as softly and smoothly as a summer zephyr."[48]

Although most of the women's planks were incorporated into the platform, there was no mention of the Child Labor Amendment or Section 213. Since the Republican platform had included a general statement supporting repeal of Section 213, women were especially disappointed that the Democratic platform ignored the issue. Dewson downplayed the Republican plank, claiming it was so carefully worded as to be practically meaningless. She said facetiously, "We are against man eating sharks, too."[49]

On the whole, Dewson was pleased with the reception of the Women's Advisory Committee on the Platform and with the recognition that women's new roles on the Platform Committee had brought. But Dewson realized that women were far from equally represented on the party councils. Four years later, as the Women's Division prepared for another election campaign, Dewson wrote her successor at the Women's Division, Dorothy McAlister: "I had the Platform Committee in '36 because girls like Lavinia Engle wanted it. No harm and a little pleasant importance to a few. I'm not much for that sort of futile stuff but I did want to have good women ready to get themselves appointed alternates to the Platform Committee if I could pull off the scheme as a first step toward what you are now after."[50]

After the Philadelphia convention, the Women's Division swung into action. Molly Dewson reminded W. Forbes Morgan of the Democratic National Committee, "The President says we are depending on the women's vote to put us over." Molly Dewson envisioned Democratic women as "the mouth-to-mouth, house-to-house interpreters and apostles of the New Deal." Congresswoman Mary T. Norton later reminded her fellow Democratic workers of Dewson's exhortations that "we Democrats should take lessons from the Fuller Brush man" in going door-to-door to talk to voters.[51]

The campaign plans of the Women's Division were based on three assumptions, which an internal campaign memorandum described:

1. Roosevelt would be reelected if the independent voters, the deciding element, knew the achievements of his first term and the significant substantiating figures.
2. Only neighbors could and would get over this information to the individual voter.
3. Minor Democratic leaders, the backbone of the Party, would become more enthusiastic workers when in possession of these facts clearly stated on Rainbow Fliers, each flier carrying the important facts in a given field of governmental activity—as agriculture, business, labor, finance, etc.[52]

In working to implement these goals, Molly Dewson inspired a strong sense of camaraderie at the Women's Division headquarters and among Democratic women throughout the country. Anna Dickie Oleson wrote to "Queen Mollie" a month before the election, "Wherever I go the women seem more acting and alert than the men. Your division is doing great work."[53]

As in past campaigns, Molly Dewson and the Women's Division received strong support from women in the network during the 1936 election campaign. The women made speeches to Iowa Democrats, participated in radio broadcasts in New Jersey, and drafted letters for release to the newspapers, among other tasks. Marion Glass Banister wrote the Women's Division, "I only wish I could have done a hundred times more." Mary Anderson's help prompted a warm note from Dewson: "Good old Mary! That's a great contribution to the party and can we use it!"[54]

Since Mary Norton was an elected representative of the Democratic party, she was expected to take an active part in the campaign. For other women in the network with government positions, political activity was sometimes problematic. Dewson was livid that the Women's Division could not use Lucy Somerville Howorth as a political speaker unless she took a leave of absence from the Veterans' Board.[55] One compromise allowed prominent women to address supposedly nonpolitical gatherings, such as a dinner honoring Frances Perkins. While the women confined their remarks to their work in Washington, the message was clear: vote for Franklin Roosevelt so that women can continue their worthwhile initiatives in the government.

Other women in the network took unpaid leaves of absence from their jobs to speak full time during the last weeks of the campaign. Marion Glass Banister took time off from her job at the Treasury Department, receiving reimbursement from the Women's Division for her travel expenses, but no pay. Likewise, Nellie Tayloe Ross, Director of the Mint and a popular and well-known Democratic speaker, gave up her official post temporarily to volunteer full time on the campaign.[56]

Ruth Bryan Owen, who had inherited her father's gift of eloquence on the public platform, was the most prominent speaker in the Democratic women's grab bag. Molly Dewson had lined up Owen as a speaker in the spring of 1936, planning to send her from engagement to engagement in a plane piloted by Phoebe Omlie, whose appointment to the U.S. Department of Aeronautics Dewson had arranged.[57] Then on July 13, 1936, Ruth Bryan Owen married Captain Micki Rohde in the chapel at Hyde Park, New York, with Eleanor Roosevelt looking on. Owen had met Rohde, a captain in the Danish Guard, while she was Minister to Denmark. Daisy Harriman reported to Molly Dewson the State Department's contention that since Owen had married a Dane, she should no longer be allowed to serve as Minister. Some State Department members even questioned whether Owen (who they mistakenly assumed had lost her U.S. citizenship when she married a foreigner) should participate in the political campaign at all. Passing Daisy Harriman's information along to Eleanor Roosevelt, Dewson remarked, "This seems to me to be man at his smallest."[58]

Soon after, Ruth Bryan Owen voluntarily resigned as Minister to Denmark because of her marriage, but kept her plans to speak in the campaign. Since Owen no longer had a job to return to, Eleanor Roosevelt volunteered to speak to Henry Morgenthau, Sr. about special compensation for her in October and November. But Molly Dewson was not sure Owen deserved such special treatment, no matter how popular a speaker she was with the women. According to Dewson, Owen's contribution was no greater than that of other women who gave up their salary for the campaign. Dewson reminded Eleanor, "After all, Ruth went out in the last campaign for just her expenses and she certainly was taken care of in a dramatic way that must have appealed to her."[59]

Ruth Bryan Owen's speaking tour went well until early in October, when she fractured her leg and had to withdraw from the campaign. Fortunately, Anna Dickie Olesen was available to take over Owen's schedule. By then Owen had become uncomfortable about the question of compensation too, and hinted that the matter should be dropped. The final resolution was contained in a scribbled note from Eleanor to Molly: "Let's have Henry [Morgenthau] give her $1000 and let it go at that."[60]

The Ruth Bryan Owen misunderstanding was one of the few problems faced by the Women's Division during the 1936 campaign. In general, its various departments, speakers' programs, and educational projects functioned smoothly and efficiently.

Here, as elsewhere in women's political and governmental activities in the New Deal, women's experiences in the suffrage campaign twenty years earlier strongly influenced their approach to political questions. The excitement of the 1932 campaign reminded Dewson of "the suffrage days when all we asked was an opportunity to serve." Frances Perkins noted the close ties between Democratic politics and woman suffrage. Many of the same women participated in the two campaigns, and they used the same techniques in the New Deal that they had learned during the 1910s: "The women's organizations around New York and in some other states too, with a hard core of the same group that were for suffrage, have followed the same methods of organizing wherever they have gone into politics." Perkins went on to elaborate: "That is, they've done a grass roots organizing job and haven't depended upon big, overall banners and slogans, although they haven't been ashamed to use them and have been perfectly able to get up a big meeting. But they have known that the real work was done in smaller meetings, in the house to house visitation, and in the organizing." Molly Dewson's strategy, Frances Perkins noted, was to "find capable women in a community and organize around them."[61]

Molly Dewson introduced another political innovation in the 1930s that drew directly on the woman suffrage experience. One-page fact sheets, called "Rainbow Fliers" because they were printed on different-colored sheets of paper, were first introduced in Roosevelt's 1930 gubernatorial campaign, and their use greatly expanded in 1932 and 1936. The idea for the fliers came from the 1918 Massachusetts Woman Suffrage Association campaign against Republican Senator John Weeks. In that campaign the suffragists, including a much younger Molly Dewson, circulated one-page leaflets highlighting Weeks's negative voting record in Congress, especially his antisuffrage stands. Dewson described these fliers as "just the facts and no comments—a sort of, if that's what you want vote for it. Not a word about his opponent."[62]

This same technique, printing the facts and distributing them widely, was utilized by the Democratic National Committee and the Women's

Division in 1936. The Rainbow Fliers stressed concrete facts about Democratic programs without editorializing or inflated campaign rhetoric. The fliers comprised more than 80 percent of all Democratic literature in 1936, saving the Democratic National Committee an estimated $1,000,000 in publicity costs. As Dewson succinctly put it, "It paid."[63]

Even though the Women's Division pioneered the idea of Rainbow Fliers in the New Deal, wrote all the copy, and provided the illustrations, Molly Dewson did not insist that the Women's Division receive credit for the fliers. In fact, she was glad they were not specifically attributed to women: "I was still afraid some men would prefer man-made statements and I considered whatever kudos might have come to the women did not offset the risk."[64] Always the practical politician, Molly Dewson shepherded the Women's Division and the network through the intricacies of Democratic politics in the 1930s.

Molly Dewson, the Women's Division, and the other women in the network were delighted with the election results on November 3, 1936. Mary LaDame wrote to Molly Dewson, "In my humble opinion there is no one who did more to provide an intelligent basis of fact on which voters could make their decision in the campaign than you and your associates in the Women's Division."[65] The network saw the election as a vote of confidence in Roosevelt's initiatives over the past four years, and a mandate for more governmental action and reform.

The women in the network also viewed the election as a vindication of the new roles women were playing in the Democratic party. Molly Dewson spoke for all these women when she said: "In three years Roosevelt had set a new trend. At last women had their foot inside the door. We had the opportunity to demonstrate our ability to see what was needed and to get the job done while working harmoniously with men."[66] Women in the Democratic party looked forward to the second term with raised expectations and with the practical experience of the last four years to guide them.

5

WOMEN AND SOCIAL WELFARE POLICY

"You and I, Mary, made Roosevelt's labor policy," Frances Perkins once remarked to Molly Dewson.[1] Just as the network played an important role in Democratic politics in the New Deal, so too did it have a strong impact on the social welfare policies of the New Deal. Women in the network, drawing on the experiences and resources of the National Consumers' League and the Women's Trade Union League, participated in most of the Roosevelt administration's initiatives in the social welfare field in the 1930s. When the name of one woman from the network turns up in a discussion of New Deal programs, the names of several other network members are usually not far away.

Obviously no single group can claim exclusive credit for a piece of legislation or a new program, but in many cases the network of women in the New Deal played a crucial role in developing and implementing the New Deal's social welfare policies. The manner in which the network functioned as a policy-influencing group emerges from an examination of the network's impact on several areas of New Deal policy: the National Recovery Administration, the 1935 Social Security Act and the 1938 Fair Labor Standards Act, and the relief programs for women in the Works Progress Administration and its predecessors.

The National Industrial Recovery Act was one of the final measures introduced in the Congress by the Roosevelt administration in the spring of 1933. The law's purpose was clear—to get industrial production moving again—but no one quite knew how to accomplish this goal given the dire shape of the economy. Lacking a clear focus, the NIRA emerged as an "omnibus proposal that had a little for everyone." Business received government authorization to suspend the antitrust laws in order to draw up code agreements limiting production. Labor received Section 7(a), which guaranteed the right to collective bargaining. An extensive public works program was included to stimulate industrial recovery and employment.[2] Reforms long sought by women in the network were also part of the act: various sections specified minimum wages and maximum hours, outlawed child labor, and provided for consumer representation.

Not all the women in the network had joined the administration when the National Recovery Administration started up in April of 1933, but during the two years of the NRA's existence, many in the network took part in its operation. Yet unlike women's experiences in the relief agencies, where most of the initiatives came from a special women's division, women's roles in the NRA were never concentrated to any great extent. There was a Women's Section of the NRA, but its function was limited to encouraging women throughout the country to patronize only businesses that displayed the Blue Eagle, the symbol of compliance ("We Do Our Part") with NRA codes. Eleanor Roosevelt was one of the few women from the network involved in this effort, speaking on the issue and devoting a chapter of her 1933 book, *It's Up to the Women*, to women and the NRA.[3] For the most part, the involvement of women in the network with the NRA was channeled through the Labor Advisory Board, the Labor Department, and the Consumers' Advisory Board, rather than through the Women's Section.

As finally adopted, the National Industrial Recovery Act contained three major sections. Titles II and III established the Public Works Administration, which undertook extensive public works programs to stimulate industrial recovery; Harold Ickes, Secretary of the Interior, was named to administer the $3 billion PWA budget. Most public attention, however, centered on Title I of the act, which mandated the establishment of codes in each industry to set production quotas, establish prices, and allocate resources. In order to ensure representation of various points of view in the NRA code formulation process, three separate advisory boards were established to consult on the codes for each industry. The Industrial Advisory Board and the Labor Advisory Board were named by the Secretaries of Commerce and Labor respectively. The Consumers' Advisory Board was chosen by and directly responsible to the administrator of Title I of the NRA, General Hugh Johnson.[4]

Women had little involvement with the initial code formulation within the various industries, and they were not represented on the Industrial Advisory Board. Occasionally, however, women in the network did play small roles. In the case of the coal code, the Roosevelt administration had experienced trouble winning final approval from the coal industry, and in the hope of breaking the impasse, coal operators were invited to spend an evening at the White House. At the last minute, Frances Perkins suggested to President Roosevelt that Josephine Roche, herself a coal operator from Colorado and soon to become Assistant Secretary of the Treasury, be invited. Roche could talk to the reluctant coal operators and try to win them over to the administration's point of view. Perkins's tactic succeeded. "Miss Roche came, cooperated, handled herself with skill, and gathered around herself a little group of coal operators who saw the advantage of having a code to protect them against the unfair competition of the large coal operators."[5]

Frances Perkins was responsible for naming the Labor Advisory Board. She charged the group with a broad mandate to represent labor interests in the code-framing process, and to ensure that safety and health provisions (such as banning homework and child labor) were included in the codes. Headed by economist Dr. Leo Wolman, the Labor Advisory Board included labor leaders such as William Green of the American Federation of Labor, John L. Lewis of the United Mine Workers, and Sidney Hillman of the Amalgamated Clothing Workers. To represent the interests of women workers, Perkins named her long-time New York colleague, Rose Schneiderman, then president of the National Women's Trade Union League.[6] Reflecting her own Consumers' League training, Perkins realized that women's special interests had to be represented. Her friend Rose Schneiderman was the perfect choice for the job.

Rose Schneiderman, in turn, was proud and honored to serve on the committee. Schneiderman, who worked as a labor leader and activist for women's causes for more than fifty years, called her two-year service on the NRA Labor Advisory Board "the high spot" of her career.[7] As part of her duties, she attended code hearings for industries with substantial numbers of women workers and offered advice on how the women workers would be affected by the provisions under discussion.

In early 1934, Schneiderman spent ten weeks in Puerto Rico representing the interests of Puerto Rican women affected by the code covering the needle trades. Schneiderman was accompanied on part of this trip by Eleanor Roosevelt, who used the occasion to investigate conditions of industrial homework on the island while enjoying a short vacation with her friend Schneiderman and several women journalists who were covering the trip. Eleanor wrote Rose right before their departure: "I am counting on you to tell me what you think I really ought to see. It will be grand to see you." The only obligation of the Labor Advisory Board that Schneiderman declined was the monthly invitation to dinner with members of the Industrial Advisory Board. Schneiderman thought that the presence of a woman at these otherwise all-male gatherings might "cramp their style" and prevent them from becoming "chummy" with each other.[8]

The Labor Advisory Board effectively represented the general needs of labor,[9] but in industries where unions were weak (the majority of industries in the early 1930s), the board lacked information upon which to base specific code suggestions. The board, therefore, often turned to the Department of Labor for figures on working conditions, average earnings, cost of living, safety standards, and enforcement schemes. In this way the Labor Department as well as the Labor Advisory Board spoke for workers' needs in the NRA.

The staffs of the Children's Bureau, Women's Bureau, and the Bureau of Labor Statistics could often provide the best data in the entire government bureaucracy for drawing up code provisions on a sound basis. According to Frances Perkins, Mary Anderson and the Women's Bureau compiled data on more than 120 industries employing significant numbers of women during the fiscal year ending June 30, 1934.[10] The Children's Bureau likewise provided research and information for the code hearings.

Testifying at such code hearings, Rose Schneiderman and the members of the Department of Labor were aided by two organizations especially interested in labor standards for women workers. The Women's Trade Union League received frequent pleas for help and advice from women in industries affected by NRA codes, and WTUL representatives like Elizabeth Christman often testified at NRA code hearings concerned with industries employing large numbers of women workers. Representatives of the National Consumers' League also appeared before NRA code commissions. Lucy Mason, president of the National Consumers' League during this period, realized that in industries with strong union organizations the unions would supply witnesses for the hearings, so she concentrated League efforts on industries in which women were largely unorganized and unrepresented. Mason also extended her efforts beyond Washington. Molly Dewson told Eleanor Roosevelt in 1934: "Lucy Mason is in the South to help put permanent underpinning under the NRA."[11]

In addition to lobbying on behalf of women workers, the National Consumers' League and the Women's Trade Union League participated in code hearings where child labor provisions were under discussion. If necessary Molly Dewson, acting on behalf of the Consumers' League, would go straight to the President with a complaint about the NRA's child labor policy: "Do you realize what the newspaper code is doing to the child labor standards which most of your closest women assistants have worked years to establish? . . . Won't you consult the head of your own Children's Bureau, Grace Abbott; or the Director of her Child Labor Division, Clara Beyer, before signing this code? Please!" Dewson added a note to Eleanor on the same letter: "You may be too busy for this but it is rotten to put Franklin in this hole. It will make 1000's of his supporters so mad. Molly."[12]

Eleanor Roosevelt also worked behind the scenes to promote the interests of the National Consumers' League and the Women's Trade Union League in the NRA process. In late 1933, Eleanor sent General Hugh Johnson a packet of NCL material "worth your reading." And in 1934, she wrote Johnson: "I wish you would have a representative of the Consumers' League on the Committee which is reviewing the codes for inconsistencies. I think it would be most helpful."[13] This cooperative effort among women in the network and their friends in voluntary associations helped strengthen the NRA provisions affecting women and children.

Women in the network and their colleagues in groups like the National Consumers' League were not always pleased with NRA policy. For example, women were upset that one-quarter of the NRA codes allowed different (that is, lower) wage levels for women workers, reflecting the long-established custom of paying women less money for performing the same work as men. Women's wages were not the only discrepancies in the codes: a third of the codes specified lower hourly wages for workers in the South, as well as exemptions for handicapped workers, learners, and industrial home workers. As the Women's Bureau pointed out, such widespread exceptions weakened the overall impact of the code provisions.[14]

Ten national women's organizations, including the Women's Trade Union League, the National Consumers' League, the Federation of Business and Professional Women, the National League of Women Voters, the Young Women's Christian Association, and the General Federation of Women's Clubs, filed a protest with General Hugh Johnson over these aspects of the NRA codes. At Mary Anderson's request, Eleanor Roosevelt allowed representatives of these groups to speak at one of her press conferences.[15] To the women's disappointment, however, the lower wage provisions for women remained.

Even though women in government and their friends in voluntary associations were unhappy with the provisions that discriminated against women workers, for the most part they agreed with Mary Anderson that the NRA codes were such a great leap forward that this progress overshadowed whatever imperfections the codes might contain. The willingness of the federal government to regulate working conditions for men and women alike accomplished in one stroke much that voluntary associations had been struggling to accomplish piecemeal over the last thirty years. It was for this reason that Rose Schneiderman called her NRA participation the high point of her career: "Here was an opportunity to help working women such as had never existed before. As representative of the Labor Board, I helped make the codes for industries employing women, and it still thrills me that I had a part in bringing about monumental changes in the lives of working men and women."[16]

The Women's Bureau confirmed Schneiderman's personal observations in a 1935 study entitled "Employed Women under NRA Codes": "Even in this period of time, which is exceedingly short for the development of so broad a program of social reconstruction, enormous advances were made for employed women in a raising of their wages, a shortening of their hours, and an increase in their employment." The NRA codes especially benefited women workers by raising their wage levels through mandatory provisions for minimum hourly wages. Since women have traditionally been concentrated in the lowest-paying jobs, they stood to gain the most from such minimum wage standards.[17]

Many gains for women under the NRA codes were by-products of improved labor standards for all workers, not the result of specific action on behalf of women's interests. Women in the network were delighted that men were able to share in benefits that previously had been available only to women. As the women in the network correctly surmised, their work on wages and hours regulation over the past thirty years had enabled the New Deal to accomplish so much in so short a time.[18]

Concern over women workers affected by NRA codes was only part of women's involvement in the workings of the NRA; the other major area was representation of the consumer. The role of consumers in modern industrial society had continued to be an important concern for female and male reformers alike since the founding of the National Consumers' League in 1899, and women in the network had been especially active in this long fight. As it happened, representation of the consumer viewpoint in the NRA was much more difficult than that of labor or industry. Without the experience and agitation of women in the network, notably that of Frances Perkins and Mary Harriman Rumsey, the rights of consumers might have been overlooked entirely.

Women in the network concentrated their attention on the Consumers' Advisory Board (CAB) of the NRA. The idea for the Consumers' Advisory Board originated with Frances Perkins herself. Her reasoning drew directly on her past experiences in the Consumers' League: "I, remembering my old Consumers' League days, realized that the Consumers' League had been a great public influence in the state of New York and in other states where it had existed in bringing the public influence to bear on labor problems . . . The public interest will nearly always be on the moral side of any situation." In her autobiography, Perkins described the Consumers' Advisory Board as a "last minute thought of my own to protect the community against a combination of labor and industry which might have been adverse." But Perkins still had to convince General Johnson, administrator of Title I of the NRA, to go along with the idea. Johnson was not known for his sympathies with the consumer movement (he once bellowed, "Who is a consumer? Show me a consumer"), but he accepted Perkins's idea because Mary Harriman Rumsey, whom he knew and respected, agreed to serve as the committee's chairman.[19]

Frances Perkins's choice of Rumsey is revealing. Again, as with Rose Schneiderman, Perkins turned to a long-time woman associate when she needed a hard job done well. Perkins had known Rumsey since 1918 when they worked together on the New York Maternity League, a social welfare organization. During the early New Deal, Perkins and Rumsey shared a home in Georgetown, and Perkins saw firsthand that Rumsey had the time and the interest to volunteer full time for the consumer cause. Perkins further realized that Mary Harriman Rumsey's social status (she was the daughter of railroad magnate E. H. Harriman) and her wide-ranging contacts in official Washington added to her attractiveness. If necessary, Rumsey could go straight to her friends in high places, including her old acquaintances from New York, Franklin and Eleanor Roosevelt. A final asset was Rumsey's money. She enjoyed entertaining, and was willing to do so for political purposes. Johnson once asked Rumsey to host a large party for the NRA staff in Washington, and Rumsey gladly picked up the tab for dinner and champagne.[20]

Through her friendship with Johnson, Rumsey was drawn into more complicated personal matters, such as the case of Frances ("Robbie") Robinson, General Johnson's secretary at the National Recovery Administration. Because of Johnson's drinking problems, Robinson had taken over many of the policy decisions that Johnson was supposed to be handling. People then began to gossip about the personal relationship between Robinson and Johnson, and these rumors were undercutting the effectiveness of the NRA. Mary Harriman Rumsey decided to organize a theater party in honor of Robinson. Rumsey invited all the women who were important in politics and government and arranged to have the party written up in the Washington society columns. Frances Perkins, Molly Dewson, Nellie Tayloe Ross, Marion Glass Banister, and several of the women in Congress attended. Frances Perkins later said that Rumsey's theater party forestalled gossip about Robinson by "showing that respectable women of good position not only gave parties for Miss Robinson, but went to parties with her." Perkins always believed that women were better at handling such delicate matters than men.[21]

For her job at the NRA, Mary Harriman Rumsey found she needed all the tact she could muster. The Consumers' Advisory Board was in an anomalous position within the NRA bureaucracy. Unlike the Labor and Industrial Boards, which reported to independent Cabinet members, the CAB was directly responsible to General Johnson himself. All publicity releases prepared by the CAB had to be cleared by his office. The CAB was charged with representing the interests of the consuming public, but beyond that its mandate was unspecified. The CAB claimed the right to advise on every NRA matter that affected the consumer (which, broadly enough construed, could be everything the NRA did), but had no way of compelling attention to its criticisms or suggestions. Since the CAB's role was basically one of obstruction in an organization obsessed with speedy action, conflict was inevitable.[22]

The CAB had trouble making itself heard partly because it lacked a clear constituency to put pressure on the administration. Consumers' rights and the public interest proved much harder to organize than lobbies such as the National Association of Manufacturers or the Chamber of Commerce. The National Consumers' League, a likely source of support, concentrated its efforts almost entirely on labor standards during the 1930s rather than on consumer affairs. In contrast to industry or labor, there was no obvious roster of consumer leaders to consult. Attempts to build a consumer constituency on a county-wide basis throughout the nation were unsuccessful. Without vocal leaders and publicly recognized advocates, the consumer was often overlooked.[23]

The legacy of the CAB was not entirely negative. In the early period of the NRA, to be sure, the CAB's advice was often ignored and neglected. But as opposition to the business-oriented approach of the NRA increased, the CAB served as a rallying point for much of the criticism. The CAB supplied documentation that price fixing, markups, and unjustifiably high price increases cut into the purchasing power of the consumer while industry earned larger and larger profits. When the NRA was unwilling to release the figures collected by the CAB, the board learned to leak such material to the press and Congress through highly placed friends.[24]

The activities of the Consumers' Advisory Board further demonstrate the convergence of women in the network in particular areas of the government. This concentration increased the effectiveness of consumer representation in the New Deal. For example, Eleanor Roosevelt lent the prestige and support of the President and his wife to the consumer cause by inviting the Consumers' Advisory Board to hold a Consumers' Conference at the White House in December of 1933. The Roosevelt's old friend, Mary Harriman Rumsey, gratefully presided at a conference in such grand surroundings.[25]

Other members of the network also participated in CAB activities. At times, the offices of the Consumers' Advisory Board resembled a network headquarters. Both Grace Abbott of the Children's Bureau and Molly Dewson, representing the National Consumers' League, served on the citizens' advisory board that met monthly to deal with consumer issues and the NRA. Sue Shelton White was Mary Harriman Rumsey's assistant at the NRA, and the two developed a close working (and personal) relationship. White devoted most of her time to the abortive nationwide consumers' councils set up to monitor prices and conditions under the Blue Eagle. Emily Newell Blair served on the informal executive committee of the Consumers' Advisory Board throughout its two-year existence. In addition, Blair ran the Complaints Bureau for the NRA. Finally, other members of the network like Josephine Roche participated in NRA matters on an informal basis.[26]

The CAB was saddened by the unexpected death of Mary Harriman Rumsey in December 1934. Emily Newell Blair was the obvious choice as her successor, but several months passed before Blair's formal appointment. By then, the NRA was in a state of flux. Critics complained that the codes were too sympathetic to big business, and that they encouraged monopoly instead of competition. Public hostility to the price-fixing aspects of the codes was especially intense. As criticism grew, Roosevelt decided to remove Hugh Johnson as administrator, replacing him with Donald Richberg in the fall of 1934. In early 1935 rumors circulated that the NRA, and especially its Consumers' Division, faced a major reorganization. Given this uncertainty about the future, Richberg delayed naming the new head of the Consumers' Advisory Board until the reorganization question had been resolved.[27]

In the meantime, members of the network mobilized to fill Rumsey's place. Emily Newell Blair wrote Molly Dewson about Rumsey's job in late December; Molly passed on the letter to Eleanor Roosevelt, adding her approval and a note that Blair was "praying" for the job. Dewson also sent a copy of Blair's letter to Frances Perkins, thinking that Perkins would pick the successor rather than the President. (Actually, it was neither—it was Richberg.) Eleanor Roosevelt forwarded the names of Emily Newell Blair, Sue Shelton White, and Lavinia Engle to the President, although Eleanor thought Blair the most logical choice because she had worked so closely with Rumsey. Frances Perkins agreed with Eleanor Roosevelt and Molly Dewson that Blair deserved the job, but suggested that they wait until the future of the Consumers' Board was settled.[28]

The resolution was rather anticlimactic. Blair's appointment to a newly reorganized Consumers' Division was approved in February of 1935. On May 27, 1935, the Supreme Court declared the industrial code-making process an unconstitutional delegation of authority in the case of

A. L. A. Schecter Poultry Corp. et. al. v. *United States.* After *Schecter,* President Roosevelt considered new legislation to revive the NRA on a sounder legal basis, but given the Blue Eagle's unpopularity he decided against this. Roosevelt's decision left the Consumers' Division in limbo, and by the summer most of its staff had been transferred elsewhere. In July Blair wrote Dewson that she still had a secretary and an assistant, but did not expect the Consumers' Division work to amount to much anymore. She added in a postscript to Dewson, "This is all right by me. I enjoyed having my finger in the pie. I've learned a lot. The five month job saw me through a tough spot, so I'm terribly grateful to you, the Administration, and Providence."[29]

Sue Shelton White was also out of a job, but at her own choosing. White had become the Associate Director of the reorganized Consumers' Division under Emily Newell Blair, but with few illusions about the prospects for the future. White had been upset at the treatment of the Consumers' Advisory Board even before Rumsey's death. White appealed for a permanent consumer agency, but the Consumers' Division kept losing staff, funding, and power, and White finally resigned. Molly Dewson described White to Eleanor Roosevelt as "so boiling mad she sounds sun struck."[30] Dewson and Eleanor Roosevelt talked to Arthur Altmeyer about a job for White on the newly formed Social Security Administration, and White joined its legal staff in the fall of 1935.

With the dismantling of the National Recovery Administration in the spring and summer of 1935, many women in the network, especially Frances Perkins and her colleagues at the Labor Department, turned their attention elsewhere. Passage of social security legislation and the introduction of laws to make permanent the wages and hours regulation begun under the NRA were of prime concern. Sue Shelton White's switch from the NRA to the new Social Security Administration exemplifies these changing priorities.

Like the Consumers' Advisory Board of the NRA, the Department of Labor contained a large concentration of members of the network. Since the Women's Bureau and Children's Bureau were part of the Labor Department, Mary Anderson, Grace Abbott, and Katharine Lenroot all held important positions there. Clara Beyer started out in the Children's Bureau and then moved to the department's Bureau of Labor Standards. Mary LaDame joined the department as Frances Perkins's administrative assistant. Jane Hoey from the Social Security Administration and Josephine Roche from Treasury worked closely with the department on various projects. Finally, Molly Dewson and Eleanor Roosevelt actively participated in many Labor Department plans and projects.

The Department of Labor also produced many of the initiatives behind the New Deal's most lasting achievements in the social welfare field. It is no coincidence that legislation such as the Social Security Act of 1935 and the Fair Labor Standards Act of 1938 came out of a department in which the network had such strength. Molly Dewson, for one, always believed that women had special talents in the field of social welfare: "I am convinced that certain women like Frances Perkins, Clara Beyer, now Assistant Director of the United States Division of Labor Standards, and Katherine Edson, who was a member of the Industrial Commission of California, have been more successful in getting progressive labor laws passed and more effective in their administration than any men ever have been or could have been."[31] Reforms like social security, maternal and child welfare, health insurance, mothers' pensions, and minimum wage and maximum hours legislation had been top priority for women in the network throughout their long careers. The New Deal finally gave them the opportunity to implement these goals.

Behind the passage of some of the New Deal's most important social legislation stood Frances Perkins. When Franklin Roosevelt originally chose Perkins as Secretary of Labor, he pledged his support to a list of major social welfare measures she had compiled. With the exception of health insurance, all these measures were adopted in the 1930s. The question of social security was one of the first to be tackled. Many members of the Department of Labor, including Arthur Altmeyer and Katharine Lenroot of the Children's Bureau, worked almost full time for two years on the law that became the Social Security Act of 1935. Molly Dewson recalled, "To win this just measure of social decency was a great cooperative undertaking of hundreds of us," but she singled out the contributions of Frances Perkins and Arthur Altmeyer.[32]

Molly Dewson and Clara Beyer played a part in bringing Arthur Altmeyer into the Labor Department in the first place. In the spring of 1934, Clara Beyer consulted with her old friend and colleague Molly Dewson about certain administrative problems in the Labor Department. The two women decided that Arthur Altmeyer, whom they knew from his work in Wisconsin and with the National Consumers' League, would provide a perfect solution to these problems if he were appointed the next Assistant Secretary of Labor. Beyer passed the suggestion along to Frances Perkins, who thought it was a good idea, but then nothing happened. Dewson finally took matters into her own hands. One morning before breakfast, Dewson called Perkins at home to remind her about the Altmeyer appointment. According to Dewson, "This forceful presentation was effective."[33] Almost as soon as Altmeyer joined the Labor Department he began to work full time on the Social Security Act.

In addition to the pressure of the depression, several other factors made passage of a social security bill feasible in the 1930s. The years of patient research and publicity by organizations like the National Consumers' League, the American Association for Labor Legislation, and the American Association for Old Age Security laid the groundwork for the act. Molly Dewson claimed: "Roosevelt took advantage of long years of study, research and experimentation in labor legislation, and utilized those responsible for it. He brought to realization many goals striven for for over twenty years." When the depression increased awareness of old age insecurity and the needs of those unable to work, a group of experts was ready with proposals on how to put such a system of social security into operation.[34] Among these experts were many of the women in the network.

Equally important were the political pressures which made the Social Security Act not only feasible, but politically expedient as the 1936 election approached. The pension plan of Dr. Francis Townsend, a Long Beach, California country practitioner turned advocate for the elderly, struck a responsive chord among many Americans. Townsend's plan, which guaranteed a pension of $200 a month to all citizens over the age of sixty if they agreed to spend the money within the month, was immensely popular. Similarly, Huey Long's Share Our Wealth program included a pension system for old people. With popular pressure for such measures increasing dramatically, Congress and the President had to act.[35]

In this context, the Cabinet-level Committee on Economic Security, composed of the Secretaries of Labor, Agriculture, and the Treasury, the Attorney General, and Harry Hopkins of the Federal Emergency Relief Administration, was established in June of 1934. Its mandate was to draft a comprehensive social security program, including both unemployment and old age insurance, for presentation to the President by December 1934. An important consideration was drafting the law in a form likely to win constitutional approval from the Supreme Court.[36] Frances Perkins headed this committee at Franklin Roosevelt's personal insistence: "You care about this thing. You believe in it. Therefore I know you will put your back to it more than anybody else, and you will drive it through. You will see that something comes out, and we must not delay."[37]

Accepting Roosevelt's challenge, Frances Perkins provided important leadership for the committee. In addition to the Cabinet-level Committee on Economic Security, the President also formed an Advisory Committee on Economic Security. This group of concerned citizens, economists, and labor leaders included women like Grace Abbott (now back at the University of Chicago, but still quite active in national affairs), Josephine

Roche, and Molly Dewson, representing the National Consumers' League. Perkins personally chose Josephine Roche for the advisory committee on the basis of their twenty-year friendship through the Consumers' League. Once Roche joined government service as the Assistant Secretary of the Treasury in the fall of 1934, she was no longer eligible for the citizens' advisory board, so Perkins had her transferred to the technical subcommittee of the Committee on Economic Security. In addition, Roche attended many meetings of the Cabinet-level Committee on Economic Security as a substitute for Secretary of the Treasury Morgenthau.[38]

In retrospect, the Advisory Committee on Economic Security proved too large and unwieldy. The committee never had enough time to deliberate on the recommendations at hand, and certain members felt like rubber stamps for decisions already made. The advisory committee was so divided internally that it could not agree on a final report for publication until 1937, two years after enactment of the Social Security Act.[39]

In December 1934, the Cabinet-level Committee on Economic Security met at the Perkins-Rumsey home to hammer out a final report. Josephine Roche again sat in for Treasury Secretary Morgenthau. Perkins ushered the small group into the dining room, placed a bottle of whiskey on the table, and locked the door. Within six hours they had agreed on a draft, which Perkins presented to the President the next day.[40] On January 17, 1935, President Roosevelt publicly called for social security legislation; later that day, Senator Robert Wagner of New York and Representative David Lewis of Maryland introduced the administration's bill in Congress.[41]

The Wagner-Lewis bill closely followed the recommendations of the Committee on Economic Security. The draft contained both an old age insurance scheme financed by payroll deductions and a federal-state system of unemployment insurance. In addition, direct relief programs like old age assistance, pensions for the blind and handicapped, aid to dependent children, and grants-in-aid for maternal and child welfare services and the public health service were included. The months of work put in by the smaller committees of experts were evident in these detailed recommendations. The Mothers' Pensions plan incorporated into the final bill as Aid to Dependent Children, for example, was based on a report written by Katharine Lenroot and Martha M. Eliot of the Children's Bureau, with the help of the former Children's Bureau chief, Grace Abbott.[42]

The women in the network had a strong stake in the passage of the Social Security Act. Those who personally had worked on the bill naturally wanted to see the long months of research and planning translated into actual programs. In the case of mothers' pensions and maternal and child welfare programs, the bill marked the culmination of agitation dating back to the Progressive period and the 1920s. For the rest of the women in the network, their interest in the Social Security Act came from a broader perspective. Ellen Woodward later observed that the Social Security Act "has grown out of the fight in which so many women have been engaged in for the past thirty years—the fight to protect and promote the well-being of the individual and his family."[43]

As the Secretary of Labor and one of the bill's main architects, Frances Perkins tried to organize public and Congressional support for the bill. She made speeches, wrote articles, and testified before the Congressional committees assigned to report on the bill. In her campaign she received help from friends and former colleagues from voluntary associations who closely followed the bill's progress. Molly Dewson reminded Eleanor Roosevelt of the National Consumers' League's role in building support for the Social Security Act:

> Just to show the calibre of our support, when the President sent his Social Security bill to Congress the Consumers' League swung into line with complete support. We considered that the time for discussion had passed and what the President needed was wholehearted support. Every state league and the entire membership was urged to write to Congress. I think we were the first organization to give support without any criticism or further suggestions.[44]

In Lucy Mason's extensive speaking trips for the National Consumers' League in 1935, she always included statements of strong support for the Social Security bill. She also spent ten days in Washington lobbying for the legislation.

The Social Security Act was signed into law by President Roosevelt on August 14, 1935. A picture of the signing ceremony reveals a smiling (for her, at least) Secretary of Labor prominently featured among the Congressional leaders who had worked for the bill's passage. Perkins obviously was pleased at the realization of her long-term goal of social insurance. No doubt she was aware of critics' charges that the bill was too conservative and that too many workers were excluded from its benefits; she agreed with many of these criticisms herself. But Frances Perkins was what her lifelong friend Agnes Leach called "a half-loaf girl: take what you can get now and try for more later."[45] She had learned this lesson from Florence Kelley while lobbying for a 54-hour bill for the Consumers' League in New York State in 1912, and it characterized her attitude in the 1930s as well. In fact, most of the women in the network were "half-loaf girls": any piece of federal social welfare legislation was an important building block for future legislative reform.

Despite her smiles at the ceremony, Perkins was disappointed that the Department of Labor was not designated to administer the unemployment and old age insurance plans, as the law originally had been drafted. Instead, Congress created a separate Social Security Administration to administer the program. Perkins believed that Congress excluded the Labor Department from responsibility for these sections because of its view that the department was too soft on workers and threw money around, but Perkins's generally poor relations with Congress were an additional reason for the last-minute change.[46] Though creation of the Social Security Administration was a setback for Perkins and the Department of Labor, it turned into rather a boon for women in the network. Molly Dewson served on the three-member Social Security Board from 1937 to 1938 and was succeeded for a six-year term by Ellen Woodward. Jane Hoey headed the Bureau of Public Assistance for the Social Security Administration, and Sue Shelton White worked in the legal department under Jack Tate.

Frances Perkins's dissatisfaction was lessened somewhat by the fact that the Social Security Act greatly increased the functions of one of her favorite bureaus in the Labor Department, the Children's Bureau. Even though administration of Aid to Dependent Children (ADC) was concentrated in the new Social Security Administration, the Children's Bureau retained an important advisory role. In addition, the Children's Bureau was responsible for supervising and administering federal-state plans for public health, nursing, and child health welfare set up by the Social Security Administration. The Children's Bureau also took over the child welfare services for children who did not qualify for ADC assistance, such as those in institutions or in foster homes. In supervising these maternal and child health and welfare programs, the Children's Bureau drew on its experience with the first federal maternal and infancy act, the Sheppard-Towner Act, which operated from 1921 to 1929. Leadership in this area passed from Grace Abbott to her successor at the Children's Bureau, Katharine Lenroot.[47]

A related outgrowth of the passage of the Social Security Act was the creation by executive order in August 1935 of the Interdepartmental Committee to Coordinate Health and Welfare Activities. This committee was designed to facilitate cooperation between the various parts of the government given additional responsibilities under the new Social Security law, and to avoid overlap or duplication of work. The committee was composed of four Assistant Secretaries of government departments (Treasury, Interior, Agriculture, and Labor), plus the chairman of the

Social Security Board and the head of the National Youth Administration. The tone of the committee was set by the two Assistant Secretaries who took the greatest interest in the subject, Arthur Altmeyer from Labor and Josephine Roche from Treasury. Roche and Altmeyer continued their collaboration begun during the planning of the Social Security Act. For the first year and a half of its existence, the committee primarily coordinated existing health programs within the government, but after 1936 it turned its attention to the development of a national health program, a goal that was never realized. Even after Josephine Roche resigned from the Treasury in 1937, she commuted from Colorado to Washington to serve on the Interdepartmental Committee, maintaining her involvement in the social welfare policies of the New Deal. Roche also continued to receive the support and encouragement of Eleanor Roosevelt, for whom Roche provided updates on the activities of the committee.[48]

Matters of health insurance were not the only items of unfinished business for women reformers in the Labor Department and the network as a whole in the mid-1930s. With the demise of the National Recovery Administration in 1935, many of the gains won under the NRA slipped away. Since the NRA was not originally intended to last more than two years, reformers had already recognized the need to follow up its key provisions with permanent legislation. The Wagner Labor Relations Act, which expanded on the model of Section 7(a) of the NRA, and the Guffey-Snyder Act of 1935, which basically reenacted the bituminous coal code, are two examples of this process. Of special concern to women in the network was enactment of permanent legislation to prohibit the employment of children under the age of sixteen and to revive the hours and wages standards provided in the old NRA codes.

The Walsh-Healey Public Contracts Act represented an early attempt to impose these standards on a permanent basis. Passed in June of 1936, this bill provided that goods and services purchased by the government had to be manufactured under conditions that included an eight-hour day and a forty-hour week and that excluded the labor of children under sixteen. Again, Frances Perkins provided important leadership for passage of this law. Perkins and Molly Dewson had consulted noted jurist Felix Frankfurter about a similar idea for regulating government contracts years before Perkins became Secretary of Labor. Perkins explained, "Mary Dewson and I were both people committed to the Consumers' League. We were people connected with the Consumers' League and that's why we did it together."[49] Such cooperation carried over into the New Deal.

Reformers like Perkins and Dewson were not satisfied with the Walsh-

Healey Act because its scope was limited to public contracts, and they explored ways to expand its coverage. The reformers were delighted when Franklin Roosevelt pledged during the 1936 election campaign to find a way to regulate wages and hours as the NRA had done. Early in the New Deal, Frances Perkins had told President Roosevelt that in case the NRA was ruled unconstitutional, "I've got two bills which will do everything you and I think important under NRA. I have them locked up in the lower left hand drawer of my desk against emergency." After the 1936 election, Perkins reminded Roosevelt of these bills and he agreed that it was time to pull the wages and hours bill out of her drawer. Perkins's draft eventually became the Fair Labor Standards Act of 1938. Perkins's formulation covered all manufacturers whose products were involved in interstate commerce, instead of just manufacturers doing business with the federal government. The bill regulated daily and weekly hours for both men and women, set a minimum wage, and prohibited labor of children under the age of sixteen.[50]

The section prohibiting child labor was added at the strong instigation of Grace Abbott. Abbott eloquently pleaded, "You are hoping that you have found a way around the Supreme Court. If you have, why not give the children the benefit by attaching a child labor clause to the bill?"[51] Perkins readily secured Roosevelt's approval for the child labor section and inserted it into the final draft.

Katharine Lenroot also drafted sections of the bill. Lenroot devised a legal strategy for enforcing the child labor aspects of the bill which differed substantially from Perkins's formulation. Perkins agreed with Lenroot's approach and, as Lenroot remembered, "went to the President and got a reversal which sustained me in my position and that was the way it went into the Fair Labor Standards Act."[52]

Although Frances Perkins and the President's advisers had agreed on a final draft of the bill by early 1937, introduction of the wages and hours bill was held back until the controversy over Roosevelt's plan to "pack" the Supreme Court had died down. FDR's unexpected attempt to reshape the Supreme Court by expanding its membership to fifteen justices, presumably ones more sympathetic to New Deal legislation, created quite a furor throughout the country. Roosevelt's attack on the sacred institution of the Supreme Court, and his inept handling of the political considerations surrounding the bill, diverted Congressional attention in the first several months of 1937. Once it became clear that the Supreme Court plan was doomed, the Congress returned to normal business. The labor standards bill was finally introduced in May of 1937. The issue of labor standards commanded liberal Democratic support, but opposition came from the conservative coalition in Congress and from certain elements in the American Federation of Labor, who feared that the statutory minimum wage might become the maximum. Labor also feared that government authority to set the wage structure would undermine unions' collective bargaining position. Prospects for passage were unclear.[53]

During the parliamentary maneuvering on the bill in the House, Congresswoman Mary T. Norton of New Jersey, recently elevated to the chairmanship of the Labor Committee by the unexpected death of the former chairman, played a strategic role. In the fall of 1937, her efforts to win passage of the bill were unsuccessful, and the wages and hours legislation was recommitted to committee. The morning after the late-night session when the bill had been killed, Mary Norton was having breakfast in bed when the phone rang. It was Franklin Roosevelt. "Hello, Mary," he said cheerfully. "Too bad about the bill. What are you going to do now?" She replied without hesitation, "I'm going to get you a bill, Mr. President."[54] Within four months, the bill had been reported out of the Labor Committee, pried loose from the Rules Committee with a discharge petition, and passed by the Congress.

In addition to participating in the drafting of the Fair Labor Standards Act and hastening its passage in Congress, women in the network helped informally to promote this legislation. Molly Dewson reminded Clara Beyer in March of 1937: "When the 40-hour bill is introduced, remember that Ellen Woodward, Assistant Director of the WPA, is quite prominent in the District of Columbia Business and Professional Women Clubs. I think she could help you in lining them up." The Women's Division of the Democratic National Committee made passage of laws like the Fair Labor Standards Act top priority in Democratic women's educational work, and included articles on labor standards in the *Democratic Digest*. The Women's Division also pressured the Democratic party to include the Child Labor Amendment and wages and hours legislation in party platforms.[55]

Though the network's role in the planning and passage of the Fair Labor Standards Act was substantial, political considerations were equally important in determining its fate. Roosevelt's Court-packing plan originally delayed the bill's introduction, and the administration's defeat on that issue influenced the history of the wages and hours bill in Congress. The Fair Labor Standards Act became "must" legislation for the Democratic party, and its passage showed the continuing viability of a liberal New Deal coalition. Amendments to the bill, however, especially from conservative Southerners hostile to the New Deal who wanted to exempt low-paid agricultural workers from the law's provisions, significantly weakened the carefully drafted plans of Frances Perkins and her staff at the Labor Department.[56]

Political considerations aside, women in the network were pleased that the act made permanent many of the reforms first attempted under the NRA. Summing up her enthusiasm about the Fair Labor Standards Act to Eleanor Roosevelt, Rose Schneiderman exclaimed, "Thanks to the President and God bless him!" Schneiderman claimed that passage of the 1938 law was "due entirely to the experience that most employers had under the NRA." But she and her friends from the network deserved part of the credit as well. In 1941 the Supreme Court upheld the Fair Labor Standards Act. Women in the network were especially pleased because the decision in effect reversed the earlier Supreme Court decision in *Adkins* v. *Children's Hospital,* so demoralizing to reformers in the 1920s, which held that Congress did not have the power to regulate child labor in interstate commerce.[57] The women in the network had waited eighteen years for this change of heart. Yet another of their goals was finally made permanent.

The network also played an active role in the planning and implementation of the New Deal's relief programs for women in the 1930s. Unlike the NRA codes or the Fair Labor Standards Act, where the interests of women were promoted through regulation of wages and hours for all workers, the New Deal devised separate programs to address the needs of women on relief.

Although reforms such as minimum wages and the abolition of child labor had been tried in the past, granting relief to women on a national scale was unprecedented.[58] The federal government literally started from scratch. Without the knowledge, experience, and above all, the constant prodding of the women in the network, this government program would never have gotten off the ground.

Assisting women on relief was a high priority for the women in public life in Washington in the 1930s. The Women's Division of the Democratic National Committee actively promoted women's relief programs through its educational work. Eleanor Roosevelt was a special patron of the women's relief programs. She confessed that she had toured so many WPA sewing rooms that it had become "somewhat automatic." In addition to her speeches and public visits, Eleanor Roosevelt worked behind the scenes to increase awareness of the needs of women on relief. In 1935, for example, she gently nudged WPA administrator Harry Hopkins about the lack of male support for the women's programs: "I forgot today to say that I hope in some way you will impress on state administrators that the women's programs are as important as the men's. They are so apt to forget us!"[59]

More than anything else, however, Ellen Sullivan Woodward's dedication and talent shaped the government's relief policies toward women. Like Molly Dewson in the political arena and Frances Perkins in the social welfare field, Ellen Woodward, as head of the Women's and Professional Projects for the WPA, served as the network's main representative in promoting relief programs for women in the New Deal. And as did Dewson and Perkins, Ellen Woodward asked for and received help from her women friends in the network to accomplish her short- and long-term goals.

To cope with the problem of massive employment, the Federal Emergency Relief Administration (FERA) was established in May of 1933 to channel $500 million of federal money to state and local agencies. Harry Hopkins was chosen as head of this new agency, and he moved quickly to set up programs, especially in construction and public works. Although official government policy stated from the outset that "needy women shall be given equal consideration with needy men," it was late November before the women's programs really got under way.[60] A major impetus was the FERA-sponsored White House Conference on the Emergency Needs of Women held on November 20, 1933.

The possibility of holding a conference at the White House had been discussed during the fall, but the actual date for the conference was not set until just a week before it took place. Despite such short notice, more than fifty nationally prominent women leaders (including many women in the network) attended the day-long session at the White House for a "full and practical discussion with a view to formulating methods for better handling the needs of unemployed women." Eleanor Roosevelt participated in the actual planning of the conference and arranged Molly Dewson's invitation. Woodward personally invited such women's leaders as Nellie Tayloe Ross, Frances Perkins, and Congresswomen Caroline O'Day and Mary T. Norton. In addition, Rose Schneiderman, Mary Anderson, Grace Abbott, Mary LaDame, and Hilda Worthington Smith attended the conference. It is possible that other members of the network were invited but were unable to come because of the short notice.[61]

Ellen Woodward recognized the large debt the conference owed to Eleanor Roosevelt's interest and encouragement. In addition to offering the use and prestige of the White House as a setting for the conference, Eleanor Roosevelt assisted in a more fundamental way, as Woodward noted: "Mrs. Roosevelt's special interest in the emergency needs of unemployed women has served to coordinate the interests of numerous women's organizations dealing with the needs of jobless women."[62]

Eleanor Roosevelt called the conference to order and then introduced Harry Hopkins, who made the opening remarks. Hopkins described the extent of the problem: 300,000 to 400,000 women needed help from either FERA or the Civil Works Administration. In November 1933, no more than 50,000 women were on work relief in the United States. Hopkins wanted to increase that number eightfold. And he wanted to do it right away: "I am committed to a belief, a conviction on my part, that it is possible to put three to four hundred thousand women to work on good projects and do it very quickly . . . We want it done inside of twenty to twenty-five days." Regrettably, Hopkins continued, FERA had found few creative work relief programs for women anywhere in the country. As Hopkins candidly admitted, the conference had been called not to inform the women what FERA was doing, but to seek ideas from the assembled national leaders on possible work projects for women. "It can't be done unless we have the cooperation of the people who know something about it, who know how to do it."[63]

Ellen Woodward spoke next about women's needs in the depression, and how state and federal governments could meet those needs. In Woodward's opinion, the most urgent necessity was providing jobs. Unfortunately, finding half a million jobs for women was much harder than finding four million for men, because women were not considered appropriate for the heavy construction jobs that made up the bulk of the work relief projects. Difficulty in devising acceptable work projects for women was a recurring theme throughout the 1930s and undoubtedly the most important factor affecting women's experiences on relief.[64]

The rest of the conference, with Eleanor Roosevelt presiding, was devoted to discussion of specific project ideas. Ellen Woodward explained that such projects as sewing rooms, canning centers, clerical work, visiting housekeeping, public health work, emergency nursery schools, musical programs, and historical research had already proved feasible. Rose Schneiderman, Grace Abbott, and Hilda Worthington Smith suggested expanding public library services, using women in unemployment offices to help other women find work, finding jobs for unemployed teachers, setting up systems for vocational guidance, and establishing resident camps combined with relief.[65]

The White House Conference on the Emergency Needs of Women came at a propitious time. Ellen Woodward had been on her job at FERA less than two months, and women's relief programs were just getting under way. Woodward and her staff were actively looking for ideas, and the White House Conference supplied them. The conference also demonstrated the support that nationally recognized women's leaders and women's organizations such as the National Consumers' League, the League of Women Voters, the American Red Cross, and the Women's Trade Union League could place behind the women's relief projects. Many projects suggested at the conference became the mainstays of the women's relief programs for the rest of the decade.[66]

The same week of the White House Conference, Ellen Woodward and

Harry Hopkins met to discuss the approach toward women in the Civil Works Administration (CWA), a federal relief program that put four million people to work in the winter of 1933-34.[67] Two years later, when the Works Progress Administration was established, Ellen Woodward reminded Eleanor Roosevelt of the confusion that had surrounded women's initial role in the CWA:

> Won't you please ask the President to emphasize in his talk Sunday night that employable women on relief will receive their fair proportion of jobs in the new program. I think this is important, Mrs. Roosevelt, for when Civil Works was initiated, many people, including otherwise intelligent state administrators, interpreted the statement "four million men will be put to work" to mean literally men and not men and women. It took weeks of effort and thousands of wires and letters to correct the erroneous impressions . . . Since the projects mentioned in the press have been mainly projects on which only men work, there is much uneasiness felt by women all over the country.[68]

By January 1934, of the approximately four million persons on the CWA rolls, about 300,000 were women. Most of these women were concentrated in the nonconstruction Civil Works Division, while the preferred jobs customarily were reserved for men. The CWA had been planned as a temporary expedient to get the country through the winter, and it was disbanded in March 1934. Harry Hopkins made it clear, however, that women's needs would receive equal treatment with men's as the CWA programs were transferred to FERA.[69]

Ellen Woodward served as the Director of Women's Work in the Federal Work Division of the Federal Emergency Relief Administration from 1933 to 1935. She supervised a small staff at the national headquarters but spent most of her time working with the state directors of women's work who were in charge of implementing the women's programs in the states. FERA, drawing on many recommendations first put forth at the White House Conference, concluded that women were best used in two kinds of work projects: skilled workers or those with professional training could render services like nursing, teaching, homemaking, library work, and research; other women were put to work in projects involving the production and distribution of items such as food and clothing. By 1935 there were almost 300,000 women on FERA work relief jobs, 12 percent of the total.[70]

By late 1935, the Works Progress Administration had replaced FERA as the main government agency providing work relief for unemployed Americans. Unlike FERA, which only provided grants to the states, the WPA put reliefers on the federal payroll. At this time, people needing assistance were put into two categories: those certified as employable were given jobs on WPA projects, while those who were physically unable to work (such as the elderly, the blind, and dependent children) were covered by the Social Security program. During this reorganization and redefinition of the federal government's role in providing assistance, the relief programs for women were maintained.[71]

Ellen Woodward continued to direct women's projects under the WPA as she had at FERA. Her new title was Assistant Administrator of the WPA, with responsibility for all of the agency's nonconstruction programs: professional and service plans, the arts section known as Federal One (including the Federal Theater Project, Federal Writers Project, and the Federal Art Project), and the women's programs. Combining the women's and professional projects into one nonconstruction section clarified an administrative problem that had plagued the FERA. Since approximately one-fourth of the women on relief were professionals (for example, teachers, nurses, or librarians), it had been unclear whether the women's section or the general white-collar section had primary responsibility for them. In this administrative tangle, the needs of these women were often overlooked. Woodward lost control of the professional women in 1934-1935, but won it back in the WPA reorganization. In her consolidated position as head of the Women's and Professional Projects Division, Ellen Woodward became a major power in the WPA.[72]

WPA women's projects closely resembled the state-run FERA projects, although the WPA relied more heavily on sewing projects. In 1936, 56 percent of all women in the WPA worked in sewing rooms. One WPA official summarized the primary role of these sewing projects succinctly: "For unskilled men we have the shovel. For unskilled women we have only the needle."[73]

Heavy reliance on sewing rooms was part of what WPA officials euphemistically referred to as "project trouble"—finding suitable jobs for women. One regional director discussed the difficulties with Eleanor Roosevelt: "Women's projects are not easy to prosecute from any point of view . . . One can put practically all of the men eligible for work in a community to work on a couple of major work projects. Not so with women. To care for one hundred women in a county we will have perhaps a dozen projects differing in nature." Such projects usually required substantial planning and close supervision, as well as on-the-job training to equip women with necessary skills. These requirements added to the cost of providing relief for women. Through 1941, expenditures for nonlabor costs on all WPA projects including construction averaged 26 percent of total project costs. Nonlabor expenditures on sewing projects actually exceeded this ratio, averaging 27 percent of total expenditures.[74]

Woodward and her staff recognized these problems, but they also were concerned with getting as many needy women as possible on relief. Between 300,000 and 400,000 women were employed at various times on WPA projects, comprising between 12 and 19 percent of the total number employed on work relief. Scattered evidence implies that the WPA attempted to limit the number of women certified for employment to avoid possible public criticism about employing "too many women," thus undermining the traditional male role as breadwinner.[75] Another study, however, has suggested that the proportion of women among workers on relief was greater than their proportion in the total labor supply. Such women, entering the work force for the first time and often lacking the necessary skills and experience to find jobs, would probably have had difficulty even in a full-employment economy. Since they had nowhere to turn but the government, many became permanently dependent on government help.[76]

Although women's experiences on the WPA were fairly positive, many women were not helped by relief at all, a situation similar to women's experiences under the NRA. In 1938, approximately 372,000 women had WPA jobs, but more than three million women were unemployed; another one and a half million women had only part-time jobs. (There were eight million unemployed men.)[77] The positive benefits of the WPA that accrued to women on relief must be weighed against the disappointment of other unemployed women who were unable to share in this progress.

The Women's Bureau was sufficiently impressed with the WPA record on women to conclude that the "WPA has opened up many bright vistas for the woman worker today." Ellen Woodward agreed, and she planned a public relations campaign in 1936 to publicize the work of her staff: "We are ready now to render a proud account. Let us do so. A summary of the work of the Women's Division must reach the general public . . . Women as a group are not yet clearly aware of all that the Administration has done to help those who were in the greatest need."[78]

Ellen Sullivan Woodward had good reason to be proud of these accomplishments. On the whole, the relief programs of the Civil Works Administration, the Federal Emergency Relief Administration, and the Works Progress Administration produced important if small steps forward for women workers. These programs carried out most of the recommendations originally proposed at the White House Conference on the Emergency Needs of Women. The establishment of a separate women's section with a qualified administrator like Ellen Woodward to coordinate and encourage women's relief programs showed the federal government's awareness that women had special needs in the depression. To a great degree, Woodward and her staff devised plans that reflected and responded to these special needs.

When Ellen Sullivan Woodward came to Washington from Mississippi in 1933, she knew only Molly Dewson and several other Southern women in politics and government. Soon after, especially through her friendship and collaboration with Eleanor Roosevelt, Ellen Woodward moved into a central position in the women's network. Woodward worked closely with network members in the planning and implementation of the government's relief policies toward women. Except for an occasional appearance by Harry Hopkins, these New Deal programs were run almost exclusively by women, for women. When the WPA faced cutbacks in the late 1930s, women in Washington wanted to repay Woodward for her work in the relief agencies over the last five years. The network banded together and got Ellen Woodward another challenging job—this time as a member of the Social Security Board.

Hilda Worthington Smith's attempt to set up and administer camps for unemployed women is a final example of what a small subset of the network could do within the larger context of the New Deal relief agencies. This program, originally under the Federal Emergency Relief Administration and later the National Youth Administration, demonstrates the problems that women faced in winning support for their programs, and how they tried to overcome these obstacles.

The Civilian Conservation Corps, with its plans for reforestation, land reclamation, and healthy outdoor living, was one of the most popular programs of the early New Deal. By September 1935, more than half a million young men lived in CCC camps, working on projects such as thinning forests, building lookout towers and wildlife shelters, and restoring Civil War battlefields. While commending the CCC work, a few astute critics noted that the program was limited to young men and asked, where was the "she-she-she"?[79] Most Americans did not realize that the government had made a similar effort to set up resident camps for women, but on a drastically reduced scale. Various members of the network, including Molly Dewson, Frances Perkins, Ellen Sullivan Woodward, and Mary Anderson, had tossed this idea around in 1932 and 1933, but it was one woman, Hilda Worthington Smith, who gets the principal credit for the implementation of the camps for unemployed women.

Unlike the Civilian Conservation Corps, which was a national program, camps for women were run primarily by the states with FERA grants. In fact, the first women's camp had been set up in 1933 under New York State's Temporary Emergency Relief Administration. As in so many aspects of relief policy, New York was in the forefront. The camp at Bear Mountain Park (later renamed Camp Jane Addams) was admittedly experimental. Its program included recreational activities, instruction in hygiene and nutrition, experience in the responsibilities of communal living, and some vocational guidance. Unlike the CCC camps, where the young men were paid wages, the women received only small allowances.[80]

At about the same time the Bear Mountain Camp was getting under way, Hilda Worthington Smith began work as a specialist in Workers' Education at FERA. Planning resident camps for unemployed women was included in the initial description of her duties. (Smith's reaction was one of mock dismay: "This, of course, would be a whole piece of work in itself if it did not constitute at present one-sixth of my new responsibilities!") The choice of Smith, a specialist in Workers' Education, meant that the general educational aspects of these camps would be strongly emphasized. Hilda Smith's ideas for the resident camps drew heavily on the Bryn Mawr Summer School for Industrial Workers which she had directed in the 1920s.[81]

By late 1933, as instructed, Hilda Smith had drawn up a proposal for resident camps for unemployed women. The plan provided for the emergency needs of the women (food, shelter, clothing), but primarily stressed educational opportunities and experience in communal, democratic living. Though some informal counseling about employment opportunities was planned, there was no attempt to set up vocational training programs for the short period the women would be at the camps. Unlike young men at the CCC camps, young women would not perform physical labor, nor would they receive wages. The only work the women did involved the upkeep and running of their camps. Hilda Smith considered offering paid work within these camp settings, but could not think how to implement such a scheme—conservation and reforestation were not considered appropriate for women. Instead Smith stressed the educational and personal aspects of the camps.[82] Once again, a different approach was necessary to meet the needs of women in the depression—simply copying projects that had proved successful for men was not enough.

For several months, nothing was heard of Smith's proposals. Eleanor Roosevelt, Hilda Smith's close friend and adviser, finally broke the bureaucratic impasse by offering to host a White House Conference on Camps for Unemployed Women. "Then events began to move rapidly," Smith remembered.[83] Approximately seventy-five people, mostly women, attended the conference on April 30, 1934; National Youth Administration director Aubrey Williams and Ellen Woodward presided. As expected, the conference went on record strongly in favor of resident schools and camps for unemployed women.

The impact of the conference went even further. Hilda Smith wrote Eleanor Roosevelt, "The White House Conference gave impetus to this whole program and the discussion at the end of the day had brought out a definite plan of action and a unified purpose in the group."[84] The outgrowth of the Conference on Camps for Unemployed Women was strikingly similar to the results of the White House Conference on the Emergency Needs of Women. The Conference on Camps was also reminiscent of the Consumer Conference held at the White House in December of 1933 for the Consumers' Advisory Board. In all three cases, Eleanor Roosevelt's offer to sponsor a White House conference gave important outside support to the programs at crucial times; Eleanor Roosevelt's intercession (and the clout that White House support commanded) ended a bureaucratic stalemate and got the programs moving again. All three White House conferences strongly influenced the programs that emerged by bringing together experts in the field, defining the basic objectives of the programs, and making concrete suggestions for their implementation.

After the White House Conference, Harry Hopkins quickly approved the project and advised state relief administrators that limited funds were available for such camps. Since the program was experimental, a limit of forty schools was set for the first summer. During 1934, twenty-eight schools and camps for unemployed women were established. FERA grants paid for staff salaries, student maintenance expenses, and building upkeep; state and private funds covered the equipment and organizational expenses (which averaged about eight dollars per person a week). A total of 3,000 one-month terms were offered to 1,800 women. Registration in the camps was limited to young women from needy families who had been recommended by local relief administrators. The first summer produced marked improvements in health, vocational guidance, systematic training in homemaking and citizenship, and "a new feeling of social responsibility." Approximately one-fifth of the women who attended the camps found a job at the end of the session, although job placement was not a stated purpose of the program.[85]

Hilda Worthington Smith's 1934 report on the camps claimed definite success. Evidently Harry Hopkins agreed, for the camps expanded under state FERA auspices in 1935: forty-five camps were in operation, each with seventy to eighty students at a time. Later in 1935, the women's camps were transferred to the National Youth Administration's Division on Educational Camps. Dorothy DeSchwenitz of the U.S. Employment Service became the director, but Hilda Smith remained primarily in charge as head of the Advisory Committee. By March 1936, ninety camps were serving some 5,000 women.[86]

In spite of Smith's glowing reports of the participants' increased physical well-being and improved mental outlook, the experimental camps suddenly came under the attack in 1937 as part of the general Congressional disenchantment with expensive New Deal social programs. Then came the order to halt the program entirely. The expense of running the camps and maintaining the students was too great for the National Youth Administration. Since the camps were not regular work projects under the WPA, the women did not qualify for relief wages, and stipends from the National Youth Administration were too small to allow the women to take care of their own needs.[87]

Hilda Worthington Smith was upset by the sudden decision to close down the camps, as she later wrote to Eleanor Roosevelt: "I was distressed, and have been ever since, that this project should have been summarily ended, without a full chance for discussion of the results of these experiments . . . Many of the former schools were just achieving a high standard of work when they were so abruptly terminated, without a hearing." Smith was especially unhappy because she felt the National Youth Administration had used an inflated figure to compute the average costs of the project.[88] Despite Smith's impassioned pleas and Eleanor Roosevelt's strong support, the experimental program of educational camps for unemployed women was too tempting a target when relief agencies faced cutbacks in 1937. No public outcry occurred when the camps were disbanded, largely because their existence had never been widely known. The camps for unemployed women had not caught the imagination of the American public as had the Civilian Conservation Corps.

Watching the bureaucratic history of camps for unemployed women was a frustrating experience for Hilda Worthington Smith and her colleagues in the network. Expectations for camps for women were always far below the scale proposed for camps for men. Hilda Smith felt this discrepancy keenly: "The CCC camps with their millions of dollars for wages, educational work, travel, and supervision constantly remind me of what we might do for women from these same families. *As so often the case, the boys get the breaks, the girls are neglected.* Even though similar plans for women are more difficult to develop, I do not believe they should be discarded as impossible" (emphasis added).[89] Yet as a result of the efforts of women like Smith, Eleanor Roosevelt, and other prominent women administrators, the government at least made a token effort to meet the needs of these young women. While not a stunning achievement in numbers (8,500 women compared to 2.5 million men), the camps might not have materialized at all without the dedication and persistence of certain members of the network.

The network of women in politics and government in the New Deal cannot claim exclusive credit for legislation such as the Social Security Act or the Fair Labor Standards Act of 1938, nor should the network be blamed for failures like the camps. Yet the overall impact of the network on such areas is undeniable. Women's vital contributions to the development of the social welfare policies of the New Deal can no longer be ignored.

6

A GENERATION ON THE WANE

As 1936 represented the "high tide" of the fortunes of the Roosevelt administration, so did 1936 mark the high tide of women's participation in the New Deal.[1] That year witnessed women's greatest involvement in national politics, and prominent Democratic women praised the accomplishments of the New Deal throughout the 1936 campaign. At the Democratic convention, Congresswoman Mary T. Norton of New Jersey summarized what the New Deal had done for women:

> The women of America will tell you, as they have told me often, that the New Deal is a square deal for them. It has not only helped women on the farms and in industry, but they have gained a new freedom because a just President in appointing them to high offices and places of distinction has given them more courage and faith in themselves, a desire to go forward with the men of the country to a more secure and greater happiness and prosperity.[2]

The network among women in politics and government reached its zenith in 1936 as well. Almost all of the original members of the network continued to play prominent roles in the Washington community, mainly in the government's still expanding social welfare programs. Franklin Roosevelt's landslide victory in November 1936 was an inspiration to them all. Once the second term began, however, the atmosphere in Washington shifted perceptibly. The New Deal itself was changing, and this strongly affected the functioning of the network.

Franklin Roosevelt's first term produced an outpouring of legislation and reform unprecedented in American history. By 1936, however, Congressional resistance to Roosevelt as a leader and to his New Deal policies was increasing. Southern conservative Democrats joined with Republicans in a loose coalition of opposition forces, and the Roosevelt administration found itself on the defensive for the first time. Other factors contributed to the change. The economic situation in the late 1930s differed from the crisis conditions of 1933 and 1934. Many in Congress believed that the emergency was over—the time had come for the New Deal to ease up on social and economic reform. Congress did enact some reform legislation in the late 1930s, notably the Fair Labor Standards Act, but on the whole the second term was characterized by stalemate and retrenchment. As one historian observed, "a different kind of New Deal" developed after 1936.[3]

In general, developments for women followed a similar pattern. No organized coalition blocked the advancement of women, but the late 1930s represented a time of retrenchment for women as well. Since so many women in the network were involved in those social welfare aspects of the New Deal facing growing opposition in Congress, women's activities naturally were hurt.

This shrinking and tightening of New Deal programs had predictable implications for women in government. Women have tended to achieve success in newer government agencies, or during periods of government expansion; by the late 1930s just the reverse was happening. The Works Progress Administration reflected this phenomenon in the late 1930s: "The informality of Mrs. Woodward's regime, which derived from a cavalier self-assurance on her part as well as from the novelty of the subject matter of her jurisdiction, was succeeded by a more formal attitude toward procedure and toward personal relationships within the staff and between the staff and their chief."[4] After 1938 and 1939, innovative programs in the Women's and Professional Projects Division faced severe cutbacks or, in the case of the Federal Theater, total abolition because of Congressional attacks. Retrenchment occurred in other areas of the government too, as the disbanding of camps for unemployed women in 1937 demonstrated. There was even talk of abolishing the Children's Bureau and the Women's Bureau, but nothing came of either proposal.[5]

In many respects, the declining fortunes of women in public life in the United States reflected the worldwide trend in the 1930s. Women in the network had feared that Section 213 of the National Economy Act, which limited the employment of married women in the federal government, was the first manifestation of the virulent antifeminism gaining in Europe and elsewhere in the 1930s. As early as 1935, Molly Dewson wrote to Eleanor Roosevelt, "The women's organizations have the jitters on the attack on women made by Hitler and others. They feel the trend is toward prohibiting women from functioning in any other capacity than wives, mothers, and homemakers. Of course, I myself think we handled dynamite when we passed 213 of the National Economy Act."⁶

Emma Guffey Miller struck a similar note in a 1936 radio address: "We are all familiar with the tragic situation in Europe. Within the last few years, Italy, Austria and Germany have passed discriminatory legislation against women workers. It never occurred to us five years ago that such a situation would come about in our own country and yet Section 213 is almost a replica of the first steps of discriminatory legislation against women which has been passed by the Fascisti in Italy and the Nazis in Germany."⁷ After 1936, anxiety over developments in Europe intensified among the women in the network. Sometimes the concern was linked specifically with Section 213, but more often the women were voicing general fears about the constriction of opportunities for women world-wide.

There certainly was cause for alarm. In a 1935 *Harper's* article entitled "Is Feminism Dead?" Genevieve Parkhurst extensively chronicled the set-backs dealt to women in all the Western countries, with German women the greatest losers. Parkhurst was especially discouraged that German womanhood had contributed so enthusiastically to Hitler's rise. Dorothy McConnell's 1936 pamphlet, "Women, War, and Fascism," similarly noted that women had been vital to the rise of the very fascism that was drastically restricting their public roles. McConnell saw parallels to the German situation already at work in the United States, especially with Section 213: "The drive against women, a cool, steady, ruthless drive which is even more drastic than any drive against racial minorities, has become in the last three years a world movement which includes the United States." Eleanor Roosevelt reported in a 1936 "My Day" column that in Germany highly trained scientific women were told that their minds were of no use to the country; they should concentrate on bearing children and managing homes. Roosevelt concluded, "We feel like say-ing, 'It can't happen here,' but unless we face the fact that this is a by-product of the great question now before us, we may wake up to find that we have gone the way of other nations which were unable to solve this situation." This narrowing of opportunities for women was, in Dorothy McConnell's phrase, "a world menace."⁸

What could the women of America do? One proposed tactic, promo-tion of a Woman's Charter to protect and expand women's opportunities throughout the world, had been a complete failure.⁹ Consequently, since most women in public life believed that opportunities for women world-wide depended on the preservation of democracy, they concentrated their efforts on democracy at home. Dorothy McAlister articulated this theme: "As democracy succeeds, the position of women advances. When democracies are supplanted by dictatorships, women's progress is set back hundreds of years. What women have gained in this country must be jealously guarded, in order that they may go forward to greater gains. It is through political power and participation in government that women can best safeguard past and future progress."[10] If the women in America could expand the number of women holding responsible national positions at a time when their numbers were shrinking in other countries, this would be even stronger proof of democracy's vitality.

In a 1939 speech to the Federation of Business and Professional Women, an organization especially concerned with developments in Europe, Ellen Sullivan Woodward emphasized that American women should be grateful for democracy: "Another kind of freedom for which we have to thank democracy is that which permits us, as women, to live full, well rounded lives as human beings as well as homemakers. If a woman has a family, she does a better job by them when she herself is free—when she is not compelled by law or custom to bind herself to everything except 'Kinder, Kirche, and Küche.' " Trends in fascist countries such as Germany were antithetical to the beliefs of the women in the network. As women in public life, their task was to maintain democratic government and to protect the gains that women had already made.[11]

The concern for diminishing opportunities abroad helps to explain the strong sense of mission behind Molly Dewson's commitment to expand opportunities for women in public life in America in the 1930s. To some degree at least, her efforts were designed to offset the declines for women abroad; this gave Dewson's demands a special urgency that would have been missing in the 1920s or 1940s. The situation in Europe made women proud of the Roosevelt record in the 1930s, with its important yet limited gains for women. With losses for womanhood occurring in so many parts of the world, American women not only preserved their political roles but actually expanded them during the decade of the 1930s. The women in the network saw themselves as living proof that "it can't happen here."

Yet women in the network were keenly aware that the general situation for women was not as open in the late 1930s as it had been earlier in the decade. One obvious problem was lack of turnover in government positions. Women had enough trouble getting patronage when Roosevelt took office in 1933; as the New Deal wore on, deserving women found it increasingly difficult to secure positions. Ellen Woodward wrote to Carolyn Wolfe at the Women's Division in 1936: "You know how desperately hard it is to place anyone now when there is such a scramble for jobs." Frances Perkins also noticed how few new jobs were opening up, especially in the highest positions: "The President is well satisfied with the work of the people he's got in high administrative posts and he tends not to change them . . . so the turnover is slight and there is not that opportunity for the aspiring young person, the aspiring outsider who isn't yet in the government." Cutbacks in personnel and expenditures in many New Deal agencies in response to Congressional pressure in the late 1930s heightened the problem. Eleanor Roosevelt wrote a job seeker in 1937 that most government agencies were not hiring new people, adding, "Mrs. Woodward is now pledged not to take on anyone who is not a relief case."[12]

Some opportunities did materialize for women in the second term. The establishment of the Social Security Administration brought Jane Hoey to the federal government as head of the Bureau of Public Assistance; Mary LaDame left the United States Employment Service to join the Labor Department as Frances Perkins's assistant; Daisy Harriman was appointed Minister to Norway in 1937. Molly Dewson herself was named to the recently established Social Security Board in 1937. Although Dewson always publicly disavowed any interest in a government position for herself, she and Eleanor Roosevelt worked actively behind the scenes to arrange this popular appointment.[13] One of Molly Dewson's friends from the Consumers' League commented to Eleanor Roosevelt, "It is almost dramatic, isn't it, to have had her prepare for years for a job that didn't exist while she was preparing for it."[14]

When Dewson retired from the board because of ill health in 1938, she made sure that a woman was named in her place—not just any woman, but Ellen Sullivan Woodward, whose job at the Works Progress Administration was in jeopardy as a result of the cutbacks and reorganization faced by New Deal relief agencies. Dewson worked hard to get Woodward named as her successor, pleading to Franklin Roosevelt, "It would send the old war mare to the pasture so happy and confident."[15]

Dewson's designation of Woodward as her successor was accomplished without too much difficulty, but in other cases the women in the network were less successful. Attempts to promote Marion Glass Banister to Treasurer from Assistant Treasurer failed; Molly Dewson's suggestion of Josephine Roche to head the new Federal Security Agency formed by the 1939 government reorganization fell on deaf ears. In addition, although the network had successfully mobilized behind Florence Allen's appointment to the Court of Appeals in 1934, it failed to generate support for elevating Allen to the United States Supreme Court when vacancies occurred in the late 1930s.[16]

Progress in the political arena was also stalled, even as early as the second term. Molly Dewson had recognized the novelty of her plans in the early New Deal: "These changes are tentative beginnings. They have not stiffened into custom." After describing women's accomplishments in

1934 and 1935, Dewson added, "That phase is over in a sense—the pre-
paratory phase. I am not positive at all about what next." In 1938 Dewson wrote to Eleanor Roosevelt about the Reporter Plan, "I'd like to see it
go on full blast at least through 1940," but beyond that she was not sure.
In fact, 1936 marked the peak of women's participation in both the Republican and Democratic national conventions; by 1940 and 1944, a
downward trend was evident.[17]

Emma Guffey Miller's schemes to subvert Molly Dewson's influence in
the Women's Division added to the backsliding for women in politics in
the late 1930s. Miller's approach to politics had always been closer to
that of her brother, Senator Joe Guffey of Pennsylvania, than to that of
Molly Dewson or Eleanor Roosevelt. Miller wanted Dewson's job as
head of the Women's Division, but her moves were thwarted by Eleanor
Roosevelt and Dewson herself.[18] Molly Dewson complained to Eleanor
Roosevelt that such personal rivalry disrupted the plans of the Women's
Division: "Nobody would care about Emma's activities except she can
make our Women's Division's work ineffective and reduce the women
from active workers for the New Deal to a bunch of schemers for personal advancement in which none of our type are interested."[19] Emma
Guffey Miller did not win many supporters in the 1930s, but she had
more success in the 1940s when, practically single-handedly, she convinced the Democrats to endorse the Equal Rights Amendment.

A third problem for women in politics in the late 1930s was the passage
of the Hatch Act in 1939, which sharply curtailed political activity by
government workers. This legislation especially harmed the Democratic
women's campaign style, because the Women's Division relied heavily
on prominent women in government to publicize the New Deal's accomplishments. The Hatch Act's restrictions were particularly galling to old-
time politicians like Nellie Tayloe Ross, who shared her frustrations with
Eleanor Roosevelt: "I am impelled to express to you my feeling, akin to
shock, that I shall be expected to sit silent and inert while our party a few
months hence will be waging a mighty battle to keep control of the government."[20]

The Hatch Act diminished the political power of Democratic women in
another way. Since the act forbade payment to political organizations for
printed matter, the Women's Division could no longer sell subscriptions
to the *Democratic Digest*. The *Digest* was an important organ of women
in politics and government in the 1930s, and part of its success came from
its independence from the Democratic National Committee (DNC). Once
the DNC took over the fairly expensive proposition of funding the
Democratic Digest, the magazine became an inviting target for editorial
control as well as financial cutbacks.[21]

During the second term, the Women's Division broke with the Roosevelt administration for the first (and only) time. This falling-out occurred over Roosevelt's 1937 plan to "reform" the Supreme Court by increasing the number of justices to fifteen and mandating retirement for justices over age seventy. Many women in the network shared Roosevelt's frustration over Supreme Court actions blocking important social welfare legislation (after all, these women had written some of the laws in the first place), but few seemed enthusiastic about Roosevelt's unexpected attack on the Supreme Court. Frances Perkins recalled: "This was the first time that I ever really questioned the President's political good sense."[22]

Molly Dewson had similar doubts about the Court plan, and her reticence influenced the stance of the Women's Division. Dewson asked individual Democratic women to write their representatives in Congress expressing support, but stopped short of a Women's Division endorsement of Supreme Court reform in the *Democratic Digest*. Dewson explained her reasoning to Dorothy McAlister:

> I have been sort of stubborn about not having the Women's Division take a public stand in the *Digest* for the President's court plan. The reason is that forty Senators are opposed to it and I don't want forty Senators in over twenty states opposed to our organization work. I think what we can do for the Party if we do not get them opposed by taking a stand is worth more than coming out publicly, for I believe the Pres. plan will carry and we are doing a lot anyway.[23]

Dewson's ploy of encouraging individual women to support the Court plan, but keeping the Women's Division neutral, was probably a way of minimizing Democratic women's opposition to the plan. At least that was what Eleanor Roosevelt thought: "In all probability you don't think Democratic women are for it but I don't know."[24]

Dewson's personal feelings aside, the Court plan marked the first instance where the Women's Division was not 100 percent behind the New Deal. The honeymoon was not over by any means, but Dewson and the women in the network were more at ease with a New Deal that was pushing social welfare legislation than with one pursuing political vendettas. The Women's Division was not well suited, ideologically or otherwise, for mobilizing behind purely political issues.

During Roosevelt's second term, the Women's Division continued to emphasize educational work and expanded its organization among local Democratic women. But there was less for women to rally around than at the beginning of the New Deal. Once enough prominent women had been appointed to government positions, less political mileage was gained by securing patronage for women, especially if they were not "firsts" for their sex. The Women's Division kept up its work, but with less visible success than during the first term.

Changes in the character of the network itself also contributed to the shifting climate for women in politics and government after 1936. These changes were not just the result of death or retirement, because three-fourths of the women in the original network were still in government in the early 1940s.[25] Rather, the network was functioning in a different political context after 1937. The New Deal was less concerned with promoting new social reform legislation than with defending from Congressional attack the gains already won. Fewer programs, social welfare or otherwise, were initiated in the late 1930s, and thus fewer opportunities existed for the cross-departmental cooperation that had characterized the women's network in the early New Deal. The network was not dead yet, as its role in the 1938 Fair Labor Standards Act demonstrated. For the most part, however, the network redirected its energies toward preserving programs already under way, rather than expanding or developing new ones.

Scattered evidence suggests that breaks in communication among members of the network were more frequent in the second term than earlier—people moved in and out of government, illnesses struck, and official paths did not cross as often. Marion Glass Banister wrote to Lucille Foster McMillin in the early 1940s, "Your little note which came a week or more ago was a pleasant reminder to me that you are still part of this swirling Washington existence, a fact that the long silences that sometimes occur in our lines of communication would almost permit me to forget." And after Molly Dewson retired from government, Marion Glass Banister wrote: "For weeks, even months, after I got back from my fall vacation, I spent my time scurrying around trying to solve the ever deepening mystery of what had become of you."[26]

Though the network continued to operate with most of its personnel and functions intact, some crucial internal changes took place after 1936. Molly Dewson's retirement from active political work in 1937 contributed to a slowdown in initiatives for women. Dewson wrote Eleanor Roosevelt, "1931-1937 is enough to give to a cause"; she was tired, and she wanted out of the hectic political life of Washington and New York.[27] Even though President Roosevelt called Dewson back from retirement to serve on the Social Security Board from 1937 to 1938, she remained aloof from partisan politics when she returned to Washington. After 1938, she spent most of her time in Maine. Never again would Dewson be the vital force for women she had been in the early 1930s.

Frances Perkins also became less effective as a female political leader in the late New Deal. Because of Perkins's involvement in postponing the deportation of Harry Bridges, a California longshoreman and labor organizer suspected of being a Communist, several members of Congress filed articles of impeachment in 1938-1939 to remove Perkins as Secretary of Labor. Although women rallied to her support and Perkins was completely exonerated, the impeachment proceedings probably made Frances Perkins too controversial to initiate new directions, either for women or labor, in the late New Deal.[28]

Two other factors heightened the impact of Dewson's and Perkins's progressive withdrawal from leadership in the women's network. One was the increasing difficulty of reaching the President. Both men and women noticed that after presidential aide Louis Howe became ill in 1935, it was much harder to gain access to FDR. Roosevelt's inaccessibility was especially damaging for women who needed the President's active support to counter resistance from male traditionalists in politics and government. Dewson complained to Eleanor Roosevelt about this problem as early as November 1935: "Yet sometimes to be perfectly frank with you I wonder whether some of the persons the papers say he sees are more important to see than I am." Dewson renewed her complaints during the 1936 campaign, remarking, "I miss Louis Howe awfully."[29]

Of even greater significance to the network was Eleanor Roosevelt's diminished involvement with women's concerns during the second term. Patronage had been taken care of, the Women's Division was running smoothly and the women's relief programs were under the watchful eye of Ellen Woodward. Eleanor Roosevelt's strenuous career as lecturer and columnist took up considerably more of her time than in the early New Deal. Moreover, Molly Dewson's and Eleanor Roosevelt's paths crossed less frequently in the late 1930s. Since so many of the gains for women in the New Deal derived from the partnership between Dewson and Roosevelt, this change naturally had an adverse impact on women's chances for advancement.

Dewson's letters during the late 1930s took on a rather plaintive tone which reflected the distance, geographical and otherwise, that separated the two women by then. In early 1939, Dewson wrote Eleanor Roosevelt, "When you are shopping in New York City sometime couldn't I go along and hold your purse?" In mid-1940, Dewson wrote Roosevelt, "I'm writing because I just hanker to see you," and Eleanor replied two days later, "I have the same hankering to see you—it has been such a long time."[30]

Occasionally a new note of tension surfaced in the correspondence between these two old friends. Eleanor Roosevelt wrote Dewson in 1941, "I have not become hardened to saying 'no' to you. I would always make an effort to do anything you really wanted me to do. It would help if I could be in more than one place at a time, but, unfortunately, I haven't been able to manage it."[31] The slightly exasperated tone of this letter did not signify a major rift between Dewson and Roosevelt or an abandonment of women's concerns by Eleanor Roosevelt. But during the late 1930s Eleanor Roosevelt increasingly turned her attention to the problems of youth and blacks. Now that women had their "New Deal," it was time for other groups to have their chance. Moreover, after 1939 Eleanor Roosevelt focused much of her attention on the critical situation in Europe. International developments fundamentally altered the milieu in which the women's network operated, as the New Deal switched from depression to war.

The year 1940 was pivotal for women in politics and government. In many ways, this year marked the culmination of the efforts of social feminists over the last forty years. The National Institute of Government in May 1940 demonstrated the effectiveness of the issue-oriented, educational approach these women brought to government. The large number of women administrators who attended the Institute of Government testified to the unprecedented roles women were playing in government by the end of the 1930s. The negative reaction to Wendell Willkie's statement during the 1940 campaign that the Secretary of Labor was a "man's job" demonstrated public support for women in high government positions.[32]

By 1940 many of the reforms sought by women since the Progressive period had been enacted by the New Deal. Of the goals that Frances Perkins had discussed with Franklin Roosevelt in 1932 before accepting the position of Secretary of Labor, all but health insurance had been adopted. When the 1940 Republican platform endorsed the social security program, Perkins exclaimed, "God's Holy name be praised! No matter who gets elected we've won." At the 1940 Democratic convention Frances Perkins and her friend Agnes Leach realized how much had changed over the past sixteen years. In 1924, women sat outside the door of the Platform Committee and their suggestions were ignored. In 1940, women were not only official members of the committee, but their ideas were taken seriously and acted upon as well.[33]

Sixteen years is just short of a generation. Nineteen forty was a transitional year in that it marked the beginning of the transfer of power to a new, younger group of women who had not been prominent in the early New Deal. Frances Perkins described one of these newcomers: "She may have been around, but she was young and somewhere down the line."[34] In 1937 Dewson had been quite enthusiastic about the future of the Women's Division ("a swell organization and two swell girls—women of experience aged 38 & 36 to build on if the men want it"), but her hand-picked successors did not fare too well in the 1940 campaign. Edward Flynn had replaced James Farley as Chairman of the Democratic National Committee, and Flynn cooperated less with the Women's Division than Farley had. In August, Eleanor Roosevelt had to ask Dewson to come down from Maine in the last months of the campaign to help out and "do some work with the men, it would be a great help. That is where Dorothy [McAlister] is weak."[35]

After the 1940 election, Molly Dewson confided to Eleanor Roosevelt her doubts about the future of the Women's Division: "Well we both agree there is no embarrassment of riches."[36] The goals, leadership, and tactics of the Women's Division shifted during the 1940s and 1950s, but not simply because a new generation of less dynamic women took over from old-timers like Molly Dewson. Changing national priorities and a growing concern with events in Europe had a more profound influence on developments for women than generational differences.

The *Democratic Digest* illustrates this shift in emphasis. Beginning in 1940, a recurring theme was preparations for the possibility of war. The Reporter Plan, with its stress on the social and economic gains of government welfare policies, was phased out and replaced by National Defense Surveys, which assessed each community's preparedness for war. Military imagery became more prominent: "An army of voters can function no more efficiently without organization than an army of soldiers." When women in government were mentioned in the *Digest* after 1940, it was usually in connection with their defense work.[37]

The appointment of Harriet Elliott as the only woman on the seven-member National Defense Committee in 1940 exemplifies these changing priorities. Elliott first took a leave of absence from the Women's College at the University of North Carolina in 1935-1936 to direct the Reporter Plan for the Women's Division; in 1940 she returned to Washington to work on national defense. Democratic women volunteered for local defense work throughout 1941, and most probably shared Molly Dewson's reaction to the attack on Pearl Harbor: "I am glad of it. No more shilly-shallying. Now for action in behalf of our ideals."[38]

Women have traditionally expanded their activities during wartime, and in many respects World War II followed this pattern. Eleanor Roosevelt wrote that women were "an indispensable part of the life of the country" during the war.[39] Women flocked to jobs in war industries—often their first experience with high-paying, industrial work. Other women contributed on the home front through the Red Cross, bond drives, civilian defense, or volunteer service on local ration boards. The Women's Division of the Democratic National Committee shifted its attention to the war as well. Once war was declared, the Women's Division patriotically urged all women to contribute to the war effort even if it meant less time for the Democratic party.[40] Many women volunteered for war work in their communities, but when it came to planning and administering the war, women were conspicuously absent at the policy-making levels.

Whereas the New Deal emergency and the corresponding expansion of government services provided new opportunities for women in government, no such influx of women into government occurred in wartime. High-level gains were limited. Eleanor Roosevelt worked briefly at the Office of Civilian Defense in 1941 and 1942, but as the President's wife she found it too awkward to hold an official job. Harriet Elliott's appointment to the National Defense Council was mainly at Franklin Roosevelt's insistence rather than the Women's Division's, according to Frances Perkins: " 'No, we have to have a woman,' he said. 'Got to pacify the women. If there is a woman, you won't have the women's protests against actions that are too military, against giving too much help to the allies. The presence of a woman on the Commission will stop all that.' He was adamant. I never knew him to be so stubborn."[41]

On the whole, wartime patronage was confined to appointments of women as United States delegates to international conferences, or as members of governmental advisory committees. Mary Anderson of the Women's Bureau was especially disappointed about women's roles in planning the war: "The emphasis was on the 'advisory' function and women were not really allowed to have a voice in formulating policies. This was a great disappointment to me and to others who hoped that the time had come when women would be given a real place in determining policies." Some prominent women charged that the government had completely ignored women leaders when setting up war agencies on production, manpower, and food.[42]

Women were especially concerned with the Office of Price Administration (OPA) because it directly affected American housewives. The Women's Division had suggested that the OPA send a housewife around the country to "sell" rationing to American women, but the male administrators thought this was unnecessary. (One woman dryly noted that these men "were not themselves confronted with the problems of stretching those ration books out to feed a family.")[43] Only much later under Chester Bowles did the OPA adopt this suggestion. Likewise, when the Office of Production Management was established under William S. Knudsen and Sidney Hillman, Mary Anderson asked her old friend Hillman to appoint a woman to a prominent position to give advice on women's issues. Hillman replied that research jobs might be available for women, but Mary Anderson persisted: "It is policymaking that we want a woman to be in on." Hillman never acted on Anderson's suggestion.[44]

The experience of the Women's Advisory Committee to the War Manpower Commission showed the prejudice and lack of support that women faced in wartime Washington. Women's groups felt a strong interest in wartime employment, because large numbers of women were working in defense plants and other industrial settings. Mary Anderson and others had hoped for full participation on the War Manpower Commission, but the men threatened to resign if women were appointed. Under such inauspicious circumstances, the Women's Advisory Committee was established. Mary Anderson was not terribly optimistic about its chances for success, as she confided to Rose Schneiderman: "The Manpower Women's Policy Committee met yesterday all day and I was there for their first meeting. It will be interesting to see if those boys over there will let them do anything. Some of them are quite skeptical but they are going to try it out."[45] For the most part, Anderson's fears were confirmed.

The Women's Advisory Committee's mandate was to evaluate problems and make suggestions as to the needs of women war workers, but it had no research staff and its advice was usually ignored. Although Mary Anderson had been promised that the Chairman of the Women's Advisory Committee, Margaret Hickey, would be a voting member of the Labor Advisory Committee, Hickey was only allowed to observe. The members of the Women's Advisory Committee resented their treatment: "If we are an advisory committee, somebody ought to ask us for advice sometimes."[46] The experience of the Women's Advisory Committee to the War Manpower Commission suggests what happens when women are relegated to special advisory committees outside the mainstream of the bureaucracy—they are ignored.

Opportunities for women in Washington in the 1940s did not entirely disappear. The Women's Bureau played a larger role in wartime than it had during the depression, because its research and fact-finding facilities could aid in the most efficient utilization of women workers in war industries. For certain younger women, wartime jobs marked the beginning of successful public careers. Katie Louchheim, head of the Women's Advisory Committee for the Democratic National Committee in the 1950s and later a Deputy Assistant Secretary of State under President John F. Kennedy, worked in the United Nations Relief and Rehabilitation Administration and its predecessors in the 1940s. Oveta Culp Hobby, a politician-journalist from Texas, came to Washington as a consultant for the Women's Interests Section of the War Department and later organized the Women's Auxiliary Army Corps (the WACs). Hobby was named Secretary of Health, Education, and Welfare by President Dwight Eisenhower in 1953. Anna Rosenberg gained important experience with the War Manpower Commission and the Advisory Board of the Office of

War Mobilization. She was appointed Assistant Secretary of Defense by President Harry Truman in 1950.[47]

Probably any woman who rose to national prominence in the 1950s or 1960s played some part in the war effort. But the opportunities for women in government in wartime were not nearly equal to those for women in the early New Deal. During wartime no influx of women into high government positions occurred, nor did a new network develop among women who did join the government in the 1940s.

Perhaps if Molly Dewson and Eleanor Roosevelt had actively promoted women's concerns in the early 1940s, further advancements might have occurred, but this is unlikely. Fundamental differences existed between the depression of the 1930s and the war period of the 1940s. To solve the crisis of the depression, the skills of trained social workers had been necessary. Women dominated that field, and they made important inroads in government. Women's potential contributions to the planning and management of the war effort were less obvious. Women like Mary Anderson and others in the network knew from their own experience in World War I what vital roles women could play in wartime.[48] But they could not convince the men, at least not the men in the war agencies. The fighting and planning of the war effort remained primarily a man's job.

The underutilization of women in Washington during the war was not entirely the fault of men, however. As the women in the network prepared for retirement, they did not foresee the need to recruit younger women to take their places once they left government. Instead of planning how to perpetuate the gains won in the 1930s, these older women naively believed that since they had done so well in government, conditions would continue to improve for women who wanted to pursue careers in government and politics. As Eleanor Roosevelt said in the *Democratic Digest* in 1938, "It seems to me that the best way to advance the equal rights of women is for every woman to do her job in the best possible way so that gradually the prejudice against women will disappear."[49] Setting an example—that was what the feminism of the women in the network was all about.

This kind of public feminism was well suited to a group of women with strong, individual talents who had been brought up in exceptional circumstances. Though the women in the network recognized that women faced discrimination in many areas (especially in entrance to the professions), they had not felt hampered by their sex in their own careers. (Frances Perkins's widely quoted statement that being a woman in government was a handicap "only in climbing trees" comes to mind.)[50] Yet such an approach to feminism was not going to produce basic changes for women in American society, no matter how impressive an example these women set. Being a "good woman" in government merely showed that some women could make it to the top; it did nothing to change the basic conditions that kept the great majority of women out.

Because the women in the network saw themselves as exceptional, they failed to question women's second-class status in American society. Never did they delve deeply into the causes of discrimination against women. Never did they challenge the stereotypes of women as "family-oriented" which have contributed so significantly to the continued oppression of women.[51] Because the feminist impact of women in the network was so dependent on their individual contributions, it was difficult to institutionalize even the limited gains that were won in the 1930s.

At the same time, the women in the network need not shoulder the entire blame for the gradual waning of their network. Many observers of American culture have noted that Americans are often more concerned with individual practice than with ideology, whether it be feminist or otherwise. Women in the network were not alone in their lack of vision.[52] Moreover, American society has rarely been openly sympathetic to women's concerns. Beyond a token commitment to equality for all Americans, few symbolic or substantive steps have encouraged wider roles for women in American life. Lack of support from the society at large made it difficult for the network to take root as an ongoing phenomenon.

One final factor contributed to the network's demise. Younger women, the next generation, appeared to be less interested in pursuing careers in public service than were women of Molly Dewson's and Frances Perkins's generation. Expanding career opportunities for women in the professions in the first third of the twentieth century provided alternatives to careers in social welfare and politics. This younger group of women also lacked the experience in social reform and suffrage that had so profoundly influenced their elders during the Progressive era. The old reformers, with their concern for the dispossessed and the downtrodden, especially the female dispossessed, were now being replaced by younger, professionally trained women whose visions were considerably narrower.

Since this younger generation of women came of age after the battle for woman suffrage, feminism and women's issues were less important to them. Although from today's perspective the feminism of women in the network was rather limited, from Katie Louchheim's perspective Eleanor Roosevelt and her friends from the 1930s were "ardent feminists." Anna Rosenberg's career reflected women's changing approach to politics, according to Eleanor Roosevelt and Lorena Hickok: "Trained as she was in the tough, realistic school of the district club, the idea of a women's division, set up as a separate, minority group within the party organization, may have seemed to her impractical and the women themselves academic, ineffectual and rather silly . . . In her own experience, politics had meant fighting your way up by yourself." The experiences and expectations of this younger generation of women did not lead them along the paths charted by their predecessors in the 1930s.[53]

As World War II drew to a close, the women's network was nearing its end as well. Deaths and retirements had taken their toll since the network's peak in 1936.[54] Many women in government reached resolutions similar to Mary Anderson's: "And so, after twenty-five years, I came to the decision that it was time for me to step out and make way for someone else." Mary Anderson's friends gathered in Washington for her retirement party in 1944, and when Frances Perkins resigned in July of 1945, many of the same old friends returned to give Perkins an affectionate farewell. Molly Dewson, who was unable to attend the latter occasion, wrote to Clara Beyer: "I am so glad they gave Frances a good send off. How I should have enjoyed being there to see all the old gang."[55]

The affection and friendship that united the network in the 1930s stayed with the women for the rest of their lives. But other conditions that had fostered their network were on the wane by the 1940s. The final blow came on April 12, 1945, when the world learned that Franklin Roosevelt had died. At the White House, Eleanor Roosevelt and Frances Perkins "went out in a hall and sat on a bench like two schoolgirls" and cried. Eleanor Roosevelt expressed the country's sense of loss when she said simply, "The story is over."[56] That epitaph applied to the network of women in politics and government as well.

EPILOGUE

The women's network was no longer influential after 1945, but the stories of individual network members in government and politics continued into the late 1940s and 1950s. Eleanor Roosevelt served with great distinction in the United Nations. Frances Perkins was a member of the Civil Service Commission from 1946 to 1953. Ellen Woodward worked in the Office of International Relations in the Federal Security Administration until 1955. Clara Beyer and Mary LaDame continued their work in the Labor Department. Lucille Foster McMillin, Marion Glass Banister, and Katharine Lenroot stayed in the government until 1950;[1] Nellie Tayloe Ross and Jane Hoey remained until forced out by the Republicans after 1952.[2] And Congresswoman Mary T. Norton retired from Congress in 1950 after serving for twenty-six years. On the whole, however, the late 1940s and early 1950s were times of retirement for those women who stayed in government past the New Deal.

The transition from the Roosevelt to the Truman administration had not been entirely smooth. According to Lucy Somerville Howorth, women in public life were worried that the end of the war would bring another economic depression and a renewal of the old prejudice against women workers. After Roosevelt died, Howorth remembered, a "kind of panic hit women in Washington":

> One of those curious waves went through the Government, petty persecution of women began, they were denied access to phones, they were pulled off inter-departmental committees, they were denied promotions. . . . About this time I saw a member of the staff of the Bureau of the Budget . . . I said to this man, "It looks as if the bureau is trying to abolish every position held by a woman." He

laughed and said, "Maybe." Probably he was teasing but his rather contemptuous attitude infuriated me.[3]

What a contrast to the "friendly" atmosphere in government Howorth remembered from the 1930s. Lucy Howorth probably exaggerated the extent of the change, but she firmly believed that if women had not worked together during the transition period, "much that had been gained in the Roosevelt administration would have been swept away."[4]

Conditions for women improved substantially in 1948, when India Edwards of the Women's Division won Harry Truman's confidence by being one of the few politicians to believe in Truman's chances for election. By the time Truman left office in 1952, his record of women's appointments had neared but not quite matched Roosevelt's. Truman accomplished this without the wide-open opportunities that Roosevelt had enjoyed; Harry Truman and his wife Bess were not surrounded by career-women friends as the Roosevelts had been. Moreover, less political mileage was gained by appointing women when they were not "firsts."[5]

Major credit for women's advances belongs to India Edwards. Edwards served as the 1940s' version of Molly Dewson, pushing strenuously to gain recognition for women.[6] Truman's important appointments of women included naming Georgia Neese Clark as Treasurer of the United States in 1949, Freida Hennock to the Federal Communications Commission in 1948, Georgia Lusk to the War Claims Commission in 1949, and Anna Rosenberg as Assistant Secretary of Defense in 1950. The Truman administration's concern with foreign affairs translated into several major appointments in the diplomatic field, including that of Eugenia Anderson as Ambassador to Denmark in 1949.[7]

But women faced setbacks in 1952 and 1953. Since the Republican party has traditionally been less interested in the liberal social reform measures toward which women in public life have gravitated, Republican administrations have generally been less receptive to women's talents than Democratic ones. This proved to be the case in the 1950s. Women did take on some major positions in the Eisenhower government: Oveta Culp Hobby, Secretary of Health, Education, and Welfare; Clare Booth Luce, Ambassador to Italy; Ivy Baker Priest, Treasurer of the United States; Frances Willis, Ambassador to Switzerland; and Mary Pillsbury Lord, delegate to the United Nations Human Rights Commission. However, many of Eisenhower's other female appointments were mere window dressing—to honorary commissions, international conferences, and the like.[8] While Bertha Adkins of the Republican National Committee had impressive plans for women, the Republican Women's Division was abolished in an economy move just four months after Eisenhower's inauguration. Eleanor Roosevelt and Lorena Hickok dryly observed, "Whatever Miss Adkins and the other Republican women may have thought is not a matter of public record."[9]

Women in the Democratic party were more vocal than their Republican sisters when the Democratic Women's Division was abolished in a similar economy move in 1953, but their protests were to no avail. When Democratic National Committee Chairman Stephen Mitchell announced that the separate budget, magazine, and staff of the Women's Division were being "integrated" into the existing party structure, the women were appalled. Ostensibly this was a big advancement, but India Edwards knew better—"in theory a step up for women, but actually a step way down." Frances Perkins concurred: "They've integrated the Women's Division as though they were raising them from slime to the throne . . . Most of the women that I know are very much disturbed about it." The women were especially suspicious because they had not been consulted about this so-called integration plan. Democratic women felt they were being blamed for losing the election (after all, everyone was saying women had elected Eisenhower) and were being used as scapegoats in a financial crunch. Yet with the national party in disarray after its defeat in the 1952 presidential election, Democratic women were loathe to start a public fight. The women would try to make the best out of the new situation.[10]

While younger women were exploring new avenues toward political power in the 1950s and 1960s, the tactics of women from the New Deal remained unchanged. Old habits die hard. In early 1961, a year before her death, Molly Dewson wrote to her close friend Clara Beyer, "I have high hopes about J.F.K. but he has one weakness for he does not realize what a help women can be to him." After President Kennedy's first 240 appointments included only nine women, Eleanor Roosevelt paid a call at the White House armed with a three-page list of women qualified for high administration posts.[11]

Eleanor Roosevelt's prodding encouraged President Kennedy to establish the Presidential Commission on the Status of Women in 1961. This commission, with Eleanor Roosevelt as its head, came at an important crossroads for several generations of American women. Although Eleanor Roosevelt was too ill to attend many of the meetings, her name gave the commission prestige as well as a strong link to past feminist efforts in the public sphere. Also serving on the Presidential Commission and the state commissions that were its offshoots were younger women just discovering issues of feminism and sex discrimination. These women, together with publicists like Betty Friedan, helped reawaken American interest in feminism in the 1960s and 1970s.[12] It is symbolic and fitting that Eleanor Roosevelt presided over this rebirth.

Yet women in public life still looked back fondly to women's experiences in the 1930s and 1940s. India Edwards wrote in 1977: "I want to remind women who today are working for equal rights and seeking to have more women in elective and appointive offices that Presidents Franklin D. Roosevelt and Truman were actively involving women in government years ago." According to Edwards, Eleanor Roosevelt and Molly Dewson "never let F.D.R. forget that women are first-class citizens and should be given a voice in government."[13] Because of a unique combination of factors (including the depression, that most important of all variables), the New Deal represented a time when women had more substantial roles in government and politics than they would in the 1950s, 1960s, and beyond.

There is a certain irony to this story of women in the New Deal. The history of America since 1933 has been fundamentally shaped by the legacy of the New Deal: the expansion of government services, the development of a capitalist welfare state, and the liberalism of the New and Fair Deals have all been incorporated into our way of life. But the gains for women, unlike the reforms of the New Deal, did not become a permanent part of the American political system. No legislation can mandate that women be taken seriously in government and politics. This has to come from a pervasive change in the consciousness of both men and women, a change that has not occurred. In contrast to the strong public support for the expansion of the government's roles during the depression, no widespread public demand brought about the gains for women in that decade.

That progress for women was not made permanent should not blind us to the accomplishments of women during the New Deal. This network of dynamic, intelligent, and committed women worked together as feminists for the advancement of their sex. Without them, the needs of women in government, politics, and on relief would have been overlooked. These women worked together as social reformers for the preservation of democracy in a time of economic crisis. Their expertise in social welfare substantially influenced New Deal legislation in that field. Recognition of the contributions these women made to politics and government in the 1930s is long overdue.

CRITERIA FOR SELECTION
OF THE WOMEN

I began collecting lists of women for possible inclusion in this study practically the first day I began my research, and I did not make the final selection until after I began the actual organizing and writing of this work in its original form as a dissertation. I deliberately kept the boundaries of the group loose, so I would not overlook an important woman in my research merely because she had not appeared earlier. The composition of the network remained intact in the transition from dissertation to manuscript. The exact citations of biographical sources are found in the notes, but in general the sources most useful in locating the women were promotional and background material put out by the Women's Division of the Democratic National Committee in the 1930s; *American Women: The Official Who's Who Among the Women in the Nation* (1936 to 1939); *Notable American Women*; and magazine articles from the period, especially from the *Democratic Digest* published by the Women's Division. Because of the variety of sources consulted, it is highly unlikely that any woman was completely overlooked.

Once I had compiled these lists of women (approximately sixty to seventy women), I established criteria for choosing the women for the study. One factor was availability of information. Luckily I did not exclude any women solely on this basis, but unavailability of material was a partial factor in several cases. Since I wanted to focus on the workings of the federal government in Washington itself, I limited the group to women who actually lived and worked in Washington, D.C. in the 1930s. Consistently good biographical information about women in the various states would have been too hard to get, and their widely disparate experiences would have made generalizations difficult to form.

Such a criterion automatically excluded women who were federal employees assigned to different parts of the country, such as the state and regional directors of women's work for the various relief agencies like the WPA and the many women who were named postmasters. It excluded women like Mary Ward (Massachusetts Commissioner of Immigration), Bernice Pyke (Collector of Customs for Ohio), and Elizabeth Bass (Bureau of Narcotics Regional Supervisor for Chicago), important Democratic women who did not want to leave their local bases of power to come to Washington. Women like Anna Rosenberg (with the Social Security Administration in New York) and Elinore Morehouse Herrick (with the National Labor Relations Board in New York) were also excluded because of this Washington criterion, although both were prominent women in government.

Women in the federal judiciary were also excluded. Judge Florence Allen, whom Franklin Roosevelt nominated to the United States Circuit Court of Appeals, was in close and frequent contact with many of the women in government, but she was left out of the study because she was in Ohio. One final group that was excluded consisted of New Yorkers active in Democratic state women's politics who remained primarily based in New York and did not have much impact on national affairs: Marion Dickerman, Nancy Cook, Florence Whitney, and Elinor Morgenthau. (Morgenthau, wife of the Secretary of the Treasury, was a special case because she was Eleanor's closest friend in Washington, but she did not have an official position and thus was not included.) These New York women were good friends of Eleanor Roosevelt and had many similarities in background and experience to the women in the network, but could not be included in this study.

Not all of the women in Washington in the 1930s automatically made it into the study. Obviously women who held secretarial and low-level jobs in the federal government (some 20 percent of all government employees) have not been considered. In addition, I tried to limit the study to women who had been appointed by 1936. This criterion excluded women like Florence Kerr, who took over Ellen Woodward's WPA job in late 1938 (Kerr had been a WPA regional director of women's work in the 1930s), Hallie Flanagan, who came to government in 1936 to head the Federal Theater Project, and Mary McLeod Bethune, who did not join the National Youth Administration until 1936. The one exception to this rule is Daisy Harriman; she was not named Minister to Norway until 1937, but she was important in Democratic women's politics in the early 1930s.

I also excluded women whose jobs were only middle-level civil service positions. Several examples from this category are Katharine Blackburn of the Division of Press Intelligence, Phoebe Omlie of the Aeronautical

Advisory Board of the Department of Commerce, Chloe Owings as an assistant in the Women's Division of the WPA, Ruth Lockett of the General Land Office, Maurine Mulliner as a technical adviser to the Social Security Board, and Mary Taylor with the Consumer's Guide of the Agricultural Adjustment Administration. These women were important in Washington, but they were not on the level of the presidential appointments of most of the women in the network. Some of these middle-level women, however, will figure tangentially in this study.

Two other groups of important women in Washington were not included. Private secretaries like Missy LeHand and Grace Tully (to Franklin Roosevelt), Malvina Thompson Scheider (to Eleanor Roosevelt), Frances Jurkowitz (to Frances Perkins), and Frances Robinson (to General Hugh Johnson) were prominent and visible women in official Washington, but on the whole they did not exercise power in their own right. Newspaperwomen like Ruby Black, Bess Furman, Emma Bugbee, and Lorena Hickok were also prominent in Washington, especially where Eleanor Roosevelt was concerned, but they were more involved in covering developments in politics and government than participating in them. Lorena Hickok traveled around the country observing relief conditions as a confidential aide to Harry Hopkins from 1933 to 1934 and was a close personal friend of Eleanor Roosevelt in this period, but these activities did not seem major enough to warrant her inclusion.

It was not possible to include all the women who were presidential appointees, but in only a few cases was this a problem. Some of these women were left out because there was hardly any information on them or because they played very minor roles in Washington in spite of their high-level jobs. After all, some of these presidential appointments were more an honor than a substantial policy-making assignment. If such women were not mentioned prominently or frequently in the correspondence among the women, or did not appear in magazine articles and promotional material as "women in the New Deal," they were not included here. I am certain, based on my extensive research, that none of these women was vital to the developments described in this study. I include their names solely for future reference:

Jewell Swofford, U.S. Employment Compensation Commission
Stella Akin, Special Assistant to the Attorney General
Antoinette Funk, Assistant Commissioner of the Land Office
Mrs. Carroll Stewart, Member of the Board of Appeals, Veterans Administration
Laura S. Brown, Member of the Board of Appeals, Veterans Administration

Lavinia Engle, Educational Representative on the Social Security Board

Marion Harron, Member, Board of Tax Appeals

Louise Stanley, Bureau of Home Economics, Department of Agriculture

Harriet Root, Chief of the U.S. Information Service

The women in Congress have not automatically been included in this study either—only Caroline O'Day and Mary T. Norton were chosen. Of the women in the Senate (Dixie Bibb Graves from Alabama, Rose Long from Louisiana, and Hattie Caraway from Arkansas), none was at all interested in the concerns of the other women in this study, and with the possible exception of Senator Caraway, they had a minimal effect on the Senate. These women all functioned more as members of the Southern Congressional bloc than as women. On the House of Representatives side, Isabelle Greenway of Arizona and Nan Wood Honeyman of Oregon, both good friends of Eleanor Roosevelt, were possibilities, but neither was in Washington long enough to have an impact either on Congress or on women's issues. A third Democratic Congresswoman, Virginia Jenckes of Indiana, was in Congress for three terms, but I could find little information about her or her potential impact.

Finally, there were three women in Washington who did not hold official government jobs but whose experiences add substantially to our understanding of women in the New Deal. Carolyn Wolfe and Dorothy McAlister as heads of the Women's Division (Molly Dewson makes it into the regular categories because she served on the Social Security Board) and Emma Guffey Miller as National Committeewoman from Pennsylvania were important forces in official Washington. Since the study was concerned with both politics and government in the 1930s, political women deserved inclusion as well.

The women chosen for this study were, with the few exceptions mentioned above, *all of the women* in important government positions in the New Deal. Luckily for my purposes, this group of women was practically the same as the network of women that I have described. I should add that I did not begin my research consciously looking for a network of women in the New Deal—I conceived of the study as a conventional collective biography. Only after I had immersed myself in the public and private papers of these twenty-eight women and started to piece together the myriad interconnections among them did I realize that I had discovered a network. Equally exciting was my realization that I had the sources to reconstruct and analyze how the network had operated in the New Deal.

APPENDIX A

One further aspect was involved in defining the network. All of the women took part in the New Deal, but for varying amounts of time. The extremes were represented by career administrators like Mary Anderson, who served from 1920 to 1944, and women who served for only a year or two, like Emily Newell Blair or Mary Harriman Rumsey. Women like Rumsey (who died in December 1934) and Ruth Bryan Owen (who resigned in 1936) were included because their early importance overshadowed their comparatively short periods of service. The network in the New Deal is best conceived as under assembly in 1933 and 1934, at its peak in 1935 and 1936, and gradually on the wane after 1936. With a few exceptions, women who resigned from government were not replaced by other like-minded women, so the network did not pick up new members from the mid-1930s on. The reasons and implications for the changes in the late New Deal are discussed in Chapter 6.

GROUP PROFILE
AND INDIVIDUAL BIOGRAPHIES

The individual short biographies that follow show the routes to the New Deal followed by women in the network and provide details about the individual women's lives that could not be incorporated into the narrative. A composite portrait of the network shows strong patterns of experience among these twenty-eight women. The similarities in their backgrounds and careers were an important precondition for the development and operation of the network.

The typical network member was born around 1880, making her in her early fifties when she entered the New Deal. One distinctive characteristic of the network was its access to higher education: more than 70 percent of the women attended college, and a third did graduate work. At that time only a select group of American women had the opportunity to attend college, and their educational experience clearly set the network members apart from the general female population.

On graduation from college, many network members became active in early twentieth century voluntary reform organizations or the trade union movement. Network members were especially active in the woman suffrage campaign, which had a strong impact on members of that generation. The women also participated in World War I patriotic undertakings. Working in suffrage, social welfare campaigns, and other Progressive reform causes brought the women together and gave them a common outlook and vocabulary.

Along the way, the typical network member married and raised a family. Two-thirds of the women in the network were married, a significantly higher figure than the usual estimates of women who combined marriage and career in the early twentieth century. The typical married woman was also a mother: married women in the network had an average of 2.2 children. In almost all cases, however, the women's active professional careers came after their children were grown. By the 1930s, most of the network members were well past their childbearing years.

During the 1920s, the network members concentrated in two areas—Democratic politics and social welfare activities. In Democratic politics, the women led the integration of women into regular party politics after the passage of the nineteenth amendment. In the field of social welfare, the women worked predominantly in two organizations—the Women's Trade Union League and the National Consumers' League—struggling to keep alive the Progressive faith in the hostile climate of the 1920s. In the process, they laid the groundwork for much of the New Deal's social welfare legislation.

In the 1930s, the network was concentrated in particular areas of the government. One subgroup worked in the Democratic party: the Women's Division, the Democratic National Committee and its advisory committees, and elected members of Congress. Another was found in the Labor Department, where Frances Perkins gathered talented women around her. State and Treasury had strong representation too. A large portion of the network worked in independent agencies like the Federal Emergency Relief Administration, the Works Progress Administration, the Civil Service Commission, and the Government Printing Office. Such concentration within the government bureaucracy facilitated the operation and functions of the network.

As members of a generation born around 1880, most women in the network began to retire in the 1940s and 1950s, as the women reached their sixties. Many of the women died in the 1960s and 1970s, although several are still alive today. The women's individual stories show how each of them fits this more general portrait.

GRACE ABBOTT (1878-1939)

Grace Abbott, Chief of the Children's Bureau from 1921 to 1934, was born in Nebraska in 1878. Her father was active in Nebraska politics, and her mother was an abolitionist and early suffragist; her older sister Edith later became known for her work in social welfare, economics, and history. Grace Abbott graduated from Grand Island College in 1898 and received an M.A. in political science from the University of Chicago in 1909. She then moved to Hull House, where she was also active in Illinois woman suffrage campaigns. Abbott joined the Children's Bureau under Julia Lathrop in 1917, and after working briefly for the Illinois State Immigrants Commission from 1919 to 1921, she returned to Washington to become head of the Children's Bureau. One of her main tasks was the enforcement of the Sheppard-Towner Maternity and Infancy Act. During the 1920s and 1930s, Abbott was active in the National Consumers' League and the Women's Trade Union League, and she served as president of the National Conference of Social Work from 1923 to 1924. Knowing that her programs were safe under the new Democratic administration, Grace Abbott left the Children's Bureau in 1934 to teach at the University of Chicago School of Social Service Administration, where she died in 1939.[1]

MARY ANDERSON (1872-1964)

Mary Anderson, Chief of the Women's Bureau from 1920 to 1944, emigrated to the United States from Sweden at the age of sixteen. She worked in the garment and shoe industries in Chicago and became involved in union activities. In 1905 Anderson began her lifelong association with the Women's Trade Union League, whose national headquarters were in Chicago. She formed an especially close relationship with the WTUL president, Margaret Dreier Robins. Naturalized in 1905, Anderson served with the Women in Industry Service during World War I, and in 1920 she was named director of the newly created Women's Bureau. While she was in Washington, she kept up close contacts with her labor and trade union friends until her retirement in 1944.[2]

MARION GLASS BANISTER (1875-1951)

Assistant Treasurer of the United States from 1933 to 1951, Marion Glass Banister was from a distinguished Virginia family that included Senator Carter Glass and Meta Glass, president of Sweet Briar College. In the early 1900s Marion Glass married Blair Banister, a member of another old Virginia family, and they had one daughter. Marion Glass Banister came to Washington during World War I to write publicity for the Committee on Public Information, and she stayed in Washington in the 1920s. She became active in Democratic women's politics in the early 1920s, assisting Emily Newell Blair with publicity in the 1924 campaign. Banister was also a founder of the Women's National Democratic Club in 1924-1925. After being widowed in the mid-1920s, Banister found it necessary to support herself and took a job handling publicity for Washington's Mayflower Hotel from 1924 until it closed during the depression in 1931. Banister was active in the 1932 campaign, and in return, Franklin Roosevelt appointed her to the Treasury position. She served there until her death in 1951.[3]

CLARA MORTENSON BEYER (1892-)

Clara M. Beyer, Associate Director of the Division of Labor Standards from 1934 to 1957, was born in California. Her parents had emigrated to America from Denmark. She attended the University of California, receiving a B.A. in 1915 and an M.S. in 1916. She then taught labor economics at Bryn Mawr for a year. During World War I she worked on the War Labor Policies Board and the District of Columbia Minimum Wage Board. In 1920 she married Otto Beyer, also an economist, and they had three sons (1921, 1924, 1925). While her children were young, Clara Beyer worked part-time as the executive secretary of the National Consumers' League; during this period she began her lifelong friendships with Molly Dewson and Frances Perkins. In 1928 Beyer joined the staff of the Children's Bureau; from 1931 to 1934, she was the director of its Industrial Department. In 1934 Beyer became the associate director of the newly created Division of Labor Standards in the Department of Labor, where she worked until her retirement from government in 1957.[4]

EMILY NEWELL BLAIR (1877-1951)

Emily Newell Blair, Assistant to the Chairman of the Consumers' Advisory Board of the National Recovery Administration (NRA) in 1933 and 1934, was born in Joplin, Missouri. She attended Goucher College and the University of Missouri. She married Harry Blair in 1900, and they had two children (1903 and 1907). Blair was very active in suffrage work after 1910 and served on the Women's Committee on National Defense under suffragist Anna Howard Shaw from 1917 to 1918. Blair was one of the first women to attain a prominent position in Democratic party politics, serving as Vice-Chairman of the Democratic National Committee from 1922 to 1928. She was also a founder of the Women's National Democratic Club, and served as its president in 1928. During the 1920s Blair lectured and wrote widely on women's new political roles. She was active in the 1932 campaign, but did not want a major patronage position for herself. While she joined the Consumers' Advisory Board of the NRA on a part-time basis, her husband was named an Assistant Attorney General. After the NRA was disbanded Blair was less prominent in Democratic women's circles, but she did work in the War Department's Public Relations Bureau briefly during the 1940s.[5]

JO COFFIN (c. 1880-1943)

Jo Coffin, Assistant to the Public Printer, Government Printing Office, 1934-1941, was born in the Midwest (probably Iowa) but spent most of her life in New York. She learned the printing trade in travels around the country and was a copy cutter for the New York *World* from 1916 to 1931. Coffin was active in the International Typographical Union and was an important part of the New York Women's Trade Union League, where she became friends with Rose Schneiderman and Mary Anderson. In the winter of 1932-33, Coffin helped Eleanor Roosevelt set up centers for unemployed women in New York City under WTUL auspices; in return, Roosevelt lobbied to get Coffin her job at the Printing Office. In 1941 Coffin had to resign the job she loved so much because of ill health, and she died in Tucson in 1943.[6]

MARY W. ("MOLLY") DEWSON (1874-1962)

Head of the Women's Division of the Democratic National Committee from 1932 to 1937 and member of the Social Security Board from 1937 to 1938, Molly Dewson was born in Quincy, Massachusetts. She graduated from Wellesley College in 1897 and then did economic research for the Women's Educational and Industrial Union in Boston. From 1900 to 1912, Dewson was Superintendent of the Parole Department of the Massachusetts State Industrial School for Girls, and she helped to draft the state's model minimum wage law in 1912. Dewson was also very active in the suffrage campaign, and she worked with the Red Cross in France during World War I. Grace Abbott asked Dewson to be her assistant at the Children's Bureau in 1921, but Dewson took a job instead as research secretary with the National Consumers' League in New York under Florence Kelley. From 1924 to 1927, Dewson was executive secretary of the Women's City Club of New York, a women's reform group. She also served as president of the New York Consumers' League from 1925 to 1931. In 1928 Dewson entered Democratic politics at Eleanor Roosevelt's request, and from 1932 to 1934 she was head of the Women's Division of the Democratic party. She kept up her Democratic work until 1937, serving as Chairman of the Advisory Committee to the Women's Division and as a Vice-Chairman of the Democratic National Committee. She also served on the Consumers' Advisory Board and the Committee on Economic Security in the National Recovery Administration. Dewson was appointed a member of the Social Security Board in 1937, but resigned in 1938 because of ill health. She then retired to Maine, where she kept up her interest in the New Deal by corresponding with her old friends from the 1930s.[7]

APPENDIX B

FLORENCE ("DAISY") JAFFRAY HARRIMAN (1870-1967)

Daisy Harriman, United States Minister to Norway from 1937 to 1941, was born in New York City. In 1889 she married J. Borden Harriman, a cousin of E. H. and Averill Harriman; she had one daughter, born in 1897. Harriman was a founder of the Colony Club in New York City in 1904, and became involved in politics and suffrage. An avid Wilsonian all her life, she ran the women's side of Woodrow Wilson's campaign in 1912. In return, he appointed her to the Federal Industrial Relations Committee. Widowed in 1914, Harriman moved permanently to Washington. She worked with the Red Cross in England during World War I and joined the National Consumers' League Board of Directors. During the 1920s she co-founded the Women's National Democratic Club and started her "Sunday Night Suppers," which became a Washington institution. Because Harriman had supported Newton Baker in 1932, she did not play an active role in Roosevelt's first term. Her banishment ended in 1937 when President Roosevelt appointed her Minister to Norway. An ordinary tour of duty was interrupted when seventy-year-old Harriman had to flee the Nazi invasion of Norway in April 1940. Harriman returned safely to this country, lecturing and writing widely about her experiences in wartime Norway.[8]

JANE MARGUERETTA HOEY (1892-1968)

Director of the Bureau of Public Assistance from 1936 to 1953, Jane Hoey came from a large Irish Catholic family (nine children) in New York, although she had spent the early part of her life in Nebraska. Jane Hoey's brother Jim was a Tammany political leader. Hoey attended Hunter and Trinity Colleges, receiving a B.A. in 1914; she received an M.A. in political science from Columbia and a diploma from the New York School of Philanthropy in 1916 under Mary Richmond. Her first social work position was under Harry Hopkins on the Board of Child Welfare in New York City from 1916 to 1917; from 1926 to 1936, she was Assistant Director of the Health Division of the Welfare Council of New York. Hoey was president of the National Conference of Social Work from 1940 to 1941. She organized the Bureau of Public Assistance within the Social Security Administration in 1936 and stayed there until November 1953, when she was forced out by Oveta Culp Hobby of Health, Education, and Welfare. From 1953 to 1957 Hoey served as Director of Social Research for the National Tuberculosis Association.[9]

LUCY SOMERVILLE HOWORTH (1895-)

Lucy Somerville Howorth, member of the Board of Appeals of the Veterans Administration from 1934 to 1950, was born in Mississippi. She was the daughter of noted suffragist Nellie Nugent Somerville, the first woman elected to the Mississippi legislature. Howorth graduated from Randolph-Macon College in 1916, did graduate work at Columbia in economics and sociology from 1918 to 1920, and received a law degree from the University of Mississippi Law School in 1922. She married another attorney in 1928, and they set up a joint practice as Howorth and Howorth; they had no children. Howorth was involved in Mississippi Democratic politics in the 1920s, and was elected to the Mississippi legislature for a term lasting from 1932 to 1934. She came to Washington in 1934 to serve on the Veterans Administration Board, and she remained there until she retired from government in 1950.[10]

MARY LADAME (c. 1885- ?)

Mary LaDame, Associate Director of the United States Employment Service in New York and Special Assistant to the Secretary of Labor from 1938 to 1945, graduated from Pembroke (Brown) in 1906. She did graduate work at Harvard, Columbia, and Carnegie Tech, and for nine years did industrial research studies for the Russell Sage Foundation. She also gained practical experience by working for a time as a clerk and manager in a department store. LaDame had been Associate Director of the Clearing House for Public Employment for New York City since the early 1920s when her friend Frances Perkins tapped her for work in the Labor Department.[11]

KATHARINE FREDRICA LENROOT (1891-)

Katharine Lenroot, Chief of the Children's Bureau from 1934 to 1949, was the daughter of Wisconsin Senator Irvine Lenroot. She graduated from the University of Wisconsin in 1912, and got her first job with the Industrial Commission of Wisconsin. She joined the Children's Bureau in 1914 as a special investigator, became Assistant Chief in 1922, and then took over as Chief on Grace Abbott's resignation in 1934. In 1935 Lenroot served as president of the National Conference of Social Work.[12]

DOROTHY MCALISTER (c. 1900-)

Director of the Women's Division of the Democratic National Committee from 1936 to 1940, Dorothy McAlister was the wife of a Michigan supreme court judge and the mother of two daughters. A graduate of Bryn Mawr, she had been involved in the drives for prohibition repeal and the Child Labor Amendment. She joined the Michigan Young Democrats and later became the state director for the Michigan Democratic State Committee before Molly Dewson brought her to Washington in 1936. McAlister resigned from the Women's Division after the 1940 election, and was active in the anti-Equal Rights Amendment campaign. She also served as Chairman of the Board of Directors of the National Consumers' League from 1947 to 1954.[13]

LUCILLE FOSTER MCMILLIN (c. 1870-1949)

Lucille McMillin, Civil Service Commissioner from 1933 to 1949, was born in Tennessee and educated by private tutors. Around 1898 she married Congressman Benton McMillin, who was twenty years her senior; she served as his hostess during his term as governor of Tennessee from 1899 to 1903 and accompanied him to the American Embassy in Peru from 1913 to 1922. They had one daughter. During the 1920s McMillin became involved in politics as the National Committeewoman from Tennessee, as the regional director of Democratic women in the Southern states in 1924, and with the League of Women Voters. Widowed in 1933, her appointment to the Civil Service Commission was in part a tribute to her late husband.[14]

EMMA GUFFEY MILLER (1874-1970)

Emma Guffey Miller, National Committeewoman from Pennsylvania from 1932 until her death, was an 1899 graduate of Bryn Mawr, where she majored in history and political science. She married Carroll Miller in 1902, and they had four sons. Emma Guffey Miller had been very active in the suffrage fight, but she became disillusioned with protective and social welfare legislation. By the 1920s she had joined the National Women's Party and was an ardent supporter of the Equal Rights Amendment. She seconded Al Smith's nomination at the 1924 Democratic convention, and by 1936 she had risen to Vice-Chairman of the Democratic National Committee. Miller held no paid position during the New Deal (she chaired the Pennsylvania National Youth Administration Advisory Board from 1935 to 1943), but her husband, Carroll Miller, was named to the Interstate Commerce Commission. Emma Guffey Miller also exercised political power through her brother, Senator Joseph Guffey of Pennsylvania, a bachelor with whom she and her husband (plus her two unmarried sisters) shared a house in Washington. In addition to her political activities, Miller's main field of interest was education.[15]

MARY T. NORTON (1875-1959)

Democratic Congresswoman from New Jersey from 1925 to 1950, Mary T. Norton was in her forties—a Jersey City housewife—before she entered politics. When her only child died, she became involved in setting up a day nursery system for Jersey City. This eventually led Norton into contact with Mayor Frank Hague, Jersey City's influential political boss. Hague redirected Norton's energies toward politics, and in 1924 she became the first Democratic woman elected to Congress. During her tenure in Congress, she was Chairman of the District of Columbia Committee and, after 1937, Chairman of the Labor Committee. From this powerful position, she played a large role in the passage of the 1938 Fair Labor Standards Act. Widowed in 1934, Norton continued serving in Congress until her term expired in 1950.[16]

CAROLINE O'DAY (1869-1943)

Congresswoman-at-large from New York from 1935 to 1942, Caroline O'Day was born on a Georgia plantation. She was trained as an artist both in New York and abroad, but she gave up painting in 1901 when she married Daniel O'Day, the son of an associate of John D. Rockefeller and himself an independent oil operator. Her children were born in 1904, 1906, and 1908; Daniel O'Day died in 1916. As a pacifist, Caroline O'Day was opposed to both World Wars I and II. In addition to doing social welfare work, O'Day was very active in the Democratic Women's Committee of New York, where she worked closely with Eleanor Roosevelt, Marion Dickerman, and Nancy Cook. In 1934 O'Day won easy election to Congress, with Eleanor Roosevelt campaigning in her behalf. Caroline O'Day did not seek a fifth term in 1942 because of ill health, and she died in 1943.[17]

RUTH BRYAN OWEN (1885-1954)

Ruth Bryan Owen, United States Minister to Denmark from 1933 to 1936, was the daughter of William Jennings Bryan, noted orator and presidential candidate. She attended the University of Nebraska from 1901 to 1903. An early marriage to Homer Leavitt, which produced two children, ended in divorce. In 1910 she was married again, this time to Major Reginald Owen of the British Army; the Owens had two children of their own. During World War I, Ruth Bryan Owen was a volunteer nurse with the British Army in Egypt and Palestine. In order to support her invalid husband and children, she became a Chautauqua lecturer as well as a member of the faculty of the University of Miami, Florida, in the 1920s. Owen was elected to Congress from the Fourth District in Florida in 1928 and 1930, but she was defeated in 1932 because of her stand on prohibition. Her appointment as Minister to Denmark, a first for women, was unanimously confirmed by the Senate the same day it was submitted. Owen had been widowed in 1927, and in 1936 (at the church in Hyde Park, New York where the Roosevelts worshiped) she married Borge Rohde, a captain in the Danish Royal Guards, whom she had met in Denmark. Because of the possible complications of her dual citizenship, Ruth Bryan Owen resigned her ministerial position in 1936 and returned to America.[18]

FRANCES PERKINS (1880-1965)

Secretary of Labor from 1933 to 1945, Frances Perkins grew up in Worcester, Massachusetts, and graduated from Mount Holyoke in 1902. Perkins was interested in social welfare and spent time at Hull House and Chicago Commons, two Chicago settlement houses. Perkins came to New York in 1910 with a fellowship from the Russell Sage Foundation to do a study of Hell's Kitchen; at the same time, she studied for her Master's degree in sociology and economics at Columbia. She joined the Consumers' League as a lobbyist, working for the fifty-four-hour bill for women and investigating the 1911 Triangle Shirtwaist fire. In 1913 she married Paul Wilson, an economist active in New York City reform politics; they had one daughter, born in 1916. Perkins (she kept her given name) was appointed to the State Industrial Commission in 1918 by Governor Al Smith, and in 1926 she became its chairman; in 1928 Governor Franklin Roosevelt made her Industrial Commissioner of New York, another promotion. In 1933 Perkins was named Secretary of Labor, the first woman to serve in the Cabinet. She resigned from that position when Roosevelt died in 1945, but Harry Truman appointed her to the Civil Service Commission from 1946 to 1953. After her retirement from government, Perkins was a highly successful lecturer at Cornell and other universities.[19]

JOSEPHINE ASPINWALL ROCHE (1886-1976)

Assistant Secretary of the Treasury from 1934 to 1937, Josephine Roche graduated from Vassar in 1908 and received an M.A. from Columbia in 1910, where she became friends with fellow graduate student Frances Perkins. From 1915 to 1918, she was director of the girls' department of Judge Ben Lindsey's Juvenile Court in Denver. In 1920 she married Edward Hale Bierstadt, but they were divorced two years later; they had no children. From 1924 to 1927 Roche was the Editorial Director of the Children's Bureau. In 1927 she returned to Colorado to run the coal mines she inherited from her father, where her enlightened approach to labor relations gained her nationwide publicity. Roche was narrowly defeated in the Democratic primary for the Colorado senate nomination in 1934. President Roosevelt appointed her to the Treasury position later in 1934, where she was in charge of health service and welfare work, specifically overseeing the United States Public Health Service which was then part of the Treasury Department. In 1935 Roche added to her duties by becoming Chairman of the Executive Committee of the National Youth Administration. Roche resigned her Treasury position in 1937 but continued to commute to Washington for meetings of the Interdepartmental Health Committee, which she had chaired since 1936. Roche served as president of the National Consumers' League from 1938 to 1944, and at John L. Lewis's suggestion, she served from 1947 to 1971 as director of the United Mine Workers Union Welfare and Retirement Fund.[20]

ELEANOR ROOSEVELT (1884-1962)

Born into a socially prominent New York family, Eleanor Roosevelt was orphaned at an early age. Although she did not attend college, Roosevelt profited from a stimulating period at the Allenswood School in England in her teens. Eleanor returned to New York to make her debut in 1902, and in 1905 she married Franklin Roosevelt; she had six children over the next ten years, of whom five survived infancy. World War I and the discovery of her husband's affair with Lucy Mercer were crucial turning points for Eleanor Roosevelt: during the 1920s she expanded her public activities dramatically. She worked in Democratic women's politics in New York and on the national level, taught at the Todhunter School, ran the Val-Kill furniture industry with two friends, and was active in organizations like the League of Women Voters, the National Consumers' League, and the Women's Trade Union League. She feared the captivity of the White House, but was able to expand her activities even further in the 1930s. After her husband's death in 1945, President Truman appointed Eleanor Roosevelt to the United Nations delegation where she served with great distinction from 1946 to 1953.[21]

NELLIE TAYLOE ROSS (1876-1977)

Director of the United States Mint from 1933 to 1952, Nellie Tayloe Ross was born in Missouri but is more closely identified with the state of

Wyoming. She married William Bradford Ross in 1902, and they had three children, one of whom died. She succeeded her husband as governor of Wyoming when he died in office in 1924, and was elected to a two-year term of her own from 1925 to 1927. Ross was narrowly defeated for reelection in 1927. In 1928 Nellie Tayloe Ross became a vice-chairman of the Democratic National Committee, and she seconded Al Smith's nomination. Ross was very active in the women's end of the 1932 campaign, and Roosevelt named her Director of the Mint in 1933, where she served until 1952.[22]

MARY HARRIMAN RUMSEY (1881-1934)

Mary Harriman Rumsey, Chairman of the Consumers' Advisory Board of the National Recovery Administration, was the daughter of E. H. Harriman, the railroad magnate, and the sister of Averill Harriman, later governor of New York. This made her a first cousin by marriage to Daisy Harriman, who was also a good friend of hers. Raised in comfortable surroundings, she also developed a social conscience: she was one of the founders of the Junior League in 1901. Mary Harriman was the first woman in her family to attend college, graduating from Barnard in 1905. In 1910 she married Charles Cary Rumsey, a sculptor; they had three children (1911, 1913, 1917). Rumsey was widowed in 1927. Mary Harriman Rumsey worked as a volunteer in World War I consumer activities, and in the 1920s she and her brother Averill broke with family tradition by declaring themselves Democrats. Rumsey was a close friend of both the Roosevelts and Frances Perkins; while serving on the NRA, Rumsey and Perkins shared a home. Rumsey's career came to a premature end when she died from complications incurred when she fell from her horse while riding to the Piedmont Hounds at Middleburg, Virginia, in December 1934.[23]

ROSE SCHNEIDERMAN (1882-1972)

Rose Schneiderman, member of the Labor Advisory Board of the National Recovery Administration, was born in Russian Poland and came to New York in 1890. She began working in various garment trades at age thirteen, and by 1900 she was an active trade unionist. Her lifelong association with the Women's Trade Union League began in 1905, and in 1910 she became a full-time paid organizer for the New York branch. She also worked as a national organizer for the International Ladies Garment Workers Union from 1915 to 1916, but found it too difficult to work with the male unionists. During this time, she often spoke out in favor of woman suffrage for the National American Woman Suffrage Association. In 1919, she and Mary Anderson were sent by the National Women's Trade Union League to the Paris Peace Conference to represent the interests of women workers. During the 1920s Schneiderman served as president both of the New York and National Women's Trade Union Leagues, and became a close friend of Eleanor Roosevelt. She was also one of the original organizers of the Bryn Mawr Summer School for Industrial Workers. After her interval on the National Recovery Administration (which included an investigation of the needle trades in Puerto Rico), Schneiderman returned to the WTUL and served as the New York Secretary of Labor from 1937 to 1943. She continued as president of the Women's Trade Union League until the National and New York Leagues disbanded in 1950 and 1955, respectively.[24]

HILDA WORTHINGTON SMITH (1888-)

Hilda Worthington Smith, Director of the Workers' Service Program in the Federal Emergency Relief Administration and the Works Progress Administration from 1933 to 1943, was a 1910 graduate of Bryn Mawr. She received an M.A. from Bryn Mawr in 1911 and also did graduate work at Columbia and the New York School of Social Work. During this period she was active in the suffrage movement. She returned to Bryn Mawr as a dean, and in the 1920s she set up the Bryn Mawr Summer School for Industrial Workers. Her main interest from then on was workers' education, which her job at the WPA allowed her to pursue; she also was in charge of the FERA-WPA camps and schools for unemployed women from 1934 to 1937. From 1943 until her retirement from government in 1945, she worked at the Federal Public Housing Authority.[25]

SUE SHELTON WHITE (1887-1943)

Sue Shelton White, Assistant Chairman of the Consumers' Advisory Board of the National Recovery Administration and a member of the legal staff of the Social Security Board, was born in Tennessee. She was very active in the Tennessee suffrage fight as a member of the radical wing of the suffrage movement from 1913 to 1920. In 1920 White went to Washington as secretary to Senator Kenneth McKellar; while there, she took night classes and received a law degree in 1923. She returned to Tennessee in 1926 to practice law and Democratic politics. White served as Nellie Tayloe Ross's executive assistant at the Women's Division from 1930 to 1933. Her New Deal career included positions at the NRA, on the National Emergency Council (where she worked under Mary Harriman Rumsey), and the Social Security Board, where by 1938 she was special assistant to the board's general counsel, Jack Tate. She became ill in the early 1940s, and died in 1943 at the home she shared with government economist Florence Armstrong.[26]

CAROLYN WOLFE (1890- ?)

Director of the Women's Division from 1934 to 1936, Carolyn Wolfe attended the University of Chicago before she married James F. Wolfe in 1916. Her husband was a supreme court justice in Utah, and they had five children (1919, 1920, 1922, 1924, 1928). Wolfe became involved in politics through the Red Cross, the Parent-Teacher Association, and the League of Women Voters in Utah. She was the vice-chairman of the Utah State Democratic Committee when Molly Dewson tapped her for the position in Washington. An attempt to get her husband named to a vacancy on the Federal bench during the 1930s was unsuccessful.[27]

ELLEN SULLIVAN WOODWARD (1887-1971)

Ellen Sullivan Woodward, WPA administrator from 1933 to 1938 and member of the Social Security Board from 1938 to 1946, was a native of Mississippi. She was the daughter of William Sullivan, an important politician and lawyer who served briefly as U.S. Senator from that state. Woodward received a diploma from Sans Souci College in Greenville, South Carolina in 1905 and a music certificate from Washington (D.C.) College. At the age of nineteen she married Albert Woodward, a lawyer and politician. They had one son, born in 1909. After Woodward was widowed in 1925, she chose jobs that reflected her interests in politics and social welfare. In 1926, she was elected to the Mississippi legislature; in 1928, she became executive director of the Mississippi State Board of Development. She also became quite involved in Democratic politics, and Senator Pat Harrison, her close friend and political ally, kept a watchful eye on her career. In 1932 Woodward was named to the Mississippi State Board of Public Welfare, where she built up a national reputation for her expertise in relief administration. During the 1932 campaign Woodward's activities caught Molly Dewson's eye, and Harry Hopkins brought Woodward to Washington in 1933 to set up the women's divisions of the Civil Works Administration and the Federal Emergency Relief Administration; in 1936 Woodward became head of Women's and Professional Projects for the Works Progress Administration. In late 1938, when the relief programs were winding down, Woodward took Molly Dewson's place on the Social Security Board. From 1943 to 1946, she was a member of the U.S. delegation to the United Nations Relief and Rehabilitation Administration. In 1946 Woodward joined the Federal Security Agency, where she was director of the Office of Inter-Agency and International Relations until her retirement in 1954.[28]

SUMMARY OF BIOGRAPHICAL MATERIAL

	Birth date	Date of death	Home state	Age in 1933	Marital status	Children	Political family	Political affiliation
Grace Abbott	1878	1939	Neb.	55	S		X	D
Mary Anderson	1872	1964	D.C.	61	S			R
Marion Glass Banister	1875	1951	Va.	58	W	1	X	D
Clara Beyer	1892		N.Y.	41	M	3		D
Emily Newell Blair	1877	1951	Mo.	56	M	2	X	D
Jo Coffin	c. 1880	1943	N.Y.	53	S			D
Molly Dewson	1874	1962	N.Y.	59	S			D
Daisy Harriman	1870	1967	D.C.	63	W	1		D
Jane Hoey	1892	1968	N.Y.	41	S		X	D
Lucy S. Howorth	1895		Miss.	38	M	0	X	D
Mary LaDame	1885	?	N.Y.	48	S			D
Katharine Lenroot	1891		Wis.	42	S		X	R
Dorothy McAlister	1900		Mich.	33	M	2	X	D
Lucille F. McMillin	1870	1949	Tenn.	63	W	1	X	D
Emma Guffey Miller	1874	1970	Pa.	59	M	4	X	D
Mary T. Norton	1875	1959	N.J.	58	W	1		D
Caroline O'Day	1869	1943	N.Y.	64	W	3		D
Ruth Bryan Owen	1885	1954	Fla.	48	W	4	X	D
Frances Perkins	1880	1965	N.Y.	53	M	1		D
Josephine Roche	1886	1976	Colo.	47	D	0		D
Eleanor Roosevelt	1884	1962	N.Y.	49	M	5		D
Nellie Tayloe Ross	1876	1977	Wyo.	57	W	3	X	D
Mary Harriman Rumsey	1881	1934	N.Y.	52	W	3		D
Rose Schneiderman	1882	1972	N.Y.	51	S			D
Hilda Worthington Smith	1888		N.Y.	45	S			D
Sue Shelton White	1887	1943	Tenn.	46	S			D
Carolyn Wolfe	1890	?	Utah	43	M	5	X	D
Ellen S. Woodward	1887	1971	Miss.	46	W	1	X	D

S = single; M = married; W = widowed; D = divorced
D = Democrat; R = Republican

APPENDIX C

College	"Seven Sisters" college	Graduate work	Suffrage	World War I	Settlement house or welfare activities	National Consumers' League	Women's Trade Union League	League of Women Voters	Women's Nat. Dem. Club	Still in government in 1940s	
X		X	X		X	X					Grace Abbott
		X	X	X	X	X	X	X		X	Mary Anderson
		X	X						X	X	Marion Glass Banister
X		X		X	X	X		X		X	Clara Beyer
X			X	X			X	X	X	X	Emily Newell Blair
					X		X			X	Jo Coffin
X	X		X	X	X	X					Molly Dewson
			X	X	X	X			X	X	Daisy Harriman
X		X	X	X						X	Jane Hoey
X		X	X			X			X	X	Lucy S. Howorth
X		X		X	X					X	Mary LaDame
X					X					X	Katharine Lenroot
X	X				X	X					Dorothy McAlister
						X		X		X	Lucille F. McMillin
X	X		X		X	X		X			Emma Guffey Miller
X				X	X					X	Mary T. Norton
X			X		X	X	X	X		X	Caroline O'Day
X				X	X	X					Ruth Bryan Owen
X	X	X	X		X	X				X	Frances Perkins
X	X	X		X	X	X	X	X			Josephine Roche
				X	X	X	X	X		X	Eleanor Roosevelt
										X	Nellie Tayloe Ross
X	X			X	X						Mary Harriman Rumsey
		X	X	X	X		X			X	Rose Schneiderman
X	X	X	X		X		X			X	Hilda Worthington Smith
X		X	X							X	Sue Shelton White
X								X			Carolyn Wolfe
X					X	X		X		X	Ellen S. Woodward

MANUSCRIPT COLLECTIONS CITED

FRANKLIN D. ROOSEVELT LIBRARY, HYDE PARK, NEW YORK

Democratic National Committee papers
Democratic National Committee, Women's Division papers
Mary W. Dewson papers
Harry Hopkins papers
Official File
Frances Perkins papers
President's Personal File
President's Secretary's File
Eleanor Roosevelt papers
Hilda Worthington Smith papers

ARTHUR AND ELIZABETH SCHLESINGER LIBRARY ON THE HISTORY OF WOMEN IN AMERICA, RADCLIFFE COLLEGE, CAMBRIDGE, MASSACHUSETTS

Florence Allen papers
Mary Anderson papers
Clara Mortenson Beyer papers
Biography File
Mary W. Dewson papers
Elinore Morehouse Herrick papers
Lucy Somerville Howorth papers
Emma Guffey Miller papers

National League of Women Voters papers
National Women's Trade Union League papers
New York Women's Trade Union League papers
Frances Perkins papers
Belle Sherwin papers
Hilda Worthington Smith papers
Mary N. Winslow papers
Women's Rights Collection
Ellen Sullivan Woodward papers

COLUMBIA UNIVERSITY, NEW YORK, NEW YORK

Frances Perkins papers

REMINISCENCES, ORAL HISTORY COLLECTION, COLUMBIA UNIVERSITY

Eveline Burns (1965)
Florence Jaffray Harriman (1950)
Katharine Lenroot (1965)
Maurine Mulliner (1967)
Frances Perkins (1955)

NATIONAL ARCHIVES, WASHINGTON, D.C.

Frances Perkins, Office of the Secretary, Department of Labor records
Social Security Administration records
Works Progress Administration records
  Civil Works Administration, 1933-1934
  Federal Emergency Relief Administration, 1933-1936
  Works Progress Administration, 1935-1944
Interview with Clara Beyer, 1965, on file at the Historical Office, Department of Labor

LIBRARY OF CONGRESS, WASHINGTON, D.C.

Florence Allen papers
Marion Glass Banister papers
Bess Furman papers
Florence Jaffray Harriman papers
National Consumers' League papers

NOTES

INTRODUCTION

1. See, for example, William L. O'Neill, *Everyone Was Brave: A History of Feminism in America* (Chicago, 1971), 264-294. Historians such as J. Stanley Lemons have extended the story of feminism into the 1920s, but left open what happened after that: "If, indeed, feminism 'failed,' the tombstone will have to bear another date, perhaps the 1930s or 1940s." J. Stanley Lemons, *The Woman Citizen: Social Feminism in the 1920s* (Urbana, 1975), vii. For general background on the 1930s, see Lois W. Banner, *Women in Modern America: A Brief History* (New York, 1974), 171-210; William H. Chafe, *The American Woman: Her Changing Social, Economic, and Political Role, 1920-1970* (New York, 1972), chaps. 1, 4, and 5. For a contemporary view, see Genevieve Parkhurst, "Is Feminism Dead?" *Harper's*, 170 (May 1935), 735-745.

2. Chafe, *The American Woman*, 111; Parkhurst, "Is Feminism Dead?" 742-743.

3. See Ruth Milkman, "Women's Work and Economic Crisis: Some Lessons of the Great Depression," *The Review of Radical Political Economics*, 8 (Spring 1976), 73-97; and the as yet unpublished work in this area by Alice Kessler-Harris, "A History of Women Workers: The Great Depression as a Test Case," March 1977, Radcliffe Institute.

4. The work of several other historians is also relevant here. Joseph P. Lash, *Eleanor and Franklin: The Story of Their Relationship, Based on Eleanor Roosevelt's Private Papers* (New York, 1971) contains a wealth of material on women in politics and government in the 1930s, but its main focus is on Eleanor Roosevelt. Likewise, George Martin's *Madam Secretary: Frances Perkins* (Boston, 1976) concentrates on the Secretary of Labor. Two unpublished theses also treat this area. Elsie George, "The Women Appointees of the Roosevelt and Truman Administrations: A Study of Their Impact and Effectiveness" (Ph.D. dissertation, American University, 1972) concentrates on Molly Dewson, Ellen Wood-

ward, Marion Glass Banister, and Hilda Worthington Smith only, but still is an important source. Paul Taylor, "The Entrance of Women in Party Politics: The 1920's" (Ph.D. dissertation, Harvard University, 1966) contains much helpful background on the 1920s and the problem of generations, as well as material on the 1930s.

5. Examples include Mary P. Ryan, "The Power of Women's Networks: A Case Study of Female Moral Reform in Antebellum America," *Feminist Studies*, 5 (Spring 1979), 66-85; Blanche Wiesen Cook, "Female Support Networks and Political Activism: Lillian Wald, Crystal Eastman and Emma Goldman," *Chrysalis*, 3 (Autumn 1977), 43-61; Carroll Smith-Rosenberg, "The Female World of Love and Ritual: Relations between Women in Nineteenth-Century America," *Signs: Journal of Women in Culture and Society*, 1 (Autumn 1975), 1-29; Rayna Reiter, "Men and Women in the South of France: Public and Private Domains," in Rayna Reiter, ed., *Toward an Anthropology of Women* (New York, 1975), 252-282.

1. THE WOMEN'S NETWORK

1. *Time* Magazine, May 13, 1940, 22-23.

2. Dorothy McAlister form letter to Democratic women leaders, March 27, 1940, Women's Division of the Democratic National Committee papers (hereafter cited as WD-DNC), Franklin D. Roosevelt Library, Hyde Park, New York (hereafter cited as FDRL). See also the official program of the National Institute of Government, May 2-4, 1940, WD-DNC, FDRL.

3. Mary W. Dewson, "An Aid to the End" (unpublished autobiography, 1949), II, 191, Mary Dewson papers, Schlesinger Library, Radcliffe College. See "Speakers' Table List," Institute of Government material, 1940, WD-DNC, FDRL.

4. Dewson, "An Aid to the End," I, 20.

5. Carrie Chapman Catt to Eleanor Roosevelt, August 15, 1933, Eleanor Roosevelt papers (hereafter cited as ER), FDRL.

6. Quoted in Lois W. Banner, *Women in Modern America: A Brief History* (New York, 1974), 131.

7. Ibid., 135.

8. For general background on women in the 1920s, see J. Stanley Lemons, *The Woman Citizen: Social Feminism in the 1920s* (Urbana, 1975); William H. Chafe, *The American Woman: Her Changing Social, Economic, and Political Role, 1920-1970* (New York, 1972); Clarke A. Chambers, *Seedtime of Reform: American Social Service and Social Action, 1918-1933* (Minneapolis, 1963).

9. Lemons, *The Woman Citizen*, 153-180, discusses the Sheppard-Towner Act.

10. Ibid., 228-244.

11. My interpretation of the New Deal has been influenced by Frank Freidel, *Franklin D. Roosevelt: Launching the New Deal* (Boston, 1973).

12. For several examples, see Chafe, *The American Woman*, 232-233; Ann

Scott and Andrew Scott, *One Half the People: The Fight for Woman Suffrage* (Philadelphia, 1975), 49-50; Eleanor Flexner, *Century of Struggle: The Woman's Rights Movement in the United States* (New York, 1970), 204; June Sochen, *Movers and Shakers: American Women Thinkers and Activists, 1900-1970* (New York, 1973), 163.

13. Dewson, "An Aid to the End," II, 191. Molly Dewson mentions the figure of forty, but according to the list put together by the Women's Division, there were seventy women seated at the Speakers' Tables.

14. In its broadest sense, network can mean an interconnected or interrelated group, but in the context of women in the federal government in the 1930s, the term is used more specifically to emphasize the aspects of communication. In general, the purpose of the network was the transmission of information and requests for assistance through relatively regularized channels of communication among its members. The communication was informal or formal depending on the specific situation and structure of the relationship in which the members were working, but was fairly frequent. Obviously personal preference played a role in determining which members of the network were in more or less active communication with others, but often women who were personal friends began to seek each other out on professional matters through the network. Alternatively, professional contact often led to personal friendships outside of regular government channels. None of the women, however, dealt only with other women, or spent all of their time on women's issues. What this study seeks to do is isolate these women's dealings with other women in the network, and make that the focus of extended examination.

This definition of network has been drawn from several sources. A standard dictionary was consulted. Of special help were two dictionaries of sociology: George A. Theodorson and Achilles G. Theodorson, *A Modern Dictionary of Sociology* (New York, 1969), especially the sections on communication channel and communication net or network, 62-63; and John T. Zadrozny, *Dictionary of Social Science* (Washington, 1959), especially the sections on communication organization, communication theory, and communications system, 56-57. *The International Encyclopedia of the Social Sciences* does not have a listing for network, and the entries on communication were not of much assistance.

15. Joseph P. Lash, *Eleanor and Franklin* (New York, 1971), 512.

16. Molly Dewson to Eleanor Roosevelt, June 30, 1939, ER, FDRL. For the affection and respect that the women reporters had for Eleanor Roosevelt, plus good information on how the press conferences operated, see Ruby Black, "New Deal for Newswomen in Capital," *Editor and Publisher*, February 10, 1934, 11, 33. For other information on the press conferences, see Mary Anderson, *Woman at Work, The Autobiography of Mary Anderson, As Told to Mary N. Winslow* (Minneapolis, 1951), 217-218; Ellen Woodward to Harry Hopkins, December 4, 1933, Federal Emergency Relief Administration (FERA) Old Subject Files, Box 85, National Archives (hereafter cited as NA); Katharine Lenroot to Malvina Schneider, November 30, 1937, ER, FDRL.

A complete set of the "My Day" columns is found in Eleanor Roosevelt's papers at FDRL. Reading the column every day was an excellent way to keep up with the work of women friends in various areas of government and politics. Molly Dewson wrote Eleanor, "I have just had to subscribe to . . . 'My Day' and keep in touch with you" (August 16, 1941, ER, FDRL). Rose Schneiderman wrote Eleanor along the same lines, "I read your column and so I know all the things you are doing" (August 6, 1937, ER, FDRL). This might also be evidence for the loosening of the network by the late 1930s and early 1940s (see Chapter 6).

17. Dewson, "An Aid to the End," I, 2; Anderson, *Woman at Work*, 178.

18. Rose Schneiderman to Eleanor Roosevelt, November 6, 1936, ER, FDRL; Molly Dewson to Eleanor Roosevelt, July, 1936, ER, FDRL; Ellen Sullivan Woodward to Eleanor Roosevelt, June 28, 1939, ER, FDRL. Dewson expressed remarkably similar sentiments eight years later on the occasion of her seventieth birthday: "Not that you and Franklin have not given me a life present, so immense, it would celebrate every future birthday if I lived to be Methuselah, for you have given me fifteen years so interested and satisfying that all my previous years seem pale things in comparison. It was like touching Mother Earth to see you again and always just as I think of you" (February 4, 1944, ER, FDRL).

19. See Appendix B for biographical material on Dewson and the other members of the network.

20. See Appendix A for the criteria used for selecting the women for this study.

21. Rackham Holt, *Mary McLeod Bethune: A Biography* (Garden City, N.Y., 1964), 205. Other sources on Bethune include Catherine Owens Peare, *Mary Mc-Leod Bethune* (New York, 1951), and Emma Gelders Sterne, *Mary McLeod Bethune* (New York, 1957). Mary McLeod Bethune showed that while her main commitment was to blacks, she was proud to be a pioneer for women as well: "I felt that if these talented white women were working at such responsible jobs at a time of national crisis I could do the same thing. I visualized dozens of Negro women coming after me, filling positions of high trust and strategic importance." "My Secret Talks with F.D.R.," *Ebony*, 4 (April 1949), 42-51, reprinted in Bernard Sternsher, ed., *The Negro in Depression and War: Prelude to Revolution, 1930-1945* (Chicago, 1969), 58.

22. Frances Perkins to Molly Dewson, February 16, 1929, Frances Perkins Papers (hereafter cited as FPP), Columbia University. The fact that this letter was written in 1929 shows how aspects of the network had begun to operate before 1933. The specific luncheon the letter refers to, and the existence of the network in the 1920s, are treated at greater length in Chapter 2.

23. Dewson, "An Aid to the End," I, 89-90.

24. Frances Perkins to Daisy Harriman, January 4, 1937, FPP, Columbia. Emily Newell Blair wrote to Harriman in a similar vein: "It is rather wonderful, I think, to be able to leave such a hole in Washington as you do." Blair to Harriman, January 31, 1939, in Florence Jaffray Harriman papers, Library of Congress (hereafter cited as LC); Mary Harriman Rumsey to Sue Shelton White, July 31, 1934, in Sue Shelton White papers, Schlesinger.

25. Molly Dewson to Ellen Woodward, February 14, 1934, WD-DNC, FDRL; Dewson to Josephine Roche, October 7, 1936, WD-DNC, FDRL; Dewson to Clara Beyer, August 7, 1933, Clara Mortenson Beyer papers, Schlesinger; Dew-

son to Ellen Sullivan Woodward, February 6, 1935, WD-DNC, FDRL; Dewson to Josephine Roche, March 20, 1935, WD-DNC, FDRL.

26. Frances Perkins to the Cosmopolitan Club, February 10, 1933, FPP, Columbia; Jo Coffin to Eleanor Roosevelt, October 11, 1937, ER, FDRL; Florence Jaffray Harriman, *Mission to the North* (Philadelphia, 1941), 23-24; George Martin, *Madam Secretary: Frances Perkins* (Boston, 1976), 278-279; Ellen Sullivan Woodward to Eleanor Roosevelt, December 19, 1937, ER, FDRL.

27. For discussion of the Equal Rights Amendment, see Chapter 4.

28. Eleanor Roosevelt, *It's Up to the Women* (New York, 1933), 202, 204; Daisy Harriman speech, early 1930s, in Florence Jaffray Harriman papers, LC; *Democratic Digest*, September 1937, 18; Ellen Sullivan Woodward speech, "Businesswomen in a Democracy," October 21, 1939, in Ellen Woodward papers, Schlesinger.

29. Dewson, "An Aid to the End," I, 110; Emily Newell Blair, "What's She Up To Now? Something New—Women Are Playing Politics for Social Betterment," *Today*, June 2, 1934, in WD-DNC, FDRL; Eleanor Roosevelt, "Women in Politics," *Good Housekeeping*, 110 (March 1940), 45.

30. Eleanor Roosevelt, *If You Ask Me* (New York, 1946), 84; Marion Glass Banister to Laura Burmaster, February 14, 1937, Marion Glass Banister papers, LC, quoted in Elsie George, "The Women Appointees of the Roosevelt and Truman Administrations" (Ph.D. dissertation, American University, 1972), 235; Mary T. Norton, "What Politics Has Meant to Me," *Democratic Digest*, February 1938, 19; *The Reminiscences of Frances Perkins* (1955), III, 644, in The Oral History Collection of Columbia University (hereafter cited as Perkins, OHC). Another example of Perkins's strong feminism was the active role she took in 1936 to have a woman named as Mary Woolley's successor as president of Mount Holyoke, Perkins's alma mater. For a good discussion of this episode, see Martin, *Madam Secretary*, 369-377.

31. Perkins, OHC, I, 183. But Lucy Somerville Howorth showed the reverse of Perkins's dilemma when she talked about the commitment to women taking precedence over human concerns: "I know we sometimes tire of forever pushing and tugging in behalf of our sex when deep within us, all we ask is to be a human being, a very ordinary human being at that, and we would like to be permitted to show our concern for all humanity." Lucy Somerville Howorth speech, "The Trained Woman's Responsibility for Leadership," May 15, 1937, Lucy Somerville Howorth papers, Schlesinger.

32. Anderson, *Woman at Work*, 133; *Democratic Digest*, October 1938; Eleanor Roosevelt, *If You Ask Me*, 62.

33. Elinore Herrick quoted in Rose Feld, "The Woman Who Unravels Labor Knots," *New York Times Magazine*, March 25, 1934, 16, found in Elinore Herrick papers, Schlesinger; Florence Allen, "Participation of Women in Government," in the American Academy of Political and Social Science, *Women's Opportunities and Responsibilities* (Philadelphia, 1947), 94-103.

34. Eleanor Roosevelt, "Women in Politics," *Good Housekeeping*, 110 (April 1940), 45, 203.

35. Molly Dewson to Eleanor Roosevelt, July 25, 1936, Dewson papers, FDRL; Molly Dewson to Charl O. Williams, July 10, 1936, Dewson papers,

FDRL. Another delightful example of Dewson's desire to have women treated like everyone else in politics was this statement from a letter she sent to Jim Farley on March 21, 1934: "I think myself it is a little antiquated to say that women make you nervous. I don't think it would sound like much of an argument to you to say that the men make me nervous sometimes" (WD-DNC, FDRL).

36. Ruby Black interview with Molly Dewson in *Equal Rights*, 2 (August 8, 1936), 179-180, in Dewson papers, Schlesinger.

37. Eleanor Roosevelt quoted in *Equal Rights*, 21 (June 1, 1935), 3; Frances Perkins speech at the Second Congress of International Federation of Business and Professional Women, July 30, 1936, in Perkins folder, Women's Rights Collection, Schlesinger; Emily Newell Blair, "Putting Women into Politics," *The Woman's Journal*, 16 (March 1931), 14.

38. Mary Anderson, "Tribute to Jane Addams," June 19, 1935, Mary Anderson papers, Schlesinger.

39. The term was originally proposed by William L. O'Neill in *Everyone Was Brave: A History of Feminism in America* (Chicago, 1971), 51-52. See also Lois Banner's definition in *Women in Modern America: A Brief History* (New York, 1974), vi; and J. Stanley Lemons, *The Woman Citizen: Social Feminism in the 1920s* (Urbana, 1973), 180.

40. Frances Perkins to Molly Dewson, May 6, 1953, Dewson papers, Schlesinger.

2. A GENERATIONAL APPROACH

1. Molly Dewson to Mrs. Borden, November 11, 1952, Mary Dewson papers, Schlesinger Library, Radcliffe College.

2. Alan Spitzer, "The Historical Problem of Generations," *American Historical Review*, 75 (December 1973), 1385. My definition draws heavily on Karl Mannheim, *Essays on the Sociology of Knowledge* (London, 1959), 286-320. Mannheim's classic definition of generations is stated on page 292: "The social phenomenon of 'generations' represents nothing more than a particular kind of identity of location, embracing related 'age-groups' embedded in a historical-social process."

3. Examples of a generational approach applied to women include Paul Taylor, "The Entrance of Women into Party Politics: The 1920's" (Ph.D. dissertation, Harvard University, 1966); Jill Ker Conway, "The First Generation of American Women Graduates" (Ph.D. dissertation, Harvard University, 1969); Barbara Miller Solomon, "Historical Determinants in Individual Life Experiences of Successful Professional Women," *Annals of the New York Academy of Sciences*, 208 (March 15, 1973), 170-178. The importance of generations had occurred to Franklin Roosevelt as well. See his well-known speech of June 27, 1936: "There is a mysterious cycle in human events. To some generations much is given. Of other generations much is expected. This generation of Americans has a rendezvous with destiny." Quoted on the title page of Eric F. Goldman, *Rendezvous with Destiny: A History of Modern American Reform* (New York, 1955).

4. Hilda Worthington Smith, "The Remembered Way" (unpublished auto-biography, 1936), 436, in Hilda Worthington Smith papers, Schlesinger; Sue Shelton White speech to the Jackson Business and Professional Women's Club, 1929, quoted in *Equal Rights*, 29 (July-August 1943), 58.

5. Lois W. Banner, *Women in Modern America: A Brief History* (New York, 1974), covers this period and its concerns on pages 146-154. See also the chapter entitled "New Generations" in Peter Filene, *Him/Her/Self: Sex Roles in Modern America* (New York, 1974), 118-152; and Paula S. Fass, *The Damned and the Beautiful: American Youth in the 1920's* (New York, 1977). For a contemporary view, see Charlotte Perkins Gilman, "The New Generation of Women," *Current History*, August 1923, 731-737.

6. Lillian Hellman, *An Unfinished Woman: A Memoir* (Boston, 1969), 29-30.

7. The material for this table, as well as all statements in this chapter concerning biographical information about the twenty-eight women in the study, is drawn from Appendixes B and C.

8. Dorothy McAlister reversed the pattern of many of these women by starting out in politics and then going on to be president of the National Consumers' League in the 1940s. At the other extreme, Grace Abbott (born 1878), who was quite near the average age for the group, was in many ways closer to the first generation of women reformers.

9. Rachel Nyswander and Janet Hooks, "Employment of Women in the Federal Government, 1923-1939," *Women's Bureau Bulletin*, no. 182 (Washington, 1941), 5.

10. The figures are from Filene, *Him/Her/Self*, 20-21.

11. For general background on higher education for women, see Mabel Newcomer, *A Century of Higher Education for American Women* (New York, 1959). The material about percentage distribution between women's colleges and coeducational institutions is found on page 49.

12. Frances Perkins, *The Roosevelt I Knew* (New York, 1946), 9, 13; *The Reminiscences of Frances Perkins* (1955), V, 303-306, in The Oral History Collection of Columbia University (hereafter cited as Perkins, OHC).

13. Thomas A. Kreuger and William Glidden, "The New Deal Intellectual Elite: A Collective Portrait," in Frederic Cople Jaher, ed., *The Rich, the Well Born, and the Powerful: Elites and Upper Classes in History* (Secaucus, N.J., 1973), 354. They concluded from their study of 380 individuals: "Drawn from every section of the country, the New Deal elite was initially processed through a diverse group of colleges and universities, then further refined at about 40 prestigious graduate and professional schools. The end product was an educated elite remarkably similar in outlook, training, and lifestyle."

14. Molly Dewson to Lorena Hickok, November 21, 1952, Dewson papers, Schlesinger; Jane Addams, *Twenty Years at Hull House* (New York, 1910; reprinted, New York, 1960), especially the chapters entitled "The Snare of Preparation" and "The Subjective Necessity for Social Settlements."

15. Dewson worked at a variety of welfare activities in the early 1900s before she came to New York in the 1920s; as late as 1911, she was still living at home with her mother. Frances Perkins spent almost five years teaching before she reoriented her life toward social welfare.

16. Smith, "The Remembered Way," 226, 294, 373.

17. Ibid., 373.

18. Filene, *Him/Her/Self*, 24.

19. Smith, "The Remembered Way," 490-491. Smith continued: "Although I had no conscious feeling of hostility to men, and indeed was working closely with many of my own age at the center, my relations to them had always been based on our common professional interest . . . Busy as I was, I was not in the least depressed by this absence of male companionship or by the evident lack of marital prospects . . . True, I often envied my friends their comfortable sense of an established home, and especially their growing families of charming young children . . . If ever I could plan where I would be for more than a year, I reflected, and had sufficient income, I would adopt a few children" (p. 491). To the best of my knowledge, Smith never carried out this plan.

20. Mary Anderson, *Woman at Work: The Autobiography of Mary Anderson, As Told to Mary N. Winslow* (Minneapolis, 1951), 65.

21. Sue Shelton White, "Mother's Daughter," reprinted from *The Nation* in Elaine Showalter, ed., *These Modern Women: Autobiographical Essays from the Twenties* (Old Westbury, N.Y., 1978), 51-52.

22. Jill Ker Conway, "Grace Abbott," in Edward T. James, ed., *Notable American Women, 1607-1950: A Biographical Dictionary* (Cambridge, Mass., 1971), I, 4; Edward T. James, "Mary Anderson," in Barbara Sicherman and Carol Hurd Green, eds., *Notable American Women: The Modern Period* (Cambridge, Mass., 1980), 23-25; James P. Louis, "Sue Shelton White," in *Notable American Women*, III, 592.

23. Elsie George, "The Women Appointees of the Roosevelt and Truman Administrations" (Ph.D. dissertation, American University, 1972), 101-102, 130. I am also indebted to Marion Hunt for sharing her recollections of Dewson and her godmother, Polly Porter.

24. Helen Howe cited several "Boston marriages" (female couples living together in a union similar to marriage) in her book, *The Gentle Americans, 1864-1960: Biography of a Breed* (New York, 1965). The relationship between Olive Chancellor and Verena Tarrant in Henry James, *The Bostonians* (1888) is a none-too-flattering fictional portrayal of one such couple. For discussion of another "Boston marriage," that between novelist Sarah Orne Jewett and Annie Fields, see Josephine Donovan, "The Unpublished Love Poems of Sarah Orne Jewett," *Frontiers: A Journal of Women Studies*, 4, no. 3 (Fall 1979), 26-31.

25. Ann Gordon, Mari Jo Buhle, and Nancy Schrom, "Women in American Society," *Radical America* (July-August 1971), 48. See also Linda Gordon, *Woman's Body, Woman's Right: A Social History of Birth Control in America* (New York, 1976), 193-194.

26. Molly Dewson to Sue Shelton White, October 13, 1939, Sue Shelton White papers, Schlesinger; "Wellesley '97 Class Book," 1927, in Dewson papers, Schlesinger.

27. George, "Women Appointees," 136. The career of Nellie Tayloe Ross followed a similar pattern. She said in an interview that until she was widowed, "My life had been made up of those domestic and social activities that engage the time of the average American woman"—marriage, three children (one of whom

died), the Cheyenne Women's Club. She had been opposed to her husband's running for governor of Wyoming in 1922, but gave in because she did not want to stand in the way of his career. With her husband's unexpected death in 1923, Ross found the strength to take over where he had left off, much to the surprise of the state Democratic leaders who had hoped to ease her out. Ross then began a career of her own, winning election in 1924. After suffering defeat in 1926, she became a prominent leader in Democratic women's politics on the national level. For information about Ross's life, see Paul A. Carter, *Another Part of the Twenties* (New York, 1977), 103-112. The quotation is from page 104.

28. Filene, *Him/Her/Self*, 10; Daniel Scott Smith, "Family Limitation, Sexual Control, and Domestic Feminism in Victorian America," in Mary Hartman and Lois W. Banner, eds., *Clio's Consciousness Raised: New Perspectives on the History of Women* (New York, 1974), 123.

29. This conforms to the conclusions in Fass, *The Damned and the Beautiful*, 60-65, which found patterns of smaller family size and choice of numbers of children most prevalent in middle-class professional families (which would apply to most of the married women in the network).

30. Perkins, OHC, III, 489; Perkins, OHC, I, 245-247. This is the complete quotation: "When I did [marry], Pauline Goldmark lamented, 'Oh, Frances, why did you marry? Oh, dear, you were such a promising person. Why did you marry?' She felt I would be more of a loss to the social work movement and the Consumers' League. I remember saying to her, 'It's hard to say, Pauline, but I thought I better marry and get it off my mind, because I was always being challenged by somebody who thought it would be a good idea to marry me or who wanted to recommend that I should marry. The matter was always being put up to me, and I spent so much time, in the course of a year, considering it and analyzing the reasons for and against as I saw them. I just thought, I just better marry. I know Paul Wilson well. I like him. I've known him for a considerable time. I enjoy his society and company, and I might as well marry and get it off my mind.' I remember Pauline saying, 'That's a strange reason for marrying—to get it off your mind.' "

31. Perkins, OHC, I, 244, 272.

32. This speech was published as Frances Perkins, "My Job," *The Survey*, March 15, 1929; a copy of the speech can be found in the Women's Rights Collection, Schlesinger. Molly Dewson attended the testimonial luncheon and reported on it to Eleanor Roosevelt, who had been unable to attend. Dewson called the luncheon "one of the great occasions of my life" (Molly Dewson to Eleanor Roosevelt, February 7, 1929, ER, FDRL).

33. George Martin, *Madam Secretary: Frances Perkins* (Boston, 1976), 135-137.

34. Molly Dewson to Clara Beyer, August 10, 1920, Clara M. Beyer papers, Schlesinger; Molly Dewson to Clara Beyer, October 12, 1931, Beyer papers, Schlesinger; Clara Beyer to Molly Dewson, October 9, 1931, Beyer papers, Schlesinger.

35. Molly Dewson to Clara Beyer, October 7, 1931, Beyer papers, Schlesinger; interview with Clara Beyer, August 4, 1964, Beyer papers, Schlesinger.

36. A basic source on the woman suffrage movement remains Eleanor Flexner, *Century of Struggle: The Woman's Rights Movement in the United States* (New York, 1970). Aileen S. Kraditor, *The Ideas of the Woman Suffrage Movement, 1890-1920* (Garden City, N.Y., 1971) provides good biographical information on the leaders and their ideology.

37. Molly Dewson to Annie Olesen, November 12, 1932, quoted in Mary W. Dewson, "An Aid to the End" (unpublished autobiography, 1949), I, 72, in Dewson papers, Schlesinger; Molly Dewson to Carrie Chapman Catt, March 19, 1934, in Women's Division, Democratic National Committee papers (hereafter cited as WD-DNC), FDRL. For more information on the network's suffragist activities, see Sue Shelton White to Carrie Chapman Catt, July 25, 1918, Sue Shelton White papers, Schlesinger; Emma Guffey Miller speech to the American Woman's Association, May 20, 1940, Emma Guffey Miller papers, Schlesinger.

38. Perkins, OHC, I, 200-201. Perkins was referring specifically to women's groups that rallied to her defense in the late 1930s, when she faced possible impeachment by the House of Representatives for her role in postponing the deportation of Communist longshoreman Harry Bridges.

39. Perkins, OHC, III, 476-477. See also Chapter 4.

40. Smith, "The Remembered Way," 273-274.

41. William Leuchtenberg, *Franklin D. Roosevelt and the New Deal, 1932-1940* (New York, 1963), 57.

42. Joseph P. Lash, *Eleanor and Franklin* (New York, 1971), 287-301.

43. For information on which of the women were still in government in the 1940s, see Chapter 6.

44. Banner, *Women in Modern America*, 124-126.

45. J. Stanley Lemons, *The Woman Citizen: Social Feminism in the 1920s* (Urbana, 1973) contains the best description of women's activities in the 1920s. For the continuities between the Progressive period and the New Deal, both in programs and personnel, see Clarke A. Chambers, *Seedtime of Reform: American Social Service and Social Action, 1918-1933* (Minneapolis, 1963).

46. Chambers, *Seedtime of Reform*, 260-261. Not to slight the rest of the country, Nellie Nugent Somerville wrote to Ellen Sullivan Woodward when she was appointed to the Social Security Board: "You are giving proof that Mississippi has as good brain power as New York which we know but they do not" (December 23, 1938, Ellen Sullivan Woodward papers, Schlesinger).

47. Perkins, OHC, II, 87-88; Grace Abbott to Molly Dewson, February 10, 1922, Dewson papers, Schlesinger.

48. Lash, *Eleanor and Franklin*, 414-415. See also Perkins, OHC, III, 474.

49. Frances Perkins, "My Job," Women's Rights Collection, Schlesinger.

50. Information on the WTUL can be found in the autobiographies of Rose Schneiderman (*All for One*, New York, 1967), Mary Anderson (*Woman at Work*), and Agnes Nestor (*Women's Labor Leader: An Autobiography of Agnes Nestor*, Rockford, Ill., 1954). Chapter 3 in William H. Chafe, *The American Woman* (New York, 1972) contains background on the WTUL. See also Robin Miller Jacoby, "Feminism and Class Consciousness in the British and American Women's Trade Union Leagues, 1890-1925," in Berenice Carroll, ed., *Liberating*

Women's History: Theoretical and Critical Essays (Urbana, 1976), 136-160; and Gladys Boone, *The Women's Trade Union Leagues in Great Britain and the United States of America* (New York, 1942).

51. Anderson, *Woman at Work*, 35-38; Perkins, OHC, I, 131-132. The Triangle Shirtwaist fire had a lifelong impact on those who were involved. In 1961, fifty years after the fire, Frances Perkins, Rose Schneiderman, and fourteen survivors attended a memorial for the dead at the site of the fire (Martin, *Madam Secretary*, 90).

52. Lash, *Eleanor and Franklin*, 378, 438-439; Eleanor Roosevelt, *This Is My Story* (New York, 1937), 344-346. Eleanor's friendships with these women had an important effect on Franklin Roosevelt as well. Rose Schneiderman and Maud Swartz in particular contributed significantly to the broadening of Franklin's previously limited outlook on labor issues. Frances Perkins remarked, "These intelligent trade unionists made a great many things clear to Franklin Roosevelt that he would hardly have known in any other way . . . A labor leader once said, 'You'd almost think he had participated in some strike or organizing campaign the way he knew and felt about it' " (Perkins, *The Roosevelt I Knew*, 30-32).

53. For background on the NCL, see Josephine Goldmark, "Fifty Years—The National Consumers' League," *The Survey*, 85 (December 1949), 674-676.

54. This was Florence Kelley's reaction to Frances Perkins's appointment: "Glory be to God! You don't mean it. I never thought I would live to see the day when someone we had trained, who knew about industrial conditions, cared about women, cared to have things right, would have the chance to be an administrative officer" (quoted in Martin, *Madam Secretary*, 143-144). The list of women trained by the National Consumers' League includes Perkins, Nelle Swartz, Clara Beyer, Molly Dewson, Amy Maher, Marie Wing, Beatrice McConnell, Dorothy Kenyon, Josephine Roche, Elinore Herrick, Pauline Goldmark, and Emily Marconnier (Goldmark, "Fifty Years," 676).

55. Speech of Frances Perkins entitled "The Living Spirit of Florence Kelley" on the fortieth anniversary dinner of the National Consumers' League, December 8, 1939, found in Frances Perkins papers, Columbia. George Martin's biography of Perkins uses this speech as an example of how Frances Perkins downplayed her sex (see, for example, *Madam Secretary*, 210), but I think it demonstrates instead that she saw herself as a representative of a reform constituency.

56. Louise C. Wade, "Florence Kelley," in *Notable American Women*, II, 316-319.

57. Frances Perkins speech, "My Job," Women's Rights Collection, Schlesinger; Frances Perkins to Florence Kelley, January 30, 1929, National Consumers' League papers, Library of Congress; Perkins, "My Job," Women's Rights Collection, Schlesinger.

58. Perkins, OHC, II, 169.

59. Perkins, OHC, I, 21-22. Clara Beyer, Frances Perkins, and Grace Abbott received some training for social work in their graduate work; Mary LaDame and Josephine Roche were trained in addition by the Russell Sage Foundation. Molly Dewson received much of her training with the Women's Educational and Industrial Union in Boston. Jane Hoey and Hilda Worthington Smith both attended the New York School of Social Work.

60. Smith, "The Remembered Way," 275. For general background on the history of social work, see Roy Lubove, *The Professional Altruist: The Emergence of Social Work as a Career 1880-1930* (Cambridge, Mass., 1965); Frank Bruno, *Trends in Social Work 1874-1956* (New York, 1957); Kathleen Woodroofe, *From Charity to Social Work in England and the United States* (London, 1962).

61. Mary Anderson respected social work in the 1920s, but remarked that she thought the "social worker has become so professional that there is overemphasis on the profession, rather than on the work itself" (Anderson, *Woman at Work*, 207).

62. Chambers, *Seedtime of Reform*, 266-267.

63. Emily Newell Blair was perhaps the most prominent and prolific commentator on women in politics in the 1920s and 1930s, and her articles provide an excellent summary of women's major concerns after suffrage. Some of the more interesting ones include, "Are Women a Failure in Politics?" *Harper's Magazine*, 151 (October 1925), 513-522; "Men in Politics as a Woman Sees Them," *Harper's Magazine*, 152 (May 1926), 703-709; "Are Women Really in Politics?" *The Independent*, 119 (December 3, 1927), 542-544; "Wanted: A New Feminism," *Independent Woman*, 10 (December 1930), 498-499; "Why I Am Discouraged About Women in Politics," *Woman's Journal*, 16 (January 1931), 20-22; "Discouraged Feminists," *Outlook and Independent*, 158 (July 8, 1931), 302-303.

64. See Appendix B for biographical material on the political backgrounds of these women.

65. Lash, *Eleanor and Franklin*, 340. For information on women in the Republican party, see Josephine Good, *The History of Women in Republican National Conventions and Women in the Republican National Committee* (Washington, 1963); and Virginia White Speel and Burnita Shelton Matthews, "What the Republican Party Has Done for Women," no date, found in WD-DNC, FDRL. Prominent Republican women included Margaret Dreier Robins, Cornelia Bryce Pinchot, Katherine Edson Phillips, and Harriet Taylor Upton.

p. 39

66. Emily Newell Blair, "Women are Organized on Nation-Wide Scale," in "Advance of Democratic Women" (1940), 13-16, pamphlet published by the Women's Division of the Democratic National Committee, found in Dewson papers, Schlesinger.

67. "Advance of Democratic Women," 14; Emma Guffey Miller to Mrs. Borden, August 17, 1958, Emma Guffey Miller papers, Schlesinger; Democratic National Committee, *Women's Democratic Campaign Manual* (Washington, 1924), 5; Lash, *Eleanor and Franklin*, 390; Eleanor Roosevelt, *This Is My Story*, 354.

68. Nellie Tayloe Ross, "Women Carry Torch during Lean Years," in "Advance of Democratic Women," 17-20, Dewson papers, Schlesinger. See also Eleanor Roosevelt's report on the 1928 Women's Division, ER, FDRL.

69. Lash, *Eleanor and Franklin*, 374.

70. Frances Perkins to Eleanor Roosevelt, December 17, 1928, ER, FDRL; Dewson, "An Aid to the End," I, 7; Emily Newell Blair to Eleanor Roosevelt, December 19, 1928, ER, FDRL.

71. Report by Caroline O'Day on work done by women of New York State, 1928, ER, FDRL. See also Eleanor Roosevelt and Lorena Hickok, *Ladies of Courage* (New York, 1954), 280.

72. "The History of the Women's National Democratic Club," *Democratic Bulletin*, June 1928, 4-12. The Women's Division of the Democratic National Committee was less than enthusiastic about this club because it felt that women should be part of the regular party machinery rather than auxiliary clubs. During the 1930s this continued to be a troublesome issue. See Nellie Tayloe Ross form letter, December 9, 1932, WD-DNC, FDRL.

73. Chafe, *The American Woman*, 25-47; "Survey of Women in Public Office," January 1933, prepared by the National League of Women Voters, found in National League of Women Voters papers, Schlesinger.

74. Ruth Bryan Owen to Emma Guffey Miller, December 7, 1923, Emma Guffey Miller papers, Schlesinger; Emily Newell Blair to Sue Shelton White, July 15, 1924, Emma Guffey Miller papers, Schlesinger; Mary T. Norton to Emma Guffey Miller, December 16, 1926, Emma Guffey Miller papers, Schlesinger. Several years later, Nellie Tayloe Ross wrote to Sue Shelton White, "I am sure that Mrs. Owen will go far in the political field. She is her father's 'own child'—very gifted" (December 20, 1929, Sue Shelton White papers, Schlesinger).

75. Dewson, "An Aid to the End," I, 70-71.

76. Campaign Letterbook, 1932, Dewson papers, FDRL. This role put Dewson in conflict with some of the women she would later get appointed to positions in the New Deal, such as Daisy Harriman. When California switched to Roosevelt on the fourth ballot at the 1932 convention, Harriman was upset at the deal: "I'd like to have seen them fight it out. I never liked a deal." Harriman turned to Dewson, and they exchanged heated words. People nearby heard Harriman say, "I'll bet you," while Dewson shook her head as if accepting a wager. (This account comes from Dewson, "An Aid to the End," I, 37.) Daisy Harriman's lack of support for FDR before he was nominated caused some hard feelings, and it was not until 1937 that Harriman was given her post in Norway.

77. Dewson, "An Aid to the End," I, 67-76, discusses women's roles in the 1932 campaign. Dewson's quotation is found on page 69. See also Lash, *Eleanor and Franklin*, 449-465. For examples of the Rainbow Fliers pioneered in the 1932 campaign, see the papers of the Women's Division at FDRL.

78. Perkins, OHC, II, 470.

79. Molly Dewson to Arthur Altmeyer, August 25, 1935, Appointments, Chairman's Files, Records of the Social Security Board, National Archives.

3. THE CRITICAL YEAR, 1933-1934

1. For background on the 1932 election and the first hundred days, see William E. Leuchtenberg, *Franklin D. Roosevelt and the New Deal, 1932-1940* (New York, 1963); and Frank Freidel, *Franklin D. Roosevelt: Launching the New Deal* (Boston, 1973).

2. Molly Dewson to Mary Winslow, January 26, 1945, Mary Winslow papers, Schlesinger Library, Radcliffe College.

3. Mary W. Dewson, "An Aid to the End" (unpublished autobiography, 1949), I, 139-140, in Mary Dewson papers, Schlesinger; Molly Dewson to Gladys

Tillett, April 11, 1941, Women's Division of the Democratic National Committee papers (hereafter cited as WD-DNC), Franklin D. Roosevelt Library (hereafter cited as FDRL); Molly Dewson to Eleanor Roosevelt, August 21, 1933, Eleanor Roosevelt papers (hereafter cited as ER), FDRL.

4. Molly Dewson to Lucy Somerville Howorth, August 21, 1949, Lucy Somerville Howorth papers, Schlesinger.

5. Molly Dewson to Eleanor Roosevelt, April 27, 1933, ER, FDRL; Molly Dewson to Marvin McIntyre, February 5, 1934, Patronage Letterbook, Dewson papers, FDRL. For examples of some of these patronage positions, see the list of women Dewson submitted to the President for action, October 23, 1933, revised November 28, 1933, in WD-DNC, FDRL.

6. United Press, August 25, 1932, in collection of clippings sent by Molly Dewson to Franklin Roosevelt, November 24, 1932, President's Official File (hereafter cited as OF), FDRL; Clara Beyer to "Edna," June 9, 1930, Clara M. Beyer papers, Schlesinger. See also Beyer to Pauline Goldmark, June 6, 1930; Beyer to Mrs. Brandeis, July 7, 1930; plus four folders of news clippings and publicity in Beyer's papers at Schlesinger.

7. Freidel, *Launching the New Deal*, 143-144; *The Reminiscences of Frances Perkins* (1955), II, 721, in The Oral History Collection of Columbia University (hereafter cited as Perkins, OHC). Material about efforts to push Ross for the Interior position is found in the Sue Shelton White papers, Schlesinger.

8. Perkins, OHC, II, 725. This is the full quotation: "It was revealing to me because of the fact that he seemed to have come to the conclusion that he wanted to appoint me for three reasons—first, to be smarter than Al [Smith]; second, to please what he thought was a body of political influence that wasn't fully taken account of, namely the women voters; third, because it was easy. I was right there and I was trustworthy."

9. Dewson, "An Aid to the End," I, 32-33; Molly Dewson to Frances Perkins, December 26, 1932, Frances Perkins Papers (hereafter cited as FPP), Columbia University.

10. Eleanor Roosevelt, *This I Remember* (New York, 1949), 5; Perkins, OHC, III, 513; Clara Beyer to Frances Perkins, December 5, 1932, Beyer papers, Schlesinger; Molly Dewson to Franklin Roosevelt, November 24, 1932, OF, FDRL.

11. Molly Dewson to Clara Beyer, November 21, 1932, Beyer papers, Schlesinger; Democratic National Committee papers, FDRL (boxes 992 and 993); Josephine Roche to Franklin Roosevelt, January 4, 1933, DNC, FDRL; Emily Newell Blair to Franklin Roosevelt, November 29, 1932, DNC, FDRL.

12. Frances Perkins to Lillian Wald, July 11, 1932, FPP, Columbia; Perkins, OHC, III, 559. George Martin, *Madam Secretary: Frances Perkins* (Boston, 1976), 523, quotes Agnes Leach that she was sure Frances Perkins had been helped financially by several women—possibly Eleanor Roosevelt and Caroline O'Day. Leach suggested that the women were so proud of Perkins's opportunity that they were not going to let the matter of finances hold her back. Pauline Newman, another old friend of Frances Perkins, mentioned independently of Leach that she thought Caroline O'Day had helped Perkins financially.

13. Perkins, OHC, III, 525; Martin, *Madam Secretary*, 237-238, from Perkins, OHC.

14. Martin, *Madam Secretary*, 239-241. FDR asked Perkins at the beginning of this meeting if Molly Dewson had told her what he had in mind. Perkins replied rather cryptically, "Well, I never know if Molly is speaking the truth or just reflecting her own hopes and aspirations."

15. Frances Perkins to Carrie Chapman Catt, June 11, 1945, FPP, Columbia; Frances Perkins speech at the presentation of the American Women's Association Award, November 24, 1933, in FPP, Columbia.

16. "Thumbnail Sketches of Women You Hear About in the New Deal," compiled by the Women's Division, 1934, found in Dewson papers, FDRL.

17. Molly Dewson to Louis Howe, June 5, 1933, Patronage Letterbook, Dewson papers, Schlesinger.

18. Freidel, *Launching the New Deal*, 303; Molly Dewson to Mrs. Matison Boyd Jones, May 18, 1936, Dewson papers, FDRL; Molly Dewson to Jim Farley, June 13, 1933, WD-DNC, FDRL.

19. Nellie Tayloe Ross to Molly Dewson, April 1, 1933, Sue Shelton White papers, Schlesinger; Molly Dewson to Jim Farley, April 28, 1933, ER, FDRL.

20. Molly Dewson wrote this in longhand on the letter before she sent it.

21. Molly Dewson to Eleanor Roosevelt, April 27, 1933, ER, FDRL.

22. Ibid.; Molly Dewson to Eleanor Roosevelt, June 29, 1933, Patronage Letterbook, Dewson papers, FDRL; Molly Dewson to Jim Farley, July 2, 1933, OF, FDRL. It was standard practice for Dewson to send copies of her correspondence with Farley (and many other people) to Eleanor Roosevelt—often with comments penciled in like those quoted in the text.

23. Molly Dewson to Emily Newell Blair, July 2, 1933, ER, FDRL. The letter begins: "I am deeply distressed because you seem out of sorts with the administration and me." Molly Dewson passed her reply on to Eleanor Roosevelt with this notation penciled on the top: "Dear Eleanor—On account of what Emily Blair said about Frances the one outstanding appointment being of a person without political experience I decided to write her before waiting to hear whether the men would give her an appointment or was it that you were to find whether there are any good jobs left? I will let you know what she says. Molly."

24. Molly Dewson to Missy LeHand, January 5, 1934, WD-DNC, FDRL.

25. Dewson, "An Aid to the End," I, 124-141, covers patronage for women in great detail.

26. Molly Dewson to Eleanor Roosevelt, April 27, 1933, ER, FDRL.

27. Anna Grogran to Harriet Elliott, January 11, 1933, Sue Shelton White papers, Schlesinger.

28. Molly Dewson to Eleanor Roosevelt, May 3, 1933, ER, FDRL. The first time Senator Carter Glass heard of the impending nomination was when Roosevelt called him to see if the appointment was objectionable. Elsie George, "The Women Appointees of the Roosevelt and Truman Administrations" (Ph.D. dissertation, American University, 1972), 232-233.

29. Molly Dewson to Eleanor Roosevelt, May 3, 1933, ER, FDRL. Daisy Harriman had not supported Franklin Roosevelt at the 1932 convention, and this was

probably why she did not receive any recognition until the second term—after she had proved her loyalty.

30. Dewson, "An Aid to the End," I, 138-139 (see also Dewson to Eleanor Roosevelt, April 27, 1933, ER, FDRL, for several examples of husbands receiving jobs in recognition for their wives' contributions); Eleanor Roosevelt to Nellie Tayloe Ross, May 2, 1933, ER, FDRL; Dewson "An Aid to the End," I, 138-139.

31. Molly Dewson to Franklin Roosevelt, October 30, 1933, OF, FDRL; Molly Dewson to Eleanor Roosevelt, October 30, 1933, OF, FDRL.

32. Eleanor Roosevelt to Louis Howe, April 28, 1933, President's Personal File (hereafter cited as PPF), FDRL; Eleanor Roosevelt to Jim Farley, May 23, 1933, ER, FDRL; Eleanor Roosevelt to Nancy Cook, October 17, 1933, ER, FDRL; Eleanor Roosevelt to Jim Farley, February 13, 1934, ER, FDRL. Jo Coffin also did a little checking up on her own. She wrote in late 1933 to Malvina Thompson, Eleanor Roosevelt's personal secretary: "Dear Malvina— Did Mr. Farley promise Mrs. Roosevelt the job of second Assistant to the Public Printer for me? It does seem like he takes a long time in choosing the Public Printer, but I could sleep sweetly if I knew he had promised Mrs. Roosevelt that place. This is woman to woman" (ER, FDRL).

33. Molly Dewson to Eleanor Roosevelt, April 27, 1933, ER, FDRL.

34. Lucy Somerville Howorth to Molly Dewson, May 3, 1934, WD-DNC, FDRL; Molly Dewson to Oscar Chapman, December 12, 1933, WD-DNC, FDRL; Molly Dewson to Lucy Somerville Howorth, July 1, 1934, Lucy Somerville Howorth papers, Schlesinger. Perhaps Howorth could afford to be so modest: she had the strong backing of Senator Pat Harrison of Mississippi.

35. See Chapter 5 for a more detailed discussion of Perkins's role.

36. Lavinia Engle to Molly Dewson, June 27, 1934, WD-DNC, FDRL.

37. Molly Dewson to Frances Perkins, May 3, 1934, FPP, Columbia.

38. Clara Beyer to Mary Hutchinson, November 1, 1934, Beyer papers, Schlesinger.

39. Martin, *Madam Secretary*, 422; Molly Dewson to Eleanor Roosevelt, December 11, 1936, President's Secretary's File (hereafter cited as PSF), FDRL.

40. Martha H. Swain, "Ellen Sullivan Woodward," in Barbara Sicherman and Carol Hurd Green, eds., *Notable American Women: The Modern Period* (Cambridge, Mass., 1980), 747-749; Ellen Sullivan Woodward to Molly Dewson, June 8, 1933, ER, FDRL; Molly Dewson to Ellen Sullivan Woodward, October 24, 1933, WD-DNC, FDRL.

41. George, "Women Appointees," 192.

42. *The Reminiscences of Jane Hoey* (1965), 3, 86, in The Oral History Collection of Columbia University (hereafter cited as Hoey, OHC).

43. Molly Dewson to Mary Winslow, January 26, 1945, Winslow papers, Schlesinger.

44. Emily Newell Blair to Molly Dewson, December 27, 1933, WD-DNC, FDRL. For further examples of Dewson's actions on behalf of Florence Allen, see Molly Dewson to Carrie Chapman Catt, March 19, 1934, WD-DNC, FDRL; Dewson to Eleanor Roosevelt, March 1, 1934, WD-DNC, FDRL; Dewson to Florence Casper Whitney, March 5, 1934, WD-DNC, FDRL; Dewson to Louis Howe,

February 3, 1934, Patronage Letterbook, Dewson papers, FDRL.

45. Molly Dewson to Florence Allen, May 10, 1934, WD-DNC, FDRL. Perhaps this unsuccessful attempt had something to do with a changing climate for women in the late New Deal (see Chapter 6).

46. Molly Dewson to Eleanor Roosevelt, April 27, 1933, ER, FDRL; Eleanor Roosevelt to Jim Farley, September 20, 1933, ER, FDRL; Eleanor Roosevelt to Jim Farley, July 5, 1933, ER, FDRL.

47. Molly Dewson to Eleanor Roosevelt, June 22, 1937, ER, FDRL; see also "The Favored State Party Set Up for Democratic Women" (1940), Dewson papers, FDRL; Molly Dewson to Eleanor Roosevelt, June 27, 1937, ER, FDRL; Molly Dewson to Emma Guffey Miller, March 22, 1937, ER, FDRL.

48. Molly Dewson to Henry Wallace, January 18, 1934, WD-DNC, FDRL; Eleanor Roosevelt to Mrs. A. P. Flynn, October 23, 1933, ER, FDRL; Molly Dewson to Emily Newell Blair, March 14, 1934, WD-DNC, FDRL.

49. Molly Dewson to Jim Farley, April 28, 1933, ER, FDRL; Molly Dewson to Frances Perkins, December 27, 1933, FPP, Columbia; Molly Dewson to Eleanor Roosevelt, October 5, 1940, ER, FDRL.

50. Quoted in Martin, *Madam Secretary*, 237; Marvin McIntyre to Jim Farley, January 14, 1936, OF, FDRL.

51. Dewson, "An Aid to the End," II, 205.

52. Dewson, "An Aid to the End," I, 124; "Advance of Democratic Women" (1940), by the Women's Division of the Democratic National Committee, in Dewson papers, Schlesinger; Frances Perkins, *The Roosevelt I Knew* (New York, 1946), 70, 120-121, 136. Perkins wrote: "He had complete reliance on her observations. He often insisted on action that public officials thought unnecessary because Mrs. Roosevelt had seen with her own eyes and had reported so vividly that he too felt he had seen. They were partners" (p. 70).

53. Perkins, *The Roosevelt I Knew*, 9.

54. Perkins, OHC, II, 721.

55. Joseph P. Lash, *Eleanor and Franklin* (New York, 1971), 449-450, 586. McIntyre and Early were also very disturbed by Eleanor Roosevelt's racial views.

56. Perkins, OHC, III, 22; Dewson, "An Aid to the End," I, 1.

57. Quoted in Dewson, "An Aid to the End," I, 90; Molly Dewson to Franklin Roosevelt, Spring 1940, Dewson papers, FDRL.

58. In fact, one impetus for writing her autobiography seems to have been Dewson's pique at Farley for leaving women completely out of his autobiography. She claimed that she felt no resentment, "But when I read *Jim Farley's Story*, I said, 'May the Lord forgive you. I cannot' " (Dewson, "An Aid to the End," I, 53).

59. Quoted in Dewson, "An Aid to the End," II, 187; Ibid., I, 46-47; Perkins, OHC, VII, 493. Perkins continued: "He thought that if he could get his girl into Wellesley, she would be as good as Mary Dewson. It was that sort of thing."

60. Louis Howe, "Women's Ways in Politics," *Woman's Home Companion*, 62 (June 1935), 9-10; Molly Dewson to Eleanor Roosevelt, April 27, 1933, ER, FDRL.

61. Molly Dewson to Eleanor Roosevelt, May 13, 1933, ER, FDRL; Molly

Dewson to General Hugh Johnson, December 12, 1933, WD-DNC, FDRL; Mary Ward to Marie Proctor, July, 1936, Dewson papers, FDRL; Molly Dewson to Jim Farley, April 15, 1936, ER, FDRL.

62. The Women's Bureau has done several studies of women in government that are invaluable for understanding the basic trends of women's participation. See Bertha Nienburg, "Women in the Government Service," *Women's Bureau Bulletin*, no. 8 (Washington, 1920); Nienburg, "The Status of Women in the Government Service in 1925," *Women's Bureau Bulletin*, no. 53 (Washington, 1926); Rachel Nyswander and Janet Hooks, "Employment of Women in the Federal Service, 1923-1939," *Women's Bureau Bulletin*, no. 182 (Washington, 1941); Mary E. Pidgeon and Janet Hooks, "Women in the Federal Service, 1923-1947," *Women's Bureau Bulletin*, no. 230 (Washington, 1949). See also Lucille Foster McMillin, *Women in the Federal Service* (Washington, 1941).

63. This seems to have been the case with the movie industry, according to Robert Sklar in *Movie-Made America: A Cultural History of American Movies* (New York, 1975), 75, 235.

64. *Women's Bureau Bulletin*, no. 182, 50. In the independent agencies as a group, the expansion of existing agencies plus the addition of new ones between 1923 and 1939 led to an increase of 220 percent in women's employment; in the executive departments, the increase was 81 percent (*Women's Bureau Bulletin*, no. 182, 25-26; *Women's Bureau Bulletin*, no. 230, 18).

65. *Women's Bureau Bulletin*, no. 182, 24.

66. Frances Perkins speech, 1937, found in the Women's Rights Collection, Schlesinger.

67. *The Reminiscences of Katharine Lenroot* (1965), 62-63, in The Oral History Collection of Columbia University. On the other hand, Mary Anderson of the Women's Bureau was rather disappointed once Perkins took office: she had hoped for "a friend to whom I could go freely and confidentially, but it did not turn out to be that way." Anderson devotes quite a few pages of her book to detailing her disappointments with Frances Perkins as Secretary of Labor. To some degree, this was "sour grapes" on Anderson's part because the momentum on women's issues had shifted away from the Women's Bureau by the 1930s. In comparison, the Children's Bureau took a much more activist and influential role in the 1930s, which probably explains why Katharine Lenroot enjoyed the atmosphere of the Labor Department so much. See Mary Anderson, *Woman at Work: The Autobiography of Mary Anderson, As Told to Mary N. Winslow* (Minneapolis, 1951), 183-185.

68. See Rose Schneiderman (with Lucy Goldwaithe), *All for One* (New York, 1967), 194-209, and McMillin, *Women in the Federal Service*; Molly Dewson to Lucy Somerville Howorth, March 7, 1934, WD-DNC, FDRL; obituary of Jo Coffin, *Democratic Digest*, April 1943.

69. Clarke Chambers, *Seedtime of Reform: American Social Service and Social Action, 1918-1933* (Minneapolis, 1963), 268.

70. Molly Dewson to Mary Winslow, January 26, 1945, Winslow papers, Schlesinger. Winslow helped Mary Anderson write her book, *Woman at Work*, and she was writing to Dewson to ask if she had anything that should be in-

cluded. Dewson replied: "I never worked with her enough on any one specific thing to remember it, altho' we were always there in the same committee rooms. I have more memories of Grace Abbott and Clara Beyer, and of course of the N.C.L. crowd so I am no use to you."

71. Ernest Griffith, *The Impasse of Democracy* (New York, 1939), 182, quoted in Jo Freeman, *The Politics of Women's Liberation* (New York, 1975), 227-228.

72. See Chapter 5 for a more detailed discussion of the White House Conference on the Emergency Needs of Women.

73. Molly Dewson to Lavinia Engle, November 20, 1933, WD-DNC, FDRL.

4. WOMEN AND DEMOCRATIC POLITICS

1. Mary W. Dewson, "An Aid to the End" (unpublished autobiography, 1949), II, 7, in Mary Dewson papers, Schlesinger Library, Radcliffe College; Emily Newell Blair, "Are Women A Failure in Politics?", *Harper's Magazine*, 151 (October 1925), 513-522.

2. Dewson, "An Aid to the End," II, 1-2.

3. "Advance of Democratic Women" (1940), 24, Dewson papers, Schlesinger; Molly Dewson to Emily Newell Blair, August 13, 1933, Patronage Letterbook, Dewson papers, Franklin D. Roosevelt Library (hereafter cited as FDRL).

4. Eleanor Roosevelt to James Farley, late 1936, Eleanor Roosevelt papers (hereafter cited as ER), FDRL; Molly Dewson to Eleanor Roosevelt, December 11, 1936, President's Secretary's File (hereafter cited as PSF), FDRL; Molly Dewson to Lavinia Engle, May 28, 1934, Women's Division of the Democratic National Committee papers (hereafter cited as WD-DNC), FDRL.

5. Molly Dewson to Eleanor Roosevelt, January 26, 1934, Patronage Letterbook, Dewson papers, FDRL.

6. Molly Dewson to Eleanor Roosevelt, January 30, 1934, WD-DNC, FDRL; Molly Dewson to Ellen Sullivan Woodward, February 6, 1935, WD-DNC, FDRL.

7. Molly Dewson's pencil notes on a copy of the original Reporter Plan, January 1934, WD-DNC, FDRL; Dewson, "An Aid to the End," I, 1. Dewson was one of a long list of network members who discussed their work at Eleanor Roosevelt's press conferences; for example, Mary Harriman Rumsey described proposals for consumers' organizations to combat high prices, and Frances Perkins announced the formation of camps for unemployed women. Mary Anderson, Katharine Lenroot, and Hilda Worthington Smith put in frequent appearances. Ellen Sullivan Woodward made several important announcements about women's relief at the press conferences, and she was often asked to be on hand to answer questions about women's work. For a good introduction to the press conferences by one of the women journalists, see Ruby Black, "New Deal for Newswomen in Capital," *Editor and Publisher*, February 10, 1934, 11, 33.

8. Reporter Plan, January 1934, WD-DNC, FDRL.

9. "Advance of Democratic Women," 25.

10. Molly Dewson to Eleanor Roosevelt, November 10, 1940, ER, FDRL; *Democratic Digest*, June 1934, 13; Molly Dewson to Harriet Elliott, December 27, 1934, WD-DNC, FDRL.

11. Dewson, "An Aid to the End," II, 23-24. Eleanor Roosevelt said, "If we follow the study program of the Reporter Plan we will not be misled by what uninformed people sometimes say. Catchwords spread quickly. Someone may turn a phrase which sounds amusing but which is untrue. Untruths spread like wildfire. This is why the Reporter Plan is so valuable—it corrects misinformation and gives the facts" (January 7, 1939, quoted in "The Favored Party Set Up," Dewson papers, FDRL).

12. Dewson, "An Aid to the End," I, 41.

13. "Advance of Democratic Women," 21.

14. Dewson, "An Aid to the End," I, 43-44. Prejudice and unwillingness to work side by side with black women also undoubtedly played a part. There was a separate Negro Voters Division of the Democratic National Committee, and Crystal Bird Fauset was in charge of activities for black women. Such activities, however, were fairly limited in the 1930s. For more information, see the papers of the Women's Division at FDRL.

15. "Advance of Democratic Women," 21, 27.

16. Dewson, "An Aid to the End," II, 37-40; see also Eleanor Roosevelt and Lorena Hickok, *Ladies of Courage* (New York, 1954), 20; Molly Dewson to Harriet Elliott, December 27, 1934, WD-DNC, FDRL.

17. Dewson, "An Aid to the End," II, 7-12. Wolfe served from 1934 through the 1936 campaign and election. McAlister took over from 1936 to 1940.

18. Dewson, "An Aid to the End," II, 69.

19. Program of the Richmond, Georgia Regional Conference, January 28, 1935, in Dewson papers, FDRL.

20. Dorothy McAlister to Bernard Baruch, December 16, 1938, ER, FDRL.

21. Ibid.

22. See, for example, Josephine Roche on the Social Security Act, *Democratic Digest*, May 1935; Marion Glass Banister on Taxes, *Democratic Digest*, November 1935; Mary Anderson on Women Workers and the Social Security Program, *Democratic Digest*, July 1936.

23. For background on the founding of this club, see "The History of the Woman's National Democratic Club," *Democratic Bulletin*, June 1928, 4-12.

24. Carolyn Wolfe to Florence Whitney, November 23, 1936, WD-DNC, FDRL.

25. Material on this banquet is found in the Marion Glass Banister papers, Library of Congress (hereafter cited as LC).

26. Emily Newell Blair to Molly Dewson, December 1935, WD-DNC, FDRL.

27. Ellen Sullivan Woodward to Malvina Schneider, May 16, 1938, ER, FDRL; Molly Dewson to Lucy Somerville Howorth, June 18, 1938, Lucy Somerville Howorth papers, Schlesinger; Mary Ellen Hughes to Harriet Allen, April 16, 1935, WD-DNC, FDRL. Hughes worked for Dewson at the Women's Division.

28. Eleanor Roosevelt to James Farley, October 31, 1935, ER, FDRL.

29. Eleanor Roosevelt to Mrs. Francis Scott, November 1, 1934, ER, FDRL.

30. Caroline O'Day to Molly Dewson, August 28, 1936, WD-DNC, FDRL.

31. Eleanor Roosevelt to Eddie Flynn, August 9, 1940, ER, FDRL.

32. Molly Dewson to Sue Shelton White, October 13, 1939, Sue Shelton

White papers, Schlesinger.

33. Emma Guffey Miller speech to the American Woman's Association, May 20, 1946, in Emma Guffey Miller papers, Schlesinger; Emma Guffey Miller to Dorothy McAlister, August 31, 1937, Dewson papers, FDRL; Molly Dewson to Cordell Hull, June 5, 1936, Dewson papers, FDRL; *The Reminiscences of Frances Perkins* (1955), VII, 443, in The Oral History Collection of Columbia University (hereafter cited as Perkins, OHC).

34. Molly Dewson to Frances Perkins, October 23, 1936, Perkins General Subject File, Department of Labor records, National Archives (hereafter cited as NA).

35. Frances Perkins to Frieda Miller, October 24, 1936, Perkins General Subject File, Department of Labor records, NA.

36. Josephine Roche to Frances Perkins, December 9, 1936, Perkins General Subject File, Department of Labor records, NA.

37. Molly Dewson to Franklin Roosevelt, March 19, 1937, quoted in Sarah Slavin Schramm, "Section 213: Woman Overboard," paper presented to the Berkshire Conference on the History of Women, Radcliffe College, October 1974, p. 8; Molly Dewson to Eleanor Roosevelt, July 25, 1936, Dewson papers, FDRL; Carolyn Wolfe to Franklin Roosevelt, March 3, 1936, in Marion Glass Banister papers, LC.

38. Molly Dewson to Charl O. Williams, July 10, 1936, Dewson papers, FDRL; Molly Dewson to Eleanor Roosevelt, April 17, 1937, ER, FDRL; Charl O. Williams to Eleanor Roosevelt, August 4, 1937, ER, FDRL.

39. Roosevelt and Hickok, *Ladies of Courage*, 15; Molly Dewson to Caroline O'Day, March 15, 1934, WD-DNC, FDRL; see also Molly Dewson to Eleanor Roosevelt, March 11, 1936, ER, FDRL.

40. Ellen Sullivan Woodward to Molly Dewson, October 18, 1935, WD-DNC, FDRL; Molly Dewson to Harriet Elliott, December 27, 1934, WD-DNC, FDRL. Dewson said in full, "I consider we are weakest east of the Mississippi and in the South, for the South needs this program of work as much as anywhere to keep the Democrats in step with the President. The Democrats outside the biggest Eastern cities need it enormously. Their votes often decide elections." See also Dewson, "An Aid to the End," II, 187.

41. Dorothy McAlister to Mary Beard, March 13, 1940, WD-DNC, FDRL.

42. Dewson, "An Aid to the End," II, 170; Roosevelt and Hickok, *Ladies of Courage*, 18; Dewson, "An Aid to the End," II, 179.

43. Molly Dewson to Eleanor Roosevelt, June 19, 1936, ER, FDRL; Molly Dewson to Mrs. J. C. Pryor, May 21, 1936, WD-DNC, FDRL; Dewson, "An Aid to the End," II, 127-128.

44. Recommendations of the Democratic Women's Committee for Suggestions on the Democratic Platform, 1936, WD-DNC, FDRL.

45. Ibid.

46. Eleanor Roosevelt, *This Is My Story* (New York, 1937), 354, and Joseph P. Lash, *Eleanor and Franklin* (New York, 1971), 390, describe the 1924 convention; Molly Dewson to Mrs. Bennett Champ Clark, May 21, 1936, WD-DNC, FDRL.

47. Molly Dewson to Eleanor Roosevelt, June 19, 1936, ER, FDRL; Molly

Dewson to Mrs. Bennett Champ Clark, May 21, 1936, WD-DNC, FDRL.

48. Dewson, "An Aid to the End," II, 129-135. The story appeared under the by-line of Bess Furman of the Associated Press, close friend of Eleanor Roosevelt and many of the women in the network.

49. Molly Dewson to Charl O. Williams, July 10, 1936, WD-DNC, FDRL.

50. Molly Dewson to Dorothy McAlister, June 5, 1940, WD-DNC, FDRL.

51. Molly Dewson to W. Forbes Morgan, January 17, 1936, WD-DNC, FDRL; Molly Dewson, "What the Women Could and Should Do for the Democratic Party," *Democratic Digest*, March 1935; Mary T. Norton form letter, August 2, 1937, WD-DNC, FDRL.

52. Molly Dewson, "Work of the Women's Division, Campaign of 1936," Dewson papers, FDRL.

53. Anna Dickie Olesen to Molly Dewson, October 2, 1936, WD-DNC, FDRL.

54. Marion Glass Banister to Gladys Tillett, October 29, 1936, Banister papers, LC; Molly Dewson to Mary Anderson, October 21, 1936, WD-DNC, FDRL.

55. Molly Dewson to Lucy Somerville Howorth, October 13, 1936, Lucy Somerville Howorth papers, Schlesinger.

56. Marion Glass Banister to Gladys Tillett, October 29, 1936, Banister papers, LC; Nellie Tayloe Ross to Molly Dewson, August 10, 1936, Banister papers, LC.

57. Molly Dewson to Ruth Bryan Owen, March 31, 1936, WD-DNC, FDRL.

58. Molly Dewson to Eleanor Roosevelt, July 23, 1936, ER, FDRL.

59. Eleanor Roosevelt to Molly Dewson, September 21, 1936, ER, FDRL; Molly Dewson to Eleanor Roosevelt, September 15, 1936, ER, FDRL.

60. See, in succession, Ruth Bryan Owen to Molly Dewson, September 8, 1936; September 15, 1936; October 10, 1936, all in ER, FDRL; note from Eleanor Roosevelt on letter from Molly Dewson to Eleanor Roosevelt, October 13, 1936, ER, FDRL.

61. Molly Dewson to Annie Olesen, November 12, 1932, quoted in Dewson, "An Aid to the End," I, 72; Perkins, OHC, III, 474, 476-477.

62. Molly Dewson to Lorena Hickok, November 21, 1952, Dewson papers, Schlesinger. This letter supplied background for the book *Ladies of Courage* by Hickok and Eleanor Roosevelt.

63. Molly Dewson to Lorena Hickok, November 21, 1952, Dewson papers, Schlesinger. See also Molly Dewson, "Our Part in the Campaign of 1936," *Democratic Digest*, December 1936.

64. Dewson, "An Aid to the End," II, 145.

65. Mary LaDame to Molly Dewson, November 18, 1936, WD-DNC, FDRL.

66. Dewson, "An Aid to the End," I, 140.

5. WOMEN AND SOCIAL WELFARE POLICY

1. Mary W. Dewson, "An Aid to the End" (unpublished autobiography, 1949), I, 82, in Mary Dewson papers, Schlesinger Library, Radcliffe College. The occasion was a lunch, a reunion of sorts, at Washington's Cosmos Club in 1948,

attended by Perkins, Dewson, Clara Beyer, and Arthur Altmeyer.

2. William E. Leuchtenberg, *Franklin D. Roosevelt and the New Deal, 1932-1940* (New York, 1963), 57-58. For an excellent discussion of the NRA and its relation to the rest of the New Deal, see Ellis W. Hawley, *The New Deal and the Problem of Monopoly* (Princeton, 1966), 17-18.

3. Margie Neal, "Brief History of Women's Section, NRA," NRA 1934 memorandum, found in Eleanor Roosevelt papers (hereafter cited as ER), Franklin D. Roosevelt Library (hereafter cited as FDRL); E. R. Clement, "Women in the NRA," *Democratic Digest*, October 1934, 9; Eleanor Roosevelt, *It's Up to the Women* (New York, 1933), 248-257.

4. Bernard Bellush, *The Failure of the NRA* (New York, 1975), 39-40.

5. Frances Perkins, *The Roosevelt I Knew* (New York, 1946), 233.

6. Bellush, *Failure of the NRA*, 38-39; Rose Schneiderman (with Lucy Goldwaithe), *All for One* (New York, 1967), 9.

7. Schneiderman, *All for One*, 9.

8. Ibid., 203-206; Eleanor Roosevelt to Rose Schneiderman, February 26, 1934, ER, FDRL; Schneiderman, *All for One*, 197.

9. See, for example, Bellush's assessment, *Failure of the NRA*, 38-39.

10. Perkins, *The Roosevelt I Knew*, 209.

11. "Bulletin of the New York Women's Trade Union League," October 1933 and January 1934, National Women's Trade Union League papers, Schlesinger; Lucy Mason, *To Win These Rights: A Personal Story of the C.I.O. in the South* (New York, 1952), 14-16; Molly Dewson to Eleanor Roosevelt, February 5, 1934, ER, FDRL.

12. Mason, *To Win These Rights*, 14-16; Schneiderman, *All for One*, 9; "Bulletin of the New York Women's Trade Union League," October 1933 and January 1934, National Women's Trade Union League papers, Schlesinger; Molly Dewson to Franklin Roosevelt, December 14, 1933, ER, FDRL. Dewson had sent copies of this letter to Louis Howe, Eleanor Roosevelt, and Clara Beyer.

13. Eleanor Roosevelt to Hugh Johnson, December 15, 1933, ER, FDRL; Eleanor Roosevelt to Hugh Johnson, January 17, 1934, ER, FDRL.

14. Mary Elizabeth Pidgeon, "Employed Women Under NRA Codes," *Women's Bureau Bulletin*, no. 130 (Washington, 1935), 2, 111, 131-132.

15. Memo, Mary Anderson to Eleanor Roosevelt, February 19, 1934, Mary Anderson papers, Schlesinger.

16. Mary Anderson to Mary Dreier Robins, January 3, 1934, Anderson papers, Schlesinger; Mary Anderson, *Woman at Work: The Autobiography of Mary Anderson, As Told to Mary N. Winslow* (Minneapolis, 1951), 143-146; Schneiderman, *All for One*, 9.

17. *Women's Bureau Bulletin*, no. 130, 2. The improvement in women's wages led to a corresponding narrowing in the pay differential between men's and women's wages.

18. Many historians and participants have noted the general debt that the New Deal owed to the past thirty years of agitation. Molly Dewson made this a major theme in her autobiography: see "An Aid to the End," I, 17. Among historians, Clarke Chambers has emphasized the cumulative effect of social reform agitation: see *Seedtime of Reform: American Social Service and Social Action, 1918-*

1933 (Minneapolis, 1963), 182. Josephine Goldmark observed, "The truth is that New Deal legislation did not spring full blown. Its roots lie in the preceeding thirty years or more." Quoted in J. Stanley Lemons, *The Woman Citizen: Social Feminism in the 1920s* (Urbana, 1973), 244.

19. *The Reminiscences of Frances Perkins* (1955), V, 369, in The Oral History Collection of Columbia University (hereafter cited as Perkins, OHC); Perkins, *The Roosevelt I Knew*, 206; Johnson's remark quoted in Persia Campbell, *Consumer Representation in the New Deal* (New York, 1940), 31.

20. See George Martin, *Madam Secretary: Frances Perkins* (Boston, 1976), 269, 278-279, for background on the friendship between Perkins and Rumsey and their decision to share a home in Georgetown, as well as Rumsey's wide-ranging contacts in official Washington; Perkins, OHC, V, 496.

21. Perkins, OHC, V, 382-384, 574-575. See also Martin, *Madam Secretary*, 329.

22. Campbell, *Consumer Representation*, 28-29, 56-58.

23. Ibid., 40, 59-66; Bellush, *Failure of the NRA*, 39-40.

24. Perkins, *The Roosevelt I Knew*, 206-207; Hawley, *The New Deal and the Problem of Monopoly*, 75-76; Bellush, *Failure of the NRA*, 46-47, 64-65, 68-69; Campbell, *Consumer Representation*, 53-54.

25. On the White House Consumers' Conference, see Campbell, *Consumer Representation*, 66. This conference led to the famous "shouting interview" between Leon Henderson and Hugh Johnson of the NRA.

26. For the membership of the Consumers' Advisory Board, see Bellush, *Failure of the NRA*, 39-40; for material on the Consumer Councils, see Hawley, *The New Deal and the Problem of Monopoly*, 75-76, and Sue Shelton White papers, Schlesinger; Campbell, *Consumer Representation*, 42-44, 47-48, covers the areas in which Emily Newell Blair worked.

27. Campbell, *Consumer Representation*, 39, 82-84.

28. Molly Dewson to Eleanor Roosevelt, December 27, 1934, and Dewson to Roosevelt, January 9, 1935, ER, FDRL; memo, Eleanor Roosevelt to Franklin Roosevelt, January 2, 1935, ER, FDRL; memo, Franklin Roosevelt to Eleanor Roosevelt, January 12, 1935, ER, FDRL. Frances Perkins's letter was quoted in full by Molly Dewson in her letter to Eleanor Roosevelt, January 9, 1935; see also Eleanor Roosevelt to Frances Perkins, January 19, 1935, ER, FDRL.

29. Emily Newell Blair to Molly Dewson, July 12, 1935, Women's Division of the Democratic National Committee papers (hereafter cited as WD-DNC), FDRL.

30. Campbell, *Consumer Representation*, 82-84; Molly Dewson to Eleanor Roosevelt, August 30, 1935, ER, FDRL.

31. Dewson, "An Aid to the End," I, 32-33.

32. Perkins, *The Roosevelt I Knew*, 152, 288; Dewson, "An Aid to the End," II, 200.

33. Dewson, "An Aid to the End," I, 55-56.

34. Dewson, "An Aid to the End," I, 17. For background, see Chambers, *Seedtime of Reform*, 182, 257-259.

35. Leuchtenberg, *F.D.R. and the New Deal*, 98, 103-106; Chambers, *Seedtime of Reform*, 257.

36. The Supreme Court had already struck down two federal child labor laws

as unconstitutional, and getting a nationwide social insurance system through the Court looked very difficult. In this context, a conversation that Frances Perkins had at a Washington tea proved very illuminating. The tea happened to be at the home of Justice and Mrs. Harlan Stone. Perkins chatted with the Supreme Court justice about how difficult it was going to be to draw up a constitutional social security bill. Justice Stone commented that the taxing power of the federal government was indeed quite sweeping, a hint that that approach might get by the Court (Arthur Altmeyer, *The Formative Years of Social Security* [Madison, 1966], 15, 20).

37. Perkins, *The Roosevelt I Knew*, 278-281.

38. Edwin E. Witte, *The Development of the Social Security Act* (Madison, 1962), 51-53; Martin, *Madam Secretary*, 350.

39. Witte, *Development of Social Security*, 63. The report was published by the Social Security Board as *Social Security in America: The Factual Background of the Social Security Act as Summarized from Staff Reports to the Committee on Economic Security* (Washington, 1937).

40. Martin, *Madam Secretary*, 353. Mary Harriman Rumsey had died just a week earlier on December 18, 1934, a great personal loss to Perkins. In early November, Perkins had received word while in a meeting with the Committee on Economic Security that Rumsey had been badly injured in a fall from her horse; Rumsey subsequently developed pneumonia and died a month later.

41. Leuchtenberg, *F.D.R. and the New Deal*, 131.

42. Witte, *Development of Social Security*, 162-165. See also *The Reminiscences of Katharine Lenroot* (1965), 84, in The Oral History Collection of Columbia University (hereafter cited as Lenroot, OHC), which treats Lenroot's role in the Social Security Act extensively.

Mothers' pensions were designed to aid women who became dependent through no fault of their own. The thrust of mothers' pensions was preventive: give relief to allow women to stay at home rather than working, keep the family intact, and thus head off the problems of delinquency before they occur. Mothers' pensions were also a reaction against the institutionalization of children in almshouses and orphanages: a home environment, even if supported by a government dole, was preferable to having children grow up unsupervised while mothers worked. Many women in the network, especially the women in the Children's Bureau, had long given high priority to laws along the lines of mothers' pensions. For more information, see Chambers, *Seedtime of Reform*, and Roy Lubove, *The Struggle for Social Security, 1900-1935* (Cambridge, Mass., 1968).

43. Ellen Sullivan Woodward speech, "Women's Stake in Social Security," September 1, 1940, Ellen Woodward papers, Schlesinger. The emphasis of the women in the network on preserving the family and keeping the mother at home with her children at all costs shows their limited commitment to work outside the home for the majority of American women. Women in the network enjoyed their own careers, especially if they did not have children at home, but they still held fairly traditional attitudes when it came to other women.

44. Molly Dewson to Eleanor Roosevelt, April 10, 1935, ER, FDRL.

45. Martin, *Madam Secretary*, 98.

46. Perkins, *The Roosevelt I Knew*, 291; Martin, *Madam Secretary*, 355.

47. Altmeyer, *Formative Years of Social Security*, 4, 36, 41. For more information on the actual Children's Bureau roles, see Lenroot, OHC, and Eveline M. Burns, *Toward Social Security: An Explanation of the Social Security Act and a Survey of the Larger Issues* (New York, 1936).

48. Josephine Roche to Eleanor Roosevelt, April 10, 1937, ER, FDRL. For background on this committee, see Altmeyer, *Formative Years of Social Security*, 93-95, and Martha M. Eliot, "The Work of the Interdepartmental Committee to Coordinate Health and Welfare Activities," in *Proceedings of the National Conference of Social Work* (New York, 1939), 101-110.

49. Perkins, OHC, VII, 16-17. For discussion of the Walsh-Healey Act, see Frances Perkins, *The Roosevelt I Knew*, 253-255, and Martin, *Madam Secretary*, 379-381.

50. Perkins, *The Roosevelt I Knew*, 249, 255; Martin, *Madam Secretary*, 387.

51. Perkins, *The Roosevelt I Knew*, 257.

52. Lenroot, OHC, 141.

53. Perkins, *The Roosevelt I Knew*, 258-261.

54. Eleanor Roosevelt and Lorena Hickok, *Ladies of Courage* (New York, 1954), 165.

55. Molly Dewson to Clara M. Beyer, March 19, 1937, Clara M. Beyer papers, Schlesinger; for the Women's Division involvement, see Harriett Elliott to Gladys Tillett, February 13, 1935, WD-DNC, FDRL: "Miss Dewson is here today and we have been discussing ways and means to help in the Child Labor Amendment drive."

56. For an excellent discussion of the bill and its political implications, see James T. Patterson, *Congressional Conservatism and the New Deal* (Lexington, Kentucky, 1967), 214, 242-246.

57. Rose Schneiderman to Eleanor Roosevelt, October 28, 1938, ER, FDRL; Martin, *Madam Secretary*, 394.

58. Ellen Sullivan Woodward to Chloe Owings, February 19, 1936, Women's Work Section, WPA General Subject File, National Archives.

59. Eleanor Roosevelt, "My Day," November 14, 1936; Eleanor Roosevelt to Harry Hopkins, September 25, 1935, ER, FDRL.

60. Harry Hopkins quoted in speech by Ellen Woodward, September 19, 1935, in Dewson papers, FDRL. See also Donald S. Howard, *The WPA and Federal Relief Policy* (New York, 1943), 278, and William McDonald, *Federal Relief Administration and the Arts* (Columbus, Ohio, 1969), 42. The Civilian Conservation Corps was the only New Deal program officially limited to men.

61. FERA Press Release, November 16, 1933, FERA Old Subject File, National Archives; for Eleanor Roosevelt's role, see Ellen Woodward to Mr. Bookman, November 17, 1933, FERA Old Subject File, National Archives, and Edith Helm to Ellen Woodward, November 14, 1933, ER, FDRL.

62. FERA Press Release, November 16, 1933, found in White House Conference File, FERA Old Subject File, National Archives.

63. Federal Emergency Relief Administration, *Proceedings of the Conference on Emergency Needs of Women* (Washington, 1933), 8-9.

64. Ibid., 9-16, 37. Terms like "suitable" or "acceptable" are used as they would have been in the 1930s. Except in a few enlightened cases, the administrators never considered women suitable for heavy (or even light) construction work or manual labor.

65. Ibid., 11-14, 15-21, 27-29, 31.

66. McDonald, *F.R.A. and the Arts*, 46.

67. Ellen Woodward to Edith Helm, November 11, 1933, ER, FDRL.

68. Ellen Woodward to Eleanor Roosevelt, April 27, 1935, ER, FDRL.

69. Ellen Woodward, "This New Federal Relief," *Independent Woman*, 13 (April 1934), 104, 126; McDonald, *F.R.A. and the Arts*, 64.

70. *Women's Bureau Newsletter*, 15 (December 1, 1935), Schlesinger Library. See also "A Work Program for Women—A Brief Statement of Basic Theories and Working Principles—FERA," early 1935. This copy was one that Ellen Woodward had left with Molly Dewson, to be sent on to Eleanor Roosevelt (Dewson to Eleanor Roosevelt, February 20, 1935, ER, FDRL).

71. For good summaries of these changes, see Theodore E. Whiting and T. J. Woofter, Jr., *Summary of Relief and Federal Work Program Statistics, 1933-1940* (Washington, 1941), 2-16; and National Resources Planning Board, *Security, Work, and Relief Policies* (Washington, 1942), 30-33.

72. McDonald, *F.R.A. and the Arts*, 99-100, 164-168.

73. *Security, Work, and Relief Policies*, 128; *Women's Bureau Newsletter*, 16 (March 1, 1936), Schlesinger; report on Women's Work under the WPA in the Western area from Dorothy Nyswander to Eleanor Roosevelt, September 29, 1935, ER, FDRL. There is never any reference to men being employed in these sewing rooms.

74. Howard, *The WPA and Federal Relief Policy*, 279; Nyswander report to Eleanor Roosevelt, September 29, 1935; Howard, *The WPA and Federal Relief Policy*, 279n.

75. Howard, *The WPA and Federal Relief Policy*, 279-280.

76. *Security, Work, and Relief Policies*, 118. Figures from the WPA show that women did make up a more permanent element of the relief population than men. In one study, the median number of months of continuous WPA employment for women was 14.6, whereas for men it was 12.2. Only 16.1 percent of men had been on the WPA continually for more than three years, while 20.5 percent of women had been (Howard, *The WPA and Federal Relief Policy*, 283-284).

77. "Women at Work: A Century of Industrial Change," *Women's Bureau Bulletin*, no. 161 (Washington, 1939), 77.

78. Ibid., 75; Ellen Woodward memorandum to Harry Hopkins, January 22, 1936, in WD-DNC, FDRL.

79. Howard, *The WPA and Federal Relief Policy*, 282n.

80. Memorandum, May 31, 1933, Women's Camps Section, FERA Old Subject File, National Archives.

81. Hilda Worthington Smith to Marion Dickerman, October 11, 1933, ER, FDRL; Hilda Worthington Smith, "The Remembered Way" (unpublished autobiography, 1936), 850, in Hilda Worthington Smith papers, Schlesinger. The Bryn Mawr School for Working Women had begun in 1921 under the leadership of M. Carey Thomas, Mary Anderson, and Hilda Worthington Smith; Smith

served as its director from 1921 to 1934. Students were selected from the trade union movement, the WTUL, and the YWCA, and given scholarships to attend the sessions. Once at Bryn Mawr, they attended classes in economics, government, history, and the history of the trade union movement, and they also learned practical skills like public speaking and composition. Many graduates of the program became trade union leaders, and the Bryn Mawr experiment spawned similar attempts at Barnard (1927-1934), and the Vineyard Shore School for Women Workers in Industry (1929-1934). Hilda Smith seems to have envisioned the camps for unemployed women along similar lines: training in history and sociology, experimentation in communal living and democratic organization, rather than vocational training. For more background, see Chambers, *Seedtime of Reform*, 80-81, and Smith, "The Remembered Way."

82. Hilda Worthington Smith, "Report of Resident Schools and Camps for Unemployed Women, Summer of 1934," found in Smith papers, Schlesinger; Elsie George, "The Women Appointees of the Roosevelt and Truman Administrations" (Ph.D. dissertation, American University, 1972), 198-199.

83. Smith, "The Remembered Way," 850-851.

84. Hilda Worthington Smith to Eleanor Roosevelt, May 17, 1934, ER, FDRL.

85. Smith, "1934 Report," 10-13.

86. See Hilda Worthington Smith to Eleanor Roosevelt, August 2, 1935, ER, FDRL; and Smith to Roosevelt, March 17, 1936, ER, FDRL, enclosing minutes from the March 4 meeting of the Advisory Committee on Educational Camps for Unemployed Women. See also Dorothy de Schwenitz to Mary Anderson, December 2, 1936, in Frances Perkins Department of Labor files, National Archives.

It was appropriate for the camps to be put under the National Youth Administration, since it was the only government agency offering employment to out-of-school and out-of-work young women (Eleanor Roosevelt to Mrs. Edward Costigan, 1939, ER, FDRL). Unfortunately, older women (those aged twenty-five to forty), who might profit just as much from the camps, were no longer eligible (Hilda Worthington Smith to Eleanor Roosevelt, May 15, 1940, Hilda Worthington Smith papers, FDRL).

87. Hilda Worthington Smith to Eleanor Roosevelt, March 17, 1936, ER, FDRL.

88. Hilda Worthington Smith to Eleanor Roosevelt, May 15, 1940, Hilda Worthington Smith papers, FDRL. Here is what Smith said: "I was not given a chance at that time to present full and accurate figures of expense, but I was convinced that if the average figures had been discussed, rather than the highest costs —such as those at Camp Jane Addams—the expense for each girl, which was less than $30 a month, would not have been considered too high a cost for the undoubted benefits the girls received." Hilda Worthington Smith was suggesting the revival of the camps on a sounder economic basis in 1940.

89. Ibid.

6. A GENERATION ON THE WANE

1. William Leuchtenberg, *Franklin D. Roosevelt and the New Deal, 1932-1940* (New York, 1963), 167 (chapter title). See also page 196: "Franklin Roose-

velt's fortunes were at high tide."

2. Mary T. Norton, *1936 Proceedings of the Democratic National Convention*, quoted in Elsie George, "The Women Appointees of the Roosevelt and Truman Administrations" (Ph.D. dissertation, American University, 1972), 54.

3. James T. Patterson, *Congressional Conservatism and the New Deal* (Lexington, Kentucky, 1967), 333.

4. William McDonald, *Federal Relief Administration and the Arts* (Columbus, Ohio, 1969), 27, 308. Florence Kerr succeeded Ellen Woodward as head of Women's and Professional Projects. Kerr had a B.A. from Grinnell (1912) and had been active in Red Cross work during World War I. From 1922 to 1927 she taught in the English department at Grinnell, and she lectured from 1932 to 1935 on literature throughout the Midwest. She had joined the FERA as regional director of Women's Activities in the Middle West in 1935, and held the same job with the WPA until she came to Washington in 1939.

5. McDonald, *F.R.A. and the Arts*, 168. There were persistent rumors in 1937 that the Women's Bureau was to be abolished, which prompted Mary Winslow of the National Women's Trade Union League to write to Frances Perkins on January 15, 1937: "I am convinced from our conversation with you that it is not your plan to abolish the Bureau and I am writing to ask if you can give us any help in running down this rumour and putting a stop to it" (Mary Anderson papers, Schlesinger Library, Radcliffe College). See also Mary Anderson to Mary Van Kleeck, January 8, 1937, Anderson papers, Schlesinger. Molly Dewson was so concerned about keeping the Children's Bureau intact in 1939 that she wrote a long note to Franklin Roosevelt about it on her Christmas card (Dewson papers, Franklin D. Roosevelt Library [hereafter cited as FDRL]).

6. Molly Dewson to Eleanor Roosevelt, October 29, 1935, Eleanor Roosevelt papers (hereafter cited as ER), FDRL.

7. Emma Guffey Miller radio speech, March 14, 1936, Emma Guffey Miller papers, Schlesinger.

8. Genevieve Parkhurst, "Is Feminism Dead?" *Harper's Magazine*, 170 (May 1935), 735-745; Dorothy McConnell, *Women, War, and Fascism* (American League Against War and Fascism, New York, 1936), 6-7; Eleanor Roosevelt, "My Day," February 1, 1936; McConnell, *Women, War, and Fascism*, 6. There had been a decline in the number of women elected to public offices in the 1930s (as opposed to women in appointive office), and this trend worried many of the women in the network because they feared women were losing interest in public affairs. See "My Day," December 28, 1938.

9. Mary Anderson, *Woman at Work: The Autobiography of Mary Anderson, As Told to Mary N. Winslow* (Minneapolis, 1951), 210-214.

10. Dorothy McAlister speech, "Why Women Should Go into Politics," 1940, Women's Division of the Democratic National Committee papers (hereafter cited as WD-DNC), FDRL. See also Bess Furman, "What the New Deal Has Done for Women," in the *Democratic Digest*, June-July 1940, which explicitly contrasts the fascist decline compared to the "large and vital body of women administrators" who had been added in the 1930s in the United States.

11. Ellen Sullivan Woodward speech, "Business Women in a Democracy,"

October 21, 1939, Ellen Sullivan Woodward papers, Schlesinger; Lucy Somerville Howorth speech, "The Trained Woman's Responsibility for Leadership," May 15, 1937, Lucy Somerville Howorth papers, Schlesinger. For an interesting discussion of women's roles under fascism, communism, and democracy, see the first chapter of Mary R. Beard, *Woman as Force in History: A Study in Traditions and Realities* (New York, 1946).

12. Ellen Sullivan Woodward to Carolyn Wolfe, September 8, 1936, WD-DNC, FDRL; *The Reminiscences of Frances Perkins* (1955), VII, 380-381, in The Oral History Collection of Columbia University (hereafter cited as Perkins, OHC); Eleanor Roosevelt to Mary Amend, January 23, 1937, ER, FDRL.

13. See, for example, Molly Dewson to Eleanor Roosevelt, December 11, 1936, President's Secretary's File (hereafter cited as PSF), FDRL. Dewson's letter makes one a little suspicious of statements like this in Molly Dewson's autobiography: "Released from harness, I was thoroughly enjoying the summer of 1937 in Castine, Maine, when in August one of the White House staff telephoned me asking whether my legal address was New York or Maine. Something was brewing. Soon the President called me, saying, 'I am sending your name to the Senate for confirmation as a Member of the Social Security Board. I want you to come right down to be sworn in and then you can return for a few days to settle your affairs.' 'Heel Fido' is my comment on FDR's remarks" (Mary W. Dewson, "An Aid to the End" [unpublished autobiography, 1949], II, 192, in Dewson papers, Schlesinger).

14. Elinore (Geno) Herrick to Eleanor Roosevelt, August 25, 1937, ER, FDRL.

15. Molly Dewson to Franklin Roosevelt, December 7, 1938, PSF, FDRL.

16. Molly Dewson to Eleanor Roosevelt, July 6, 1939, ER, FDRL; Dorothy McAlister to Franklin Roosevelt, August 30, 1939, WD-DNC, FDRL.

17. Speech by Molly Dewson, 1936, Dewson papers, FDRL; Molly Dewson to Eleanor Roosevelt, November 5, 1935, ER, FDRL; Molly Dewson to Eleanor Roosevelt, December 23, 1938, ER, FDRL; Marguerite J. Fisher and Betty Whitehead, "Women and National Party Organization," *The American Political Science Review*, 38 (October 1944), 897-899.

18. Joseph P. Lash, *Eleanor and Franklin* (New York, 1971), 606-607, provides a convenient summary; see also Emma Guffey Miller to Eleanor Roosevelt, March 26, 1937, Emma Guffey Miller papers, Schlesinger; Miller to Eleanor Roosevelt, July 12, 1937, and Roosevelt's reply, July 15, 1937, Miller papers, Schlesinger.

19. Molly Dewson to Eleanor Roosevelt, June 22, 1937, ER, FDRL. In another letter from April 17, 1937, Dewson had complained to Eleanor Roosevelt: "But with Emma Guffey Miller hot on my trail and theirs they will be sunk unless *you* help. The men are foolish to tolerate Emma. They could tell Jo Guffey to make her confine herself to Penn." (ER, FDRL).

20. Nellie Tayloe Ross to Eleanor Roosevelt, September 25, 1939, ER, FDRL.

21. Dewson, "An Aid to the End," II, 62-68. This is exactly what happened in the 1950s. When the Women's Division was integrated into the Democratic National Committee in 1953, the men took over the *Democratic Digest*. According to India Edwards, the men wanted to turn it into a political *New Yorker*. They

were quite unsuccessful, and the *Democratic Digest* met its demise in the mid-1950s. See India Edwards, *Pulling No Punches: Memoirs of a Woman in Politics* (New York, 1977), 203; see also the Epilogue.

22. Perkins, OHC, VII, 314.

23. Molly Dewson to Dorothy McAlister, March 25, 1937, WD-DNC, FDRL.

24. Eleanor Roosevelt to Molly Dewson, May 18, 1937, ER, FDRL.

25. Grace Abbott left the Children's Bureau in 1934 and died in 1939; Emily Newell Blair left the government after her stint at the NRA and was only infrequently mentioned in Democratic women's articles; Ruth Bryan Owen left her position as a diplomat and active roles in politics after her remarriage in 1936; Josephine Roche left the Treasury Department in 1937; Mary Harriman Rumsey died in 1934; Rose Schneiderman left Washington to become the New York State Secretary of Labor in 1937; Carolyn Wolfe left the Women's Division in 1936 to return to Utah. The rest of the twenty-eight women in the network were still in government at least until the early 1940s.

26. Marion Glass Banister to Lucille Foster McMillin, February 22, 1944, Marion Glass Banister papers, Library of Congress (hereafter cited as LC); Marion Glass Banister to Molly Dewson, January 11, 1939, Banister papers, LC.

27. George, "Women Appointees," 81; Molly Dewson to Eleanor Roosevelt, April 17, 1937, ER, FDRL.

28. George Martin, *Madam Secretary: Frances Perkins* (Boston, 1976), 418, 444-445. According to Martin, this probably was one reason why Perkins was not given a prominent role in the war effort either, although she did work behind the scenes and on various committees.

29. Molly Dewson to Eleanor Roosevelt, November 5, 1935, ER, FDRL; Lash, *Eleanor and Franklin*, 573. This problem became worse during World War II, according to Frances Perkins in her autobiography (*The Roosevelt I Knew* [New York, 1946], 375) and in a letter to Harry Hopkins, June 17, 1944, Frances Perkins Papers (hereafter cited as FPP), Columbia University.

30. Molly Dewson to Eleanor Roosevelt, January 27, 1939, ER, FDRL; Dewson to Roosevelt, April 17, 1940, ER, FDRL; Roosevelt to Dewson, April 19, 1940, ER, FDRL.

31. Eleanor Roosevelt to Molly Dewson, March 19, 1941, ER, FDRL.

32. Perkins, OHC, IX, 130. Perkins made these notes of a phone conversation she had with Franklin Roosevelt in November, 1940 on this subject: " 'Now Willkie made us a lot of votes by attacking you and indicating that no woman was good enough to be in the Cabinet. I want to keep a woman in the Cabinet, and there isn't any other woman fit to be Secretary of Labor. Now, that's that, and don't talk about it anymore.' "

33. Martin, *Madam Secretary*, 431; Perkins, OHC, II, 318; *Democratic Digest*, August 1940. See also Dorothy McAlister to Eleanor Roosevelt, July 30, 1940, ER, FDRL, sending her a copy of the platform recommendations of the Women's Advisory Committee.

34. Perkins, OHC, III, 472. She was referring to India Edwards, head of the Women's Division from 1948 to 1952.

35. Molly Dewson to Eleanor Roosevelt, April 17, 1937, ER, FDRL; Roosevelt to Dewson, August 6, 1940, quoted in Dewson, "An Aid to the End," II, 201-202.

36. Molly Dewson to Eleanor Roosevelt, November 10, 1940, ER, FDRL.

37. Gladys Tillett to John Fischer, May 31, 1941, WD-DNC, FDRL, discusses the National Defense Surveys; the military image is from the *Democratic Digest*, July 1939, 8. For a good sense of how women in government and politics were preparing for war, see any issue from 1940 of the *Democratic Digest*; see also Ellen Sullivan Woodward radio speech, "Woman's Place in National Defense," April 9, 1941, Woodward papers, Schlesinger.

38. *Democratic Digest*, June-July 1940, 20; Molly Dewson, "Shall We Sell Our Birthright for a Mess of Potage?" *Democratic Digest*, January 1942, 7.

39. Eleanor Roosevelt, *This I Remember* (New York, 1949), 313. William Chafe, *The American Woman* (New York, 1972) devotes more than a quarter of the book to World War II and its impact, and the war's expansion of women's economic roles is a critical part of his argument. Lois Banner, *Women in Modern America* (New York, 1974) also gives the war a large role in twentieth-century American women's history. See also Beard, *Woman as Force in History*; and Leila J. Rupp, *Mobilizing Women for War: German and American Propaganda, 1939-1945* (Princeton, 1978). The following is not meant to be a comprehensive account of women's roles in World War II. Women's experiences are sketched briefly to show the contrast to the 1930s.

40. Eleanor Roosevelt and Lorena Hickok, *Ladies of Courage* (New York, 1954), 22.

41. Eleanor Roosevelt, *This I Remember*, 230-232, 240; Perkins, *The Roosevelt I Knew*, 356. Elliott represented consumer interests on the board, and she was assisted by Dr. Caroline Ware, an economist and consumer expert.

42. Roosevelt and Hickok, *Ladies of Courage*, 23; Anderson, *Woman at Work*, 249; Chafe, *The American Woman*, 152. The women he was referring to were Mary Van Kleeck, prominent social worker, and Minnie Maffett, head of the National Federation of Business and Professional Women.

43. Roosevelt and Hickok, *Ladies of Courage*, 249.

44. Ibid., 23; Anderson, *Woman at Work*, 249.

45. Anderson, *Woman at Work*, 249-250; Mary Anderson, "War History," draft of article on the wartime work of the Women's Bureau, 1944, Anderson papers, Schlesinger; Mary Anderson to Rose Schneiderman, October 2, 1942, Anderson papers, Schlesinger. The letter also contains a lengthy discussion of Jo Coffin's illness, which had forced her to leave the Government Printing Office and retire to Tucson. Coffin died in early 1943.

46. Chafe, *The American Woman*, 153-154; see also Anderson, "War History."

47. Anderson, *Woman at Work*, 246-254; Katie Louchheim, *By the Political Sea* (Garden City, N.Y., 1970), 17-21; Roosevelt and Hickok, *Ladies of Courage*, 222-230; Beard, *Woman as Force in History*, 50-51; Roosevelt and Hickok, *Ladies of Courage*, 198-205.

48. Mary Anderson wrote: "I knew, having had the experience of World War

I, that women would be called upon to enter every industry . . . It was very interesting to me and a bit disconcerting to find that another generation had grown up knowing practically nothing about the experiences of the last war . . . No one seemed to know anything about what women had done in World War I" (*Woman at Work*, 246-247).

49. "Dear Mrs. Roosevelt," *Democratic Digest*, February 1938, 9.

50. Martin, *Madam Secretary*, 210-211. As Martin says in his notes, Perkins's remark was so widely quoted that its original appearance has been lost. Perkins talks quite a lot in her oral history memoir about the wide opportunities that women had always enjoyed in New England, and how this had strongly influenced her perceptions: "I had been brought up in a group where the women were very well-treated, very well-advantaged and where they had their own property" (Perkins, OHC, I, 180; see also Perkins, OHC, III, 490-491). Lucy Somerville Howorth described Perkins as someone who "generally took the position that the time had passed to struggle for the advancement of women as women. She could be pushed out of this position when necessary; there were too many women around who had on occasion rallied to help her" (Lucy Somerville Howorth, "Memo to Accompany Three Clippings," 1958, Lucy Somerville Howorth papers, Schlesinger).

51. For an interesting treatment of how women reformers were trapped by the very stereotypes they were trying to subvert, see Jill Conway, "Women Reformers and American Culture, 1870-1930," in Jean E. Friedman and William G. Shade, eds., *Our American Sisters: Women in American Life and Thought* (Boston, 1976), 301-312.

52. See Carl Degler, "Revolution without Ideology: The Changing Place of Women in America," in Robert Jay Lifton, ed., *The Woman in America* (Boston, 1965), 193-210; and Ann Gordon, Mari Jo Buhle, and Nancy Schrom, "Women in American Society: An Historical Contribution," *Radical America* (July-August 1971), 43, 52.

53. Louchheim, *By the Political Sea*, 123; Roosevelt and Hickok, *Ladies of Courage*, 204-205. Betty Friedan also talks about changing expectations for women by placing the "feminine mystique" as early as the 1940s. One example she gives is her own decision to turn down a fellowship for graduate work in psychology in order to marry and raise children (*The Feminine Mystique* [New York, 1963], 62-63).

54. Mary Anderson retired in 1944; Jo Coffin died in 1943; Dewson had retired in 1938; Daisy Harriman retired after returning from Norway in 1941; Dorothy McAlister left the Women's Division in 1940; Caroline O'Day died in 1943; Sue Shelton White died in 1943. These changes are in addition to those that occurred in the mid-1930s (see note 25).

55. Anderson, *Woman at Work*, 257; Molly Dewson to Clara Beyer, July 13, 1945, Clara M. Beyer papers, Schlesinger.

56. Frances Perkins to Charles Burlingham, May 7, 1945, FPP, Columbia. Eleanor Roosevelt's statement was widely reprinted in the press. See the preface to Joseph P. Lash, *Eleanor: The Years Alone* (New York, 1972), 5.

EPILOGUE

1. When the Children's Bureau was disbanded in 1946, Clara Beyer wrote to Pauline and Josephine Goldmark, "Isn't it too bad about the Children's Bureau being broken up? Poor Katharine is heartsick over it. I believe she dreads the future in the Federal Security Administration. She has been given no assurance that her program will go on in a unified fashion. Poor Grace [Abbott] would turn over in her grave if she knew the things going on. I am so glad she is spared it all" (Clara M. Beyer papers, Schlesinger Library, Radcliffe College). The Women's Bureau is still in existence.

2. In fact, it was Oveta Culp Hobby who forced Hoey out. Hoey's position was turned into a patronage one by the Republicans, and when Hoey refused to resign, Hobby fired her. Bess Furman wrote up this incident on page one of the *New York Times*, and it got quite a lot of publicity. Hoey thought this kept Hobby from firing other people (*The Reminiscences of Jane Hoey* [1965], 96-97, in The Oral History Collection of Columbia University).

3. Lucy Somerville Howorth, "Memo to Accompany Three Clippings," 1958, in Lucy Somerville Howorth papers, Schlesinger.

4. Ibid. One example, which Howorth described as "typical" of the efforts of the women, was the campaign to keep Ellen Woodward in a top policy position after the Social Security Board was abolished in 1946. The main tactic was a letter-writing campaign to the President and to the head of the new Federal Security Administration, which was successful in getting Woodward her new job in the Office of International Relations of the FSA. For details of the campaign, see Lucy Somerville Howorth to Lucretia Grady, June 20, 1946, Howorth papers, Schlesinger.

5. India Edwards, *Pulling No Punches: A Memoir of a Woman in Politics* (New York, 1977), 7-8; Elsie George, "The Women Appointees of the Roosevelt and Truman Administrations" (Ph.D. dissertation, American University, 1972), 81-82.

6. Though India Edwards's goals and tactics were quite similar to Molly Dewson's, her career shows the differences in background between her generation and Molly Dewson's. Edwards, born in the late 1890s, had wanted to be a dancer in the 1910s, and then had entered journalism in 1918. She was the society page editor for the Chicago *Tribune* from 1931 to 1942. She lost a husband in World War I and a son in World War II, and began to get involved in politics only in 1944 when she joined the staff of the Women's Division. See Edwards, *Pulling No Punches*.

7. George, "Women Appointees," 83-85; Eleanor Roosevelt and Lorena Hickok, *Ladies of Courage* (New York, 1954), 209-216.

8. Roosevelt and Hickok, *Ladies of Courage*, 221. But appointments of women do not automatically go over well with other women. Lorena Hickok and Eleanor Roosevelt wrote of Clare Booth Luce's nomination: "No appointment was ever greeted with less enthusiasm by members of her own sex" (pp. 230-231).

9. Ibid., 34. The women were put in a "special activities group" which also

included veterans, farmers, labor, and minority groups.

10. Edwards, *Pulling No Punches*, 104; *The Reminiscences of Frances Perkins* (1955), III, 479, in The Oral History Collection of Columbia University; Roosevelt and Hickok, *Ladies of Courage*, 29-31; Edwards, *Pulling No Punches*, 203. India Edwards always blamed herself for not fighting harder, especially to save the *Democratic Digest* for the women.

11. Molly Dewson to Clara Beyer, March 9, 1961, Beyer papers, Schlesinger; Joseph P. Lash, *Eleanor: The Years Alone* (New York, 1972), 312. Emma Guffey Miller was another one who kept up her old ways. She began an August 29, 1964 letter to President Lyndon Johnson by saying, "As one who has grown old in the service of the Democratic party may I tell you, I trust without offense, of the deep disappointment of many thousands of Democratic women . . ." about the omission of the Equal Rights Amendment from the 1964 Democratic platform (Emma Guffey Miller papers, Schlesinger).

12. Jo Freeman, *The Politics of Women's Liberation* (New York, 1975), 52-53, discusses this phenomenon.

13. Edwards, *Pulling No Punches*, 8, 269.

APPENDIX B. GROUP PROFILE AND INDIVIDUAL BIOGRAPHIES

1. Jill Ker Conway, "Grace Abbott," in Edward T. James, ed., *Notable American Women, 1607-1950: A Biographical Dictionary* (Cambridge, Mass., 1971), I, 2-4; Edith Abbott, "Grace Abbott: A Sister's Memoir," *Social Service Review*, 13 (September 1939), 3.

2. Mary Anderson, *Woman at Work: The Autobiography of Mary Anderson, As Told to Mary N. Winslow* (Minneapolis, 1951); Mary Anderson papers, Schlesinger Library, Radcliffe College; Edward T. James, "Mary Anderson," in Barbara Sicherman and Carol Hurd Green, eds., *Notable American Women: The Modern Period* (Cambridge, Mass., 1980), 23-25.

3. Marion Glass Banister papers, Library of Congress; Elsie George, "The Women Appointees of the Roosevelt and Truman Administrations: A Study of Their Impact and Effectiveness" (Ph.D. dissertation, American University, 1972), 224-250.

4. Clara M. Beyer papers, Schlesinger Library; interview with Clara Beyer, 1965, on file at the Historical Office of the Department of Labor, Washington, D.C.

5. *Democratic Bulletin*, March 1933, 11-13; Estelle B. Freedman, "Emily Newell Blair," in John A. Garraty, ed., *Dictionary of American Biography: Supplement Five, 1951-1955* (New York, 1977), 61-63; Margot Jerrard, "Emily Newell Blair," in *Notable American Women: The Modern Period*, 82-83.

6. Obituary in the *Democratic Digest*, April 1943; Emily Newell Blair, "A Who's Who of Women in Washington," *Good Housekeeping*, January 1936, 38-39; "Thumbnail Sketches of Women You Hear About in the New Deal" (hereafter cited as "Thumbnail Sketches"), 1934, prepared by the Women's Division of the Democratic National Committee, found in Molly Dewson papers, Franklin D.

Roosevelt Library (hereafter cited as FDRL).

7. Molly Dewson papers, Schlesinger Library and FDRL; Dewson, "An Aid to the End" (unpublished autobiography, 1949), Dewson papers, Schlesinger; George, "Women Appointees," 98-134; James T. Patterson, "Mary Dewson and the American Minimum Wage Movement," *Labor History*, 5 (Spring 1964), 134-152; Paul C. Taylor, "Mary Dewson," in *Notable American Women: The Modern Period*, 188-191.

8. Florence Jaffray Harriman, *From Pinafores to Politics* (New York, 1923) and *Mission to the North* (Philadelphia, 1941); Florence Jaffray Harriman papers, Library of Congress; *The Reminiscences of Florence Jaffray Harriman* (1950), The Oral History Collection of Columbia University; Susan Ware, "Florence Jaffray Harriman," in *Notable American Women: The Modern Period*, 314-315.

9. *The Reminiscences of Jane Hoey* (1965), The Oral History Collection of Columbia University; obituary, *New York Times*, October 7, 1968; Blanche D. Coll, "Jane Hoey," in *Notable American Women: The Modern Period*, 341-343.

10. Lucy Somerville Howorth papers, Schlesinger Library; *Current Biography*, 12 (October 1951), 14-16.

11. *Democratic Digest*, September 1934; *Democratic Digest*, January 1940; "Thumbnail Sketches."

12. *The Reminiscences of Katharine Lenroot* (1965), The Oral History Collection of Columbia University; Women's Rights Collection, Schlesinger Library; *Democratic Digest*, February 1940.

13. *Democratic Digest*, May 1937; Women's Division, Democratic National Committee papers, FDRL.

14. Emily Newell Blair, "Who's Who . . . in Washington"; "Thumbnail Sketches."

15. Emma Guffey Miller papers, Schlesinger Library; Women's Division, Democratic National Committee papers, FDRL; Keith Melder, "Emma Guffey Miller," in *Notable American Women: The Modern Period*, 476-478.

16. Frances Parkinson Keyes, "Truly Democratic: The Life of Mary T. Norton," *The Delineator*, 122 (March 1933), 12; Eleanor Roosevelt and Lorena Hickok, *Ladies of Courage* (New York, 1954), 152-167; Paul Taylor, "The Entrance of Women into Party Politics: The 1920's" (Ph.D. dissertation, Harvard University, 1966); Carmela A. Karnoutsos, "Mary T. Norton," in *Notable American Women: The Modern Period*, 511-512.

17. Marion Dickerman, "Caroline Love Goodwin O'Day," in *Notable American Women*, II, 648-650; obituaries in the *Democratic Digest*, December-January 1943, and the *New York Times*, January 5, 1943.

18. Paola E. Coletta, "Ruth Bryan Owen Rohde," in *Dictionary of American Biography: Supplement Five, 1951-1955*, 582-583; *Democratic Bulletin*, April 1929; Roosevelt and Hickok, *Ladies of Courage*, 205-206; Louise M. Young, "Ruth Bryan Owen Rohde," in *Notable American Women: The Modern Period*, 591-593.

19. Frances Perkins papers, Columbia University, Schlesinger Library, and FDRL; Frances Perkins, *The Roosevelt I Knew* (New York, 1946); *The Reminis-*

cences of Frances Perkins (1955), The Oral History Collection of Columbia University; George Martin, *Madam Secretary: Frances Perkins* (Boston, 1976); Charles H. Trout, "Frances Perkins," in *Notable American Women: The Modern Period*, 535-539.

20. Roche biography file, Schlesinger Library; Blair, "Who's Who . . . in Washington"; Millard Milburn Rice, "Roosevelt, Roche, and Recovery," *Literary Digest*, 118 (September 1, 1934), 8; obituary in the *New York Times*, July 31, 1976.

21. Eleanor Roosevelt papers, FDRL; Eleanor Roosevelt, *This Is My Story* (New York, 1937) and *This I Remember* (New York, 1949); Joseph P. Lash, *Eleanor and Franklin* (New York, 1971); William H. Chafe, "Anna Eleanor Roosevelt," in *Notable American Women: The Modern Period*, 595-601.

22. Roosevelt and Hickok, *Ladies of Courage*, 112-115; "Thumbnail Sketches"; *Democratic Bulletin*, August 1932; Paul A. Carter, *Another Part of the Twenties* (New York, 1977), 103-112.

23. Persia Campbell, "Mary Harriman Rumsey," in *Notable American Women*, III, 208-209; "Thumbnail Sketches"; obituary in the *New York Times*, December 19, 1934.

24. Rose Schneiderman (with Lucy Goldwaithe), *All for One* (New York, 1967); obituary in the *New York Times*, August 13, 1972; Nancy Schrom Dye, "Rose Schneiderman," in *Notable American Women: The Modern Period*, 631-633.

25. Hilda Worthington Smith papers, Schlesinger Library and FDRL; Hilda Worthington Smith, "The Remembered Way" (unpublished autobiography, 1936), Smith papers, Schlesinger Library; George, "Women Appointees," 185-223.

26. James P. Louis, "Sue Shelton White," in *Notable American Women*, III, 590-592; Sue Shelton White papers, Schlesinger Library; James P. Louis, "Sue Shelton White and the Woman Suffrage Movement in Tennessee, 1913-1920," *Tennessee Historical Quarterly*, 22 (June 1963), 170-190; obituary in *Equal Rights*, 29 (July-August 1943), 58; Sue Shelton White, "Mother's Daughter" (*The Nation*, 1926), in Elaine Showalter, ed., *These Modern Women: Autobiographical Essays from the Twenties* (Old Westbury, New York, 1978), 45-52.

27. "Thumbnail Sketches"; Women's Division papers, FDRL.

28. Ellen Sullivan Woodward papers, Schlesinger Library; Works Progress Administration records, National Archives; George, "Women Appointees," 135-184; Martha H. Swain, "Ellen Sullivan Woodward," in *Notable American Women: The Modern Period*, 747-749.

INDEX

Abbott, Edith, 26, 143
Abbott, Grace, 4, 33, 46, 90; biographical, 21, 23, 26, 31, 38, 143-144, 166n8; head of Children's Bureau, 53, 55, 60, 63, 96; Consumers' Advisory Board, 95; Advisory Committee on Economic Security, 98; and Social Security Act, 99, 101; and Fair Labor Standards Act, 103; White House Conference on Emergency Needs of Women, 106, 107
Addams, Jane, 5, 17, 19, 24, 46, 47
Adkins, Bertha, 133-134
Adkins v. Children's Hospital, 105
Advisory Committee on Economic Security, 98-99
Agricultural Adjustment Act, 44
Agriculture, Department of, 60, 65, 98
Aid to Dependent Children (ADC), 100, 101
Akin, Stella, 139
Allen, Florence, 16, 31, 41, 47, 56, 57, 120, 138; appointment to Court of Appeals, 55-56
Altmeyer, Arthur, 96, 97, 102
American Association for Labor Legislation, 33, 98
American Association for Old Age Security, 98
American Federation of Labor, 34, 46, 89, 104
American Red Cross, 32, 107
Anderson, Eugenia, 133
Anderson, Mary, 4, 46, 56, 83, 106, 111; on Eleanor Roosevelt, 10; on feminism, 15, 17; biographical, 23, 25, 26, 39,

131, 144; World War I, 32, 191-192n48; Women's Trade Union League, 35, 66; head of Women's Bureau, 55, 60, 63, 96; and NRA codes, 90, 91; World War II, 127, 128, 129; on social work, 171n61; disappointment with Frances Perkins, 177n67
Anthony, Susan B., 30, 31
Anti-slavery, and women's rights, 6
Armstrong, Florence, 26, 155

Banister, Marion Glass, 79, 93, 123; on feminism, 15; biographical, 23, 32, 38, 144; in Democratic politics, 39, 73, 83, 84; Women's National Democratic Club, 40, 74; Assistant Treasurer of the U.S., 50, 63, 120, 132
Barnard College, 23
Bass, Elizabeth, 138
Bethune, Mary McLeod, 12-13, 138, 163n21
Beyer, Clara Mortenson, 13, 74, 90, 97, 104; biographical, 21, 23, 29, 32, 145; supports Grace Abbott for Secretary of Labor, 46; supports Frances Perkins for Secretary of Labor, 47; appointment to Labor Department, 53-54, 63, 96, 132; links to National Consumers' League, 66
Birth control, 27
Black, Ruby, 16, 139
Blackburn, Katherine, 138
Blacks in the New Deal, 12, 72, 125, 179n14
Blair, Emily Newell, 5, 41, 47, 50, 55, 79;

on women in politics, 14-15, 17, 68; biographical, 31, 32, 145; in Democratic politics, 39, 40, 42, 73, 75, 81; Women's National Democratic Club, 40, 74; and patronage, 49, 69; Consumers' Advisory Board and NRA, 51, 65, 67, 95-96

Blair, Harry, 51, 145

"Boston marriages," 26, 167n24

Bowles, Chester, 127

Brandeis, Elizabeth, 47

Breckinridge, Sophonisba, 47

Bridges, Harry, 124

Brown, Laura S., 139

Bryan, William Jennings, 38, 150

Bryn Mawr College, 23, 24

Bryn Mawr Summer School for Industrial Workers, 112, 186-187n81

Bugbee, Emma, 71, 139

Bureaucracy, women in, 61, 63, 117, 119-120

Bureau of Public Assistance, 55, 101, 120

Business and Professional Women, see National Federation of Business and Professional Women

Camp Jane Addams (Bear Mountain Park), 111, 112

Camps for unemployed women, 66, 111-114, 115, 117

Caraway, Hattie, 41, 140

Catt, Carrie Chapman, 4, 5, 30, 47, 55

Chambers, Clarke, 33

Child labor: under NRA codes, 88, 89, 90-91; under Fair Labor Standards Act, 102, 103

Child Labor Amendment, 19, 36, 81, 82, 104

Children's Bureau, 36, 96, 117, 193n1; network concentration in, 11, 29, 33; Grace Abbott's successor, 53-54; and NRA, 90; and Social Security Act, 97, 99, 101, 172n67, 184n42

Christman, Elizabeth, 90

Civil Service Commission, 51, 60, 65, 66, 132

Civil Works Administration, 106, 107-108, 110

Civilian Conservation Corps, 44, 111, 112, 114

Clark, Mrs. Bennet Champ, 82

Clark, Georgia Neese, 133

Coffin, Jo, 14, 42, 74, 81; biographical, 23, 145-146; links to Women's Trade Union League, 35; appointment to

Government Printing Office, 52, 65, 66, 175n32

Collective bargaining, 44, 88, 104. See also National Labor Relations Act

Columbia University, 23

Committee on Economic Security, 98, 99

Congress, United States, and growth of conservative coalition, 103-104, 114, 116-117, 120, 123, 124

Consumers' Advisory Board, NRA, 51-52, 53, 88, 92-96, 113

Cook, Nancy, 40, 58, 76, 138, 150

Cornell University, 25, 36

Court-packing, see United States Supreme Court

Dell, Jessie, 60

Democratic Digest, 71, 73-74, 104, 122, 126; fate in 1940s and 1950s, 121, 189-190n21

Democratic National Committee, 39, 49, 56, 72, 80; Rainbow Fliers, 85-86; takes over Democratic Digest, 121; abolishes Women's Division, 134. See also Women's Division

Democratic party, women in, 3, 11, 58, 68-86; 1940 campaign, 3, 125, 126; 1936 campaign, 16, 68, 80-86; in the 1920s, 39-41; 1932 campaign, 41-42; patronage, 45, 49, 54, 56; progress stalled, 120-121; setbacks in 1950s, 134

Depression, 1, 6, 43, 61, 117; attitudes about women working during, 1, 2; impact on conditions for women in New Deal, 6, 135

DeSchwenitz, Dorothy, 113

Dewson, Mary W. (Molly), 18, 97, 126, 134; National Institute of Government, 3, 4, 6; and Eleanor Roosevelt, 7, 10, 40, 42, 60, 100, 120, 124, 163n18, 174n23; biographical, 11, 21, 23-24, 26, 30-31, 33, 146; and Frances Perkins, 13, 45-48, 53-54, 102, 131, 168n32; attitudes about feminism and women's roles, 14, 16, 26-27, 48-52, 69-70, 77, 97, 165n35; and members of the network, 29, 54, 55, 66, 67, 111, 172n76; and National Consumers' League, 33, 35, 66, 90, 100; head of Women's Division, 40, 41, 68-69, 70, 72, 74, 80, 120-121, 122, 123, 125-126; on New Deal and Franklin D. Roosevelt, 42, 44, 58, 59, 70, 86, 98; patronage, 44-57, 57-58, 66; disagreements with Jim Farley, 59, 71-72, 165n35,

176n58; Consumers' Advisory Board and NRA, 65, 95-96; Social Security Board, 65, 101, 120, 189n13; introduces Reporter Plan, 70; Buenos Aires Conference and the Equal Rights Amendment, 78; Section 213 of the National Economy Act, 79, 82, 117-118; 1936 campaign, 81-82, 84-86; impact of suffrage on Democratic politics, 85; Rainbow Fliers, 86; role in New Deal social welfare legislation, 87, 96, 99, 104, 106, 111
Dickerman, Marion, 40, 58, 138, 150
Douglas, Paul, 47
Dreier, Mary, 34

Early, Stephen, 59
Edson, Katherine, 47, 97
Education, higher, for women, 21-24
Edwards, India, 133, 134, 135, 190n34, 193n6
Eisenhower, Dwight, 133, 134
Eliot, Martha M., 99
Elliott, Harriet, 53, 81, 126, 127
Engle, Lavinia, 57, 67, 69, 79, 95, 140; 1936 Platform Committee, 81, 82
Equal Rights Amendment, 5, 14, 16, 30, 77-79, 81, 121

Fair Labor Standards Act, 15, 87, 97, 103-105, 117, 123
Farley, James F., 75, 76, 80, 126; and patronage, 49, 52, 56, 57; attitudes about women in politics, 59; different approach from Women's Division, 71, 72
Fascism, and women's roles, 117-119
Federal Art Project, 109
Federal Emergency Relief Administration (FERA), 11, 54, 55, 65, 66, 75; women's relief programs, 106-107, 108-109, 110; camps for unemployed women, 111-113
Federal government, women in, 21, 60-63; and diplomatic service, 48, 50, 57, 65-66, 133
Federal Security Agency, 120, 132
Federal Theater Project, 109, 117, 137
Federal Writers Project, 109
Feminism: revival in 1960s, 2, 6, 134; and peace, 5, 16, 81; network's attitudes toward women's roles, 14-17; term applied to National Women's Party, 16; social feminism, definition and goals, 17, 125; worldwide declines, 117-119;

network's limited feminist vision, 129-130, 184n43
Ferguson, Miriam A. ("Ma"), 41
Fertility rates, 27; of women in network, 27-28
Fifty-fifty (equal) representation, 79-80
Flanagan, Hallie, 138
Flynn, Edward, 76, 126
Frankfurter, Felix, 47, 102
Freudian attitudes about sexuality, 26; Molly Dewson's reaction to, 26-27
Friedan, Betty, 134, 192n53
Funk, Antoinette, 139
Furman, Bess, 139, 181n48, 193n2

Gardener, Helen Hamilton, 60
General Federation of Women's Clubs, 30, 33, 91
Generations, 19, 20-21, 28, 38, 125, 130-131; definition, 18-19, 165n2
Glass, Carter, 38, 50, 144
Goldmark, Pauline, 46, 168n30, 183n18
Government Printing Office, 52, 65, 66
Graves, Dixie Bibb, 140
Green, William, 89
Greenway, Isabella, 140
Guffey, Joseph, 38, 121, 149
Guffey-Snyder Act, 102

Hague, Frank, 150
Hamilton, Alice, 47
Harriman, Averill, 147, 153
Harriman, E. H., 93, 147, 153
Harriman, Florence Jaffray (Daisy): Minister to Norway, 13, 50-51, 59, 63, 65-66, 120, 138, 172n76; on women's roles, 14; and Frances Perkins, 14, 46-47; biographical, 23, 27, 31, 32, 147, 153; in Democratic politics, 40, 42; Women's National Democratic Club, 40, 74; on Ruth Bryan Owen's marriage, 84
Harrison, Pat, 155
Harron, Marion, 140
Hatch Act, 121
Hellman, Lillian, 20
Hennock, Frieda, 133
Herrick, Elinore Morehouse (Geno), 15-16, 138
Hickey, Margaret, 128
Hickok, Lorena, 130-131, 134, 139
Hillman, Sidney, 89, 127
Hobby, Oveta Culp, 128, 133, 147, 193n2
Hoey, Jane, 37, 74; biographical, 23, 32,

38, 147; Bureau of Public Assistance, 55, 65, 96, 101, 120, 132, 193n2
Honeyman, Nan Wood, 140
Hoover, Herbert, 43, 46
Hopkins, Harry, 54, 55, 98, 111, 147, 155; head of New Deal relief programs, 105, 106, 108; White House Conference on Emergency Needs of Women, 106-107; camps for unemployed women, 113
Howe, Louis, 42, 48, 51, 52, 56, 124; on women in politics, 59-60
Howorth, Lucy Somerville, 13, 52, 74, 75, 83; biographical, 23, 31, 32, 38, 41, 148; appointment to Veterans' Administration, 65, 66; on Truman transition, 132-133; on Frances Perkins's feminism, 192n50
Hull, Cordell, 39
Hull House, 24, 36

Ickes, Harold, 88
Industrial Advisory Board, NRA, 88-89, 94
Inter-American Peace Conference, Buenos Aires, and Equal Rights Amendment, 78-79
Interdepartmental Committee to Coordinate Health and Welfare Activities, 101-102
Interior, Department of, 50, 88, 101
It's Up to the Women, 88

Jenckes, Virginia, 140
Johnson, Hugh, 53, 60, 88, 91, 93, 94, 95
Journalism, women in, 7, 71, 89
Jurkowitz, Frances, 139

Kelley, Florence, 19, 35, 36-37, 100, 146, 170n54
Kellogg, Paul, 33
Kennedy, John F., 128, 134
Kerr, Florence, 138, 188n4
Kingsbury, Susan, 47
Knudsen, William S., 127

Labor, Department of, 50, 88, 90, 101, 104, 120, 132; network concentration in, 11, 53-54, 63, 65, 96; Frances Perkins named as Secretary, 45-48; social welfare leadership, 97
Labor Advisory Board, NRA, 53, 66, 88, 89-90, 92, 94
Labor Standards, Division of, 54, 90, 96
LaDame, Mary, 106; biographical, 23, 32, 148; joins Labor Department, 53,

63, 120, 132; in Democratic politics, 73, 74, 86
Lathrop, Julia, 19, 46, 60, 143
Leach, Agnes, 100, 125, 173n12
League of Women Voters, *see* National League of Women Voters
LeHand, Missy, 50, 139
Lenroot, Katharine, 74; biographical, 23, 38, 39, 148; head of Children's Bureau, 54, 63, 96, 132; role in Social Security Act, 97, 99, 101; and Fair Labor Standards Act, 103
Lewis, David, 99
Lewis, John L., 89, 152
Lockett, Ruth, 139
Long, Huey, 98
Long, Rose, 140
Lord, Mary Pillsbury, 133
Louchheim, Katie, 128, 130
Lovejoy, Owen, 47
Luce, Clare Booth, 133, 193n8
Lusk, Georgia, 133

McAlister, Dorothy, 74, 118-119; biographical, 21, 23, 38, 148-149, 166n8; head of Women's Division, 51, 73, 80, 81, 82, 122, 126, 140
McConnell, Dorothy, 118
McIntyre, Marvin, 45, 58, 59
McMillin, Lucille Foster, 74, 123; biographical, 23, 27, 38, 149; appointment to Civil Service Commission, 51, 65, 66, 132
Magee, Elizabeth, 53
Mason, Lucy, 90, 100
Massachusetts Woman Suffrage Association, 85
Miller, Carroll, 51, 149
Miller, Emma Guffey, 17, 41, 51, 79, 118; biographical, 23, 30, 31, 38, 149; National Women's Party and the Equal Rights Amendment, 30, 77, 78; in Democratic politics, 39, 56, 121, 140, 194n11
Miller, Frieda, 53, 78
Minimum wage and maximum hours legislation, 15, 19, 36, 103, 104; NRA codes and, 44, 88, 92, 102
Mitchell, Stephen, 134
Morgan, W. Forbes, 83
Morgenthau, Elinor, 76, 138
Morgenthau, Henry, Jr., 99
Morgenthau, Henry, Sr., 84, 85
Moskowitz, Belle, 59
Mothers' Pensions, 99, 100, 184n42
Mount Holyoke College, 11, 23, 36

Muller v. *Oregon*, 36
Mulliner, Maurine, 139
Musser, Elise, 78, 79
"My Day," 7, 74, 118, 162-163n16

National American Woman Suffrage
  Association (NAWSA), 4, 5, 30, 31
National Child Labor Committee, 33
National Conference of Social Work, 38,
  144, 148
National Conference on the Cause and
  Cure of War, 5
National Consumers' League, 37, 55, 77,
  92, 97, 107; in New York in 1920s, 33,
  35-36; impact on network, 66, 87, 89,
  102; and Democratic politics, 75; and
  NRA codes, 90, 91; consumer repre-
  sentation in New Deal, 92, 94, 95; and
  Social Security Act, 98, 99, 100;
  women trained by, 170n54
National Defense Council, 126, 127
National Defense Surveys, 126
National Federation of Business and Pro-
  fessional Women, 33, 91, 104, 119
National Industrial Recovery Act, 44,
  87-88. *See also* National Recovery
  Administration
National Institute of Government, 3-4, 6,
  71, 73, 74, 125
National Labor Relations Act, 102
National League of Women Voters, 5,
  33, 79, 91
National Recovery Administration
  (NRA), 44, 60, 73, 87-96, 110; and
  labor, 44, 88, 102; network participa-
  tion in, 51, 65, 89, 90, 91, 92, 94-96;
  Consumers' Advisory Board, 51-52,
  88, 92-96; Labor Advisory Board, 53,
  88, 89, 90, 92; Women's Section, 88;
  Industrial Advisory Board, 88-89;
  child labor provisions, 90-91; lower
  codes for women, 90-91; Frances
  Robinson scandal, 93; and Fair Labor
  Standards Act, 102, 105
National Women's Party, 5, 16, 30, 77,
  78
National Women's Trade Union League,
  see Women's Trade Union League
National Youth Administration (NYA),
  51, 66, 102, 114; Office of Minority
  Affairs, 12; camps for unemployed
  women, 111, 112, 113, 187n86
Network of women in New Deal, 2, 6-7;
  members, 7-13, 137-141, 142-155;
  shared ideology, 14-17, 77-79; roots
  of, 18-42; attitudes on marriage and

career, 24-29; emerges in 1933 and
  1934, 66-67; and Democratic politics,
  68, 73-76, 80-86; and social welfare
  policy, 87, 88, 94-95, 96-97, 101, 105-
  111; zenith, 116-117; changes in second term, 117, 119-120, 123-125; limited feminist vision, 129-130, 184n43;
  gains not institutionalized, 130-131;
  definition, 162n14
New Deal: expanded roles for women, 1,
  2, 6-7, 61; foundations in 1920s, 32-33;
  first hundred days, 43-44; social welfare policies, 66, 87-115; educational
  basis of Women's Division plans,
  69-71; growth of conservative opposition, 103-104, 116-117, 120, 123, 124;
  high tide, 116; legacy, 135. *See also*
  Roosevelt, Franklin D.
New York Child Labor Committee, 33
New York Consumers' League, 29, 40,
  100
New York League of Women Voters, 40
New York Maternity League, 93
New York Women's Democratic Committee, 40, 76
New York Women's Trade Union
  League, 35, 40, 52
Norton, Mary T., 76, 106; on feminism,
  15; biographical, 32, 132, 150; in
  Democratic politics, 40, 41, 42, 74, 83,
  116; and Fair Labor Standards Act,
  104

O'Day, Caroline, 76, 106; biographical,
  21, 150; in Democratic politics, 40, 74,
  80, 81; influences Franklin D. Roose-
  velt, 58; Eleanor Roosevelt campaigns
  for, 75-76
Office of Civilian Defense, 127
Office of Price Administration, 127
Office of Production Management, 127
Olesen, Anna Dickie, 57, 83, 85
Omlie, Phoebe, 84, 138-139
Owen, Ruth Bryan, 4, 46; biographical,
  27, 32, 38, 150-151; in Democratic
  politics, 41, 42, 84-85; Minister to
  Denmark, 48, 63, 65-66
Owings, Chloe, 139

Parkhurst, Genevieve, 118
Patronage, 44-57; reasons for success in
  New Deal, 57-63; and Molly Dewson's
  political goals, 69; little turnover in
  second term, 119-120; limited in wartime, 127
Peace, and women, 5, 16, 81

Perkins, Frances, 4, 13, 14, 57, 93, 97, 106, 111, 127; role in network, 11, 67, 124; on feminism and women's roles, 14, 15, 17, 28, 77, 129, 164n30, 168n30, 192n50; biographical, 19, 21, 23, 24, 132, 151, 170n51; on suffrage, 31, 85; part of New York reform circles, 33, 33-34, 37; Florence Kelley and National Consumers' League, 35, 36, 36-37; and Eleanor Roosevelt, 40; on roots of New Deal, 42; in Democratic politics, 42, 74, 78-79, 84, 122, 125, 134; as Secretary of Labor, 45-48, 173n12, 174n14; patronage, 49, 50, 53-54, 55, 95, 119-120; impact on New Deal social welfare policy, 87, 97; and NRA, 89, 90, 92-93; and Social Security Act, 98-99, 100-101, 184n36; and Fair Labor Standards Act, 102-103, 104; resignation and Franklin Roosevelt's death, 131

Platform Committee, 80-82, 125

Polls, Gallup, 2

Porter, Mary (Polly), 26

Presidential Commission on the Status of Women, 134

Priest, Ivy Baker, 133

Progressive reform, 2, 5, 6, 7, 19, 20; and suffrage, 30; survival during 1920s, 32-33, 37; New Deal continuities, 42, 125

Protective legislation, 5, 34-35, 36; and Equal Rights Amendment debate, 77-78

Public Works Administration, 88

Pyke, Bernice, 138

Rainbow Fliers, 83, 85-86

Regional Conferences, 73, 74

Relief programs for women, 105-114. See also Federal Emergency Relief Administration; Works Progress Administration

Reporter Plan, 70-71, 73, 74, 80, 121, 126, 179n11

Republican National Committee, 133-134

Republican party, women in, 39, 82, 121, 125, 133-134

Richberg, Donald, 95

Robins, Margaret Dreier, 34, 47, 144

Robinson, Frances, 93, 139

Roche, Josephine, 13, 14, 47, 79, 89; biographical, 23, 27, 32, 53, 120, 151-152; Assistant Secretary of the Treasury, 53, 63, 96; Consumers' Advisory Board, 53, 95; and Social Security Act,

98-99; Interdepartmental Health Committee, 102

Rohde, Borge (Micki), 84, 151

Rohde, Ruth Bryan Owen, see Owen, Ruth Bryan

Roosevelt, Eleanor, 4, 74, 93, 102, 130-131, 134; role in network, 7, 10, 60, 67, 96, 124-125; press conferences, 7, 70, 91; "My Day," 7, 74, 118; on feminism and women's roles, 14, 15, 16, 17, 118, 129; biographical, 21, 23, 30, 32, 127, 132, 152; links to Women's Trade Union League and National Consumers' League, 35, 66; in politics before New Deal, 39, 40, 42, 81; role in patronage, 45, 46, 48, 49, 50, 51, 52, 54, 56, 57, 69, 95, 96, 120; impact on Franklin Roosevelt, 58, 59; friendship with Louis Howe, 60; in Democratic politics, 75-76, 82, 122, 126; and Ruth Bryan Owen, 84, 85; and NRA, 88, 89, 90-91, 94; and women's relief, 105, 106, 107, 108, 111; and women's camps, 112, 113, 114; on Franklin Roosevelt's death, 131

Roosevelt, Franklin D., 3, 75, 93, 96, 116, 131; attitudes on women, 4, 46, 57-58, 58-59, 79, 124; and Frances Perkins, 23, 40, 47-48, 97, 98, 125, 190n32; and labor women, 35, 170n52; and Molly Dewson, 40, 47, 72, 79, 90, 123; continuities of New Deal, 42; first 100 days, 43-44; patronage for women, 50, 51, 55, 56, 120, 123, 127; supports social welfare legislation, 98, 99, 100, 103, 104; Court-packing, 103-104, 122

Root, Harriet, 140

Rosenberg, Anna, 128, 130-131, 133, 138

Ross, Nellie Tayloe, 46, 93, 106; biographical, 23, 27, 38, 132, 152-153; 167-168n27; in Democratic politics, 39-40, 41, 42, 48, 84, 121; appointed Director of the Mint, 50, 63

Rumsey, Mary Harriman, 13, 14, 40, 67; biographical, 23, 32, 153; head of Consumers' Advisory Board, 53, 65, 93-95; death, 95, 184n40

Russell Sage Foundation, 37

A. L. A. Schecter Poultry Corp. et al. v. United States, 96

Scheider, Malvina Thompson, 139

Schneiderman, Rose, 10, 14, 67, 106, 107; biographical, 23, 31, 35, 153-154, 170n51; Labor Advisory Board, 53, 65, 66, 89-90, 91-92, 105

Section 213 of the National Economy Act, 2, 77, 79, 81, 82, 117-118
Seligman, E. R. A., 23
Settlement houses, 26, 36
Sewing rooms, WPA, 105, 107, 108, 109
Shaw, Anna Howard, 5, 145
Sheppard-Towner Federal Maternity and Infancy Act, 5-6, 101
Sherwin, Belle, 67, 79
Smith, Al, 39, 42, 59, 149, 151, 153
Smith, Hilda Worthington, 19, 37, 106, 107; biographical, 23, 24, 154; on marriage, 25, 167n19; on suffrage, 31; at FERA and WPA, 55, 65, 66; camps for unemployed women, 111-114
Smith College, 22
Social reform, and women, 4, 5, 7, 14-17, 32-37
Social Security Act, 87, 97-101, 109
Social Security Administration, 52, 65, 96, 101, 120
Social Security Board, 11, 65, 69, 75, 101, 102, 111, 120, 123
Social welfare policy, and women, 7, 14, 45; network role in, 87-115
Social Work, 37-38, 63, 129, 171n61
Somerville, Nellie Nugent, 31, 38, 148, 169n46
Stanley, Louise, 60, 65, 140
Stanton, Elizabeth Cady, 30
State, Department of, 63, 78, 79, 84
Stewart, Mrs. Carroll, 139
Stone, Lucy, 30
Suffrage: woman suffrage campaign, 4-5, 6, 19, 30-32, 56; sets generations apart, 29-30, 130; network participation in, 30-32; links to New Deal, 31, 39, 70, 85. See also Catt, Carrie Chapman; Massachusetts Woman Suffrage Association; Shaw, Anna Howard
Survey Associates, 33
Swartz, Maud, 35, 170n52
Swofford, Jewell, 139

Tate, Jack, 154
Taylor, Graham, 47
Taylor, Mary, 139
Temporary Emergency Relief Administration, 111
Tennessee Valley Authority, 44
This Is My Story, 14
Thomas, M. Carey, 19
Townsend, Francis, 98
Treasury, Department of, 63, 98, 101
Triangle Shirtwaist fire, 35, 170n51
Truman, Harry S., 129, 132-133, 135,

151, 152
Tully, Grace, 139

Unions, 34, 90. See also Collective bargaining; National Labor Relations Act
United States Circuit Court of Appeals, 31, 120
United States Employment Service, 53, 73, 120
United States Supreme Court: Florence Allen mentioned for, 56, 120; strikes down NRA, 95-96; and Social Security Act, 98, 183-184n36; Roosevelt's Court-packing plan, 103-104, 122; and Fair Labor Standards Act, 103, 105

Vassar College, 22, 23
Veterans' Administration, Board of Appeals, 31, 52, 65, 66, 83

Wagner, Robert, 99
Wagner Act, see National Labor Relations Act
Wald, Lillian, 36, 46, 47
Walsh-Healey Public Contracts Act, 102-103
War Manpower Commission, Women's Advisory Committee, 127-128
Ward, Mary, 138
Welles, Sumner, 79
Wellesley College, 11, 22, 23, 59
White, Sue Shelton, 13, 19, 79; biographical, 25-26, 30, 31, 154-155; in Democratic politics, 39, 40, 41-42, 48, 50; Consumers' Advisory Board, 51-52, 65, 95-96; Social Security Administration, 65, 96, 101; member of National Women's Party, 77, 78
White House Conference on Camps for Unemployed Women, 112-113
White House Conference on the Emergency Needs of Women, 67, 106-107, 108, 110, 113
White House Consumers' Conference, 94, 113
Whitney, Florence Casper, 76, 78, 138
Willebrandt, Mabel Walker, 46
Williams, Aubrey, 112
Willis, Frances, 133
Willkie, Wendell, 125, 190n32
Wolfe, Carolyn: biographical, 38, 155; head of Women's Division, 51, 73, 74, 79, 81, 140
Wolman, Leo, 89
Woman's Charter, 118
Women's and Professional Projects, 11,

106, 109, 117. *See also* Woodward, Ellen Sullivan; Works Progress Administration

Women's Auxiliary Army Corps (WACS), 128

Women's Bureau, 11, 55, 63, 96, 110; and NRA codes, 90, 91, 92; rumor of disbanding, 117, 188n5; larger World War II role, 128

Women's Christian Temperance Union, 33

Women's City Club, 33

Women's Division, Democratic National Committee, 3, 31, 57-58, 72-73, 78, 79-80, 104, 105; Molly Dewson heads, 11, 68, 69-70; and patronage, 45, 49, 50, 56, 57; Carolyn Wolfe heads, 51, 140; Dorothy McAlister heads, 51, 140; Reporter Plan, 70-71, 73, 74, 80; conflicts with Farley, 72; and Southern women, 72, 75, 80, 169n46; Regional Conferences, 73; *Democratic Digest*, 73-74; network participation in, 75; 1936 campaign, 80-86; Rainbow Fliers, 85-86; conflicts with Emma Guffey Miller, 120; against Court-packing plan, 121-122; work in second term, 121, 122-123, 124, 125-126; 1940 campaign, 126-127; abolished, 134

Women's International League for Peace and Freedom, 5

Women's Joint Congressional Committee, 6

Women's National Democratic Club, 40-41, 73, 74, 80

Women's Trade Union League, 33, 34-35, 77, 87, 107; links to network, 66; and NRA codes, 89, 90, 91

Woodward, Ellen Sullivan, 13, 14, 79, 100, 104, 117; cooperation with Eleanor Roosevelt, 10-11, 108; role in network, 11, 66, 67, 105-106, 111; on women's roles and feminism, 14, 119; biographical, 21, 23, 27, 38, 41, 132, 155, 193n4; shapes women's relief policy, 54, 65, 105-106, 107, 108, 109-110, 111, 112; in Democratic politics, 70, 73, 74, 75, 80, 119; appointed to Social Security Board, 101, 111, 120

Woolley, Mary, 4, 164n30

Workers Education, 24, 55, 112

Works Progress Administration (WPA), 11, 61, 65, 73, 117, 120; relief programs for women, 105-106, 108-110, 111, 114. *See also* Women's and Professional Projects; Woodward, Ellen Sullivan

World War I, women's activities, 32, 61, 129

World War II, women's activities, 32, 61, 125, 126-129

Young Women's Christian Association, 33, 91

Zimmer, Verne, 54